A Biography Compiled From His Papers and Correspondence

J. A SYMONDS — 1886

A BIOGRAPHY

COMPILED FROM HIS PAPERS AND CORRESPONDENCE

BY

HORATIO F. BROWN

With Portraits and other Illustrations

IN TWO VOLUMES

VOLUME THE FIRST

NEW YORK
CHARLES SCRIBNER'S SONS
153-157 FIFTH AVENUE
MDCCCXCV

PREFACE BY MRS. SYMONDS

MR. HORATIO F. BROWN was, by my husband's will, left his literary executor, and in a few pathetic last words to me, written in a trembling hand on the last day of his short illness at Rome, when I, unhappily, was not by his side, he reminded me of this :

"ROME, *April* 18, 1893.

"There is something I ought to tell you, and being ill at Rome, I take this occasion. If I do not see you again in this life, you remember that I made H. F. Brown the depositary of my published books. I wish that legacy to cover all MSS., diaries, letters, and other matters found in my books, and cupboard, with the exception of business papers. . . . Brown will consult and publish nothing without your consent.—Ever yours,

"J. A. SYMONDS.

"You are ill at Venice, and I have fallen here."

To make a selection among this mass of written matter of all sorts has been a difficult task. No one could have brought to it more perfect knowledge, delicacy, and sympathy than the friend of twenty years, to whom my husband had written, in almost daily letters, all the various interests and problems with which his active brain was filled, and I am well satisfied that the portrait of him which the world will read should have been drawn by that faithful hand.

J. C. S.

PREFACE

THE object which I proposed to myself in compiling this book was twofold. I desired, if possible, to present a portrait of a singular personality, and I hoped to be able to achieve this object mainly by allowing Symonds, to speak for himself—to tell his own story. The book, in short, was to be as closely autobiographical as I could make it.

The material at my disposal was unusually abundant. I imagine that few men of letters have left behind them, in addition to some thirty published volumes, such a mass of letters, diaries, note-books, and memoranda as that which has passed through my hands.

This material is of two kinds, that which came into my possession under Symonds' will, and that which has been supplied to me by relations and friends. My own material consists of (1) diaries, introspective and emotional ; (2) a series of note-books labelled ἔργα καὶ ἡμέραι, in which he recorded day by day such external facts as the books he read, the essays he wrote, the dinner parties which he gave or attended, the bare outlines of journeys

which he took ; (3) an autobiography ; (4) a miscellaneous collection of papers, including copies of
many of his letters which Symonds himself reckoned
important ; and (5) the whole of his correspondence with me, which began in 1872, and was carried
on most copiously and regularly down to the very
last.

The material supplied to me by relations and
friends consists of Symonds' voluminous correspondence with his sister Charlotte, Mrs. Green, with Mr.
W. R. W. Stephens, with Mr. H. G. Dakyns, with
Mr. Henry Sidgwick and Mr. Arthur Sidgwick,
besides smaller collections of letters addressed to
Mr. T. H. Warren, President of Magdalen College,
Oxford, to Mrs. Ross, to Mr. W. Barclay Squire, to
Mr. Edmund Gosse (who also kindly procured me
the use of the letters to Mr. R. L. Stevenson), to the
Honourable Roden Noel, to Lord Ronald Gower,
and to many others whose names will generally be
found when letters to them are quoted. My thanks
are due to all of these for so kindly allowing me
to examine their correspondence. Miss Margaret
Symonds has also written an account of her father's
last journey, when she was, as she had often
been, his companion. This is printed in the last
chapter.

It may be asked why, as an autobiography exists,
I have not confined myself to the publication of
that. Apart from the ordinary and obvious reasons
which render the immediate publication of auto-

biographies undesirable, there is a consideration
supplied by Symonds himself, which induced me to
adopt the course I have taken. "Autobiographies
written with a purpose," he says in the autobiography itself, "are likely to want atmosphere. A
man, when he sits down to give an account of his
own life, from the point of view of art or of passion
or of a particular action, is apt to make it appear as
though he were nothing but an artist, nothing but
a lover, or that the action he seeks to explain were
the principal event in his existence. The report
has to be supplemented in order that a true portrait
may be painted." Under the circumstances, it was
possible from letters and diaries to furnish such supplement. Furthermore, I felt that autobiographies,
being written at one period of life, inevitably convey
the tone of that period; they are not contempo-
raneous evidence, and are therefore of inferior value
to diaries and letters. For these reasons, then, I
have used diaries and letters wherever that was
possible; holding that they portray the man more
truly at each moment, and progressively from moment to moment. But at certain places, notably at
the very outset, the higher authorities, the letters and
diaries, are wanting; and there I have been obliged
to use the autobiography as supplying what no other
authority "could communicate with equal force." I
take the letters and diaries as soon as they appear;
but as the autobiography was written towards the
very end of Symonds' life, the reader can hardly fail

to be aware of a break in style when passing from one source to the other, from autobiography to early letters and diaries. This, however, is a defect which becomes less and less sensible as the biography advances and Symonds' style begins to form itself. The autobiography being by far the best authority for the early years of his life, I thought it advisable to accept this slight drawback.

I must now say a word as to the method which I have pursued in compiling the biography from the materials described. As I have stated, I wished to leave Symonds to tell his own story, as far as that was possible, and at the same time I desired to construct a consecutive narrative and a current page, in order to avoid the awkward breaks which result from printing in the text the superscriptions, subscriptions, and dates of letters in full. It is hoped that in this way the reader may be enabled to read straight on; but should he at any time desire to know the source of the passage which he is reading, —when that source is not already mentioned in the text, he will only have to look at the last footnote, and there he will find whether the quotation is from autobiography, diaries, or letters, and in the last case he will learn the superscription and date of the letter.

It was my desire to add as little of myself as might be; but I found, in the course of compilation, that it was impossible to disappear altogether from the page. All that I have to say, however, is marked

off between square brackets, and when that in-
cludes quotations from Symonds these are given
within inverted commas.

The biography of such a man as Symonds must
depend for its interest upon psychological development. He was a man of means, and travelled for
the sake of his health or for the accumulation of
knowledge; but his journeys were not of the kind
which led to external adventures. For a biography
of the psychological order, however, the material is
rich and varied, as rich and varied as the temperament of the man who created it. The question
is, what was the nature of that temperament? Is
it possible to find a clue to the labyrinth of this
complex human soul, laid bare with unflinching
fidelity? Can we attain to a point of view which
will embrace and also explain the varied and per-
plexing phenomena?

It is hard for a man to know himself. It is
almost impossible for a friend, however intimate, to
reach the inner truth of his friend's nature. But
a biographer is in duty bound to form and to express
some co-ordinating view upon the mass of material
which he is giving to the world, and which in some
way or other represents the man whose portrait
he is seeking to delineate.

A nature so rich, a temperament so varied as
that of Symonds, must inevitably have attracted
by different qualities, and attached by various liga-
ments, his many friends; and no doubt each one

of these would describe and explain the psychology of the man under slightly diverse aspects.

I can only say that the view I am about to put forward is one which I have held, more or less subconsciously, ever since I became his friend in 1872; and that it has been forced home upon me with irresistible conviction during the compilation of this book.

I believe that, psychologically, Symonds was constructed thus: a highly analytical and sceptical intellect, with which was connected a profound sense of the one ultimate positive fact knowable to him—himself; a rich, sensuous, artistic temperament, with which was united a natural vein of sweetness and affection: an uncompromising addiction to truth, a passion for the absolute, a dislike of compromises, of middle terms, of the *à peu près.*

The central, the architectonic, quality of his nature was religious. By religious, I mean that his major occupation, his dominating pursuit, was the interrogation of the Universe, the search for God.

"Theological" his temperament certainly was not. He had arrived early at the conviction that the "theos" about whom the current "logos" was engaged must be a "theos" apprehended, if not created, by the human intellect, therefore not the universal, all-embracing "theos" for whom he was in search. "Religious," in so far as submission is implied by that term, he was not by nature, though

I think he was being lessoned by life towards that
issue. But if the honest, courageous recognition
of the Self confronted with God, the soul with the
universe, the struggle to comprehend and be com-
prehended, is religious, then Symonds was pre-
eminently a religious man.

Emotionally he desired the warmth of a personal
God, intellectually he could conceive that God
under human attributes only, and found himself
driven to say "no" to each human presentment of
Him.

I imagine that this is a temperament not altogether uncommon, that it is even characteristic, to
some extent, of our century, post-revolutionary and
scientific; but I feel confident that the manifes-
tation of such a temperament has seldom been so
complete.

On such a psychological basis it would not in any
case have been easy to construct a thoroughly happy
or restful life. And when we take into consideration the burden of ill-health, and all the thwartings
of a powerful, ambitious, and determined nature
implied thereby, that note of depression which
marks so many pages of diary, letters, and autobiography alike, will hardly cause surprise.

But it is no ignoble melancholy which over-
shadowed so large a part of Symonds' life. The
passionate desire to reach God, to understand what
we are, and why we are here, meeting with an
equally powerful devotion to truth in its purest,

simplest form, an equally potent resolve to accept
no theory that is not absolute, final, larger than
ourselves, inevitably produced a spiritual conflict, to
witness which may make us sad, but can hardly fail
to raise both respect and love for the soul which was
its battle-field.

It is possible that many who met Symonds did
not surmise behind the brilliant, audacious exterior,
underlying the witty conversation, and the keen
enjoyment of life and movement about him, this
central core of spiritual pain.   But the old adage is
true—παθήματα μαθήματα—and I believe that he owed
much of his singular charm, his attractiveness,
his formative power over youthful character, his
wide sympathy and his unfailing helpfulness, pre-
cisely to the pain, the bitterness, the violence of
this internal struggle, which vivified and made
acutely sensitive a nature in its essence sweet and
affectionate.

It must be remembered, however, that though this
pain lay deep down at the root of his life, and finds
expression where the man is speaking to himself, as
it were, in diaries and letters to his most intimate
friends, it did not obscure the sparkling genialities
of his daily converse with the world, nor overlay the
founts of human sympathy and kindliness which
welled up within his nature.   I am sure that his intellectual equals would bear testimony to the brilliancy and vivacity of the personality which he
presented to them.   I am equally sure that the

many to whom he brought material assistance would testify to the abundance of his philanthropy. "Nemo te magis in corde amicos fovebat nec in simplices et indoctos benevolentior erat." His friend and teacher, the late Master of Balliol, wrote these words for his grave, and they are true.

I think that down to what Symonds always called "the crisis" at Cannes, in the year 1868—that is, when he was twenty-eight years of age—this long internal struggle to know, and refusal to know in part, this unceasing interrogation of the Universe, had been conducted mainly in the field of abstract thought, by a continual cloud-war within the brain. After Cannes, and down to the close of his life, this inquiry was gradually removed from the region of the abstract to the region of the concrete; but the problem remained the same, the desire to solve it quite as potent. At times his philosophy of life may have appeared very positive, almost material, but that was merely because the pure abstract had grown wearisome, not because the ideal point of view had been abandoned, the gravitation towards God arrested in its course. He seemed to me to be always studying, studying, studying, "a terrible fellow for diving to the roots of things," whether those things were the abstractions of the intellect or the concrete of daily life among the people with whom his lot was cast; in either field he was in pursuit of an answer to the riddle of existence, or, as he put it, "living in the whole." Moreover, it was only when abstractions were renounced that one large side of his nature was brought fully into play. His artistic, sensuous temperament found a satisfaction in actual life, which had been denied it in the cloud-land of speculation. The devotion to truth, the critical intellect, still maintained their old activity, but now more of the whole man became energetic, and he felt, and said he felt, wider, wiser, more humane—and on the whole happier.

I do not think that Symonds ever expected the problem to be solved, the struggle to be abandoned. The renunciation of the quest would have seemed to him spiritual death—the solution of the riddle, also, most likely, death. In December 1889, he wrote : "When will the soul be at ease? If it has to live for ever, I believe mine will never be at ease." Did he want it to be? I think so,—but upon terms which we suppose to be precluded by the limitations of human nature, by the loss of its individual self-consciousness, by absorption into the Universal consciousness. "E naufragar m'é dolce in questo mare."

This is my view as to the central point in Symonds' nature ; whether the present volumes will carry to the reader the same conviction that the work of compiling them has strengthened in me, I cannot say. They are here to speak for themselves.

These volumes have enjoyed the great advantage

of revision by Symonds' family, and by two of his older friends, Mr. H. G. Dakyns and Mr. Henry Sidgwick. I can never sufficiently thank them for the patience and pains with which they have assisted me, in a task which I might otherwise have found to be even more difficult than it has proved.

HORATIO F. BROWN.

CA TORRESELLA, VENICE,
November, 1894.

CONTENTS

CHAPTER I

CHILDHOOD

CHAPTER II

BOYHOOD

CHAPTER III

BOYHOOD

CHAPTER IV

YOUTH

CHAPTER V

MANHOOD. FROM DEGREE TO FELLOWSHIP

CHAPTER VI

MANHOOD. FELLOWSHIP TO MARRIAGE

CHAPTER VII

MANHOOD. DRAWN TOWARDS LITERATURE

CHAPTER VIII

MANHOOD. SPECULATIVE LIFE

LIST OF ILLUSTRATIONS

VOLUME THE FIRST

JOHN ADDINGTON SYMONDS

CHAPTER I

CHILDHOOD

I[1] WAS born upon the 5th of October 1840, at 7
Berkeley Square, Bristol. Here I lived until June
1851, when our home was changed for Clifton Hill
House.

I cannot say that I have a distinct memory of
my mother. She died of scarlet fever when I
was four years old, and she had been always too
weak in health to occupy herself energetically in
the household. Those who knew her intimately
were unanimous in saying that she combined
rare grace and beauty of person with singular

[1] Autobiography.

sweetness of character and distinguished mental endowments.

The one thing which I can clearly remember about her is, that we were driving alone together in my father's carriage (a chariot with glass windows at the front and sides, drawn by two horses) down a steep hill by Cornwallis Terrace to the Lower Crescent, when the horses plunged and broke into a gallop. Her fright must have made a deep impression on me. I can still see a pale face, a pink silk bonnet, and beautiful yellow hair. These have for background in my memory the glass windows of a *coupé*, and the red stone wall overhung with trees which embanked the garden of Cornwallis Terrace. I do not know now whether the road has been altered. It is long since I walked there. But the instantaneous flash of that moment on my brain persists as I describe it.

I can also remember the morning of my mother's funeral. We children were playing in our nursery with tin soldiers and clumsy wooden cannon, painted black and yellow. These were on the floor beside us. We were dressed in black. The nurses took us away to my grandmother's house in the Lower Crescent.

This is all I recollect about my mother. I have been told that my name was the last upon her lips when she was dying. But my father never spoke to me much about her, and only gave me a piece of her hair.

He sometimes took me with him to her grave. This was in the Arno Vale Cemetery, high up upon a grassy hillside, where harebells and thyme blossomed in the short turf of a down. A plane-tree spread its branches over the tomb, and the flat stone which marked her resting-place was enclosed by iron railings. My father took jealous care that these railings should be over-rioted with ivy, roses, and clematis, growing in unpruned luxuriance. He wished to withdraw the sacred spot from vulgar eyes. I could not see inside it. It was our custom to pluck leaves from the plane-tree and the creepers, and to return in silence to the carriage which stood waiting by the gate. These leaves, gathered from my mother's grave, were almost all I knew about her—all I had of her. I used to put them into a little book of texts called "Daily Food," which had belonged to her, and which I read every night, and still read at all hours of the day in the year 1889.

I cannot pretend that I greatly desired to have a clearer notion of my mother, or that I exactly felt the loss of her. It was all dreamy and misty to my mind. I did not even imagine what she might have been to me. Sometimes I thought that I was heartless and sinful because I could not want her much. But this was foolish, because I had never really felt the touch of her. My father showed no outward signs of grief, and said nothing. He was only more than usually reserved on these occasions, and inspired me with a vague awe. Death was a mystery, into which the mother I had never really known, was now for ever drawn away from me.

I doubt whether the following is worth recording. But since it is the first event of which I seem to have a distinct recollection, I must do so. My sister Charlotte, younger than myself by two years short of two months, was christened at St. George's Church, Bristol. So far as I can now recall it, the building is of pseudo Græco-Roman architecture, rectangular in the body, faced with a portico and surmounted with a nondescript Pecksniffian spire in the bastard classic style. Of its internal arrangement I remember nothing definite, and yet I seem to see this picture vividly—an area of building, dim, grey, almost empty; a few people grouped about in my immediate neighbourhood; tall enclosed pews of a light yellow colour round the groups; something going on at no great distance to our left, which makes the faces turn in that direction looking backwards; myself dressed in white, with a white hat and something blue in the trimmings of it, half standing, half supported, so as to look over the rim of the pew. This is what I remember, or think I remember, of my sister's christening.

It is surely impossible to be certain whether these very early memories, definite as they may be, and not improbable, are actual impressions of scenes left upon our senses, or whether they are not rather the product of some half-conscious act of the imagination working reflectively upon what has been related to the child.

About another of these recollections I have not the same kind of doubt. I was in the nave of Bristol Cathedral, during service time, lifted in my nurse's arms, and looking through the perforated doors of the organ screen, which then divided nave from choir. The organ was playing, and the choristers were singing. Some chord awoke in me then, which has gone on thrilling through my lifetime, and has been connected with the deepest of my emotional experiences. Cathedrals, college-chapels, "quires, and places where they sing," resuscitate that mood of infancy. I know, when I am entering a stately and time-honoured English house of prayer, that I shall put this mood upon me like a garment. The voices of choiring men and boys, the sobbing anti-phones and lark-like soaring of clear treble notes into the gloom of Gothic arches, the thunder of the labouring diapasons, stir in me old deep-centred innate sentiment.

So it is with another of my earliest experiences. When I was still a little child, my father began to take me with him on his long drives into the country. After jolting through the city streets, we broke away at his quick travelling-pace into unknown regions of field, and wood, and hedgerows, climbing the Somer-setshire hills, threading their deep lanes and bosky combes, passing under avenues of ancient parks, halting at low-roofed farm-houses. Then I used to leave the carriage and wander for a while alone in fairyland—knee-deep in meadow-sweet and willow-herb, bruising the water-mint by shallow brooks, gazing at water-lilies out of reach on sleepy ponds, wondering why all about me was so still, and who the people were who dwelt there. The hush of sickness and expected death sobered the faces of the men and women who received my father; and he was often very thoughtful when he left their home-steads, and we journeyed back in silence. It used to be late in the evening generally when we returned from these excursions. Twilight added to the mystery of the unknown, the shadow of the unin-telligible sorrow I had felt. The shimmer of moon-light blending with late sunset upon boughs of wild roses or spires of foxglove, or hyacinths in ferny hedges—a sallow western sky seen from the heathy heights of Mendip or of Dundry, the heavy scent of clematis or privet when the air is hot and moist in June, the grey front of lonely farm-buildings flanked by yew-trees, the perfume suddenly distilled from limes or laurels through darkness at some turning of the road—such things have always brought the feeling of those solemn evenings back. I used often to fall asleep in the carriage, and woke up startled by a carter's shout as we swept onward, or by the glare of the city lamps, when we broke at last away from the country roads, and rattled over the pave-ment of the city streets.

I had no love for my birthplace, 7 Berkeley

Square. I am distinctly aware of the depressing effect produced upon me by the more sordid portions of this town house, especially by a dingy dining-room, and a little closet leading through glass doors into a dusty back garden. The garden had one miracle, however, to ennoble it. That was a cherry-tree, which clothed itself in silver beauty once a year, maugre the squalor which surrounded it. I ought also not to forget, that our back windows looked out on Brandon Hill, from which a glorious prospect over city, river, meadow, distant hills and wooded slopes, could then be gained.

The front door of our house was fairly well pro-portioned, and surmounted with a pediment boldly hewn, of Bath-stone, grey and mossy. I felt a par-ticular affection for this pediment. It had style. The limes and almond-trees and bright berries of the mountain ashes in the Square garden, were also a great consolation. But certain annuals—esch-scholtzia, Virginia stock, and minor convolvulus—have always remained unpleasantly associated with the forlorn ill-cared-for flower beds. I found some difficulty in conquering my dislike for the nasturtium, on account of the innumerable earwigs which its gorgeous trumpet-blooms concealed. On the other hand, certain dusky-green and brownish-pink hawk-moths, fluttering about the limes on summer even-ings, seemed to me like angels from a distant land.

Trifling as these matters are, they indicate the spontaneous development of powerful instincts. My

long exile in the High Alps has been rendered
more than tolerable by the fact, that nothing which
man makes can wholly debase the mountains of
Graubünden. Simplicity and purity and wayward
grace in natural things, strength and solidity and
decent form in things of art, were what my temperament unconsciously demanded.

The sense of meanness which annoyed me in our
house afflicted me far more keenly in the chapel of
the Blind Asylum, where we attended service twice
on Sundays. The bastard Gothic lancets, dead-
grey, rough-cast walls and ugly painted woodwork
of that paltry building, gave me absolute pain. It
suffocated my soul, and made me loathe evangelical
Protestantism. Most of all, at night, when gas-
lamps flared in open jets upon the sordid scene, I
felt defrauded of some dimly apprehended birthright.

It is significant, in this respect, that two tales
made a deep impression at this period on my mind.
One was Andersen's story of the Ugly Duckling. I
sympathised passionately with the poor bird swim-
ming round and round the duck-puddle. I cried
convulsively when he flew away to join his beautiful
wide-winged white brethren of the windy journeys
and the lonely meads. Thousands of children have
undoubtedly done the same; for it is a note of
childhood, in souls destined for expansion, to feel
solitary and debarred from privileges due to them.
The other tale was a kind of allegory called "The
Story without an End," translated, I think, by Lucy

Duff Gordon from the German. The mystical dreamy communing with nature in wild woods and leafy places took my fancy, and begat a mood of *Sehnsucht* which became habitual.

My sisters and I were riding one day upon a rocking-horse which stood on the landing of the attic floor. I was holding on to the tail, I remember, a little anxious lest the tuft of grey horse-hair should suddenly give way and precipitate me backward, as it often did. We were screaming out Scott's lines upon the death of Marmion in chorus—

> With dying hand, above his head,
> He shook the fragment of his blade,
> And shouted "Victory."—
> "Charge, Chester, charge! On, Stanley, on!"
> Were the last words of Marmion.

Suddenly I ceased to roar. A resolve had formed itself unbidden in my mind, "When I grow up, I too will be an author."

I was a very nervous child, and subject to many physical ailments, which made me no doubt disagreeable to the people around me. It seems that I suffered from a gastric fever soon after my birth, and this left me weak. Being sensitive to the point of suspiciousness, I imagined that I inspired repugnance in others, and my own condition not unfrequently made me noisome to myself. My constitutional dislike of squalor had to suffer severe mortification. I became unreasonably shy and timid.

In connection with these childish illnesses, and what follows about night terrors, it is proper here to say that I had an elder brother, John Abdy Stephenson, who only lived seven months, and died of cerebral inflammation. He had been preceded by twin-sons, premature and still-born. My elder sister Mary Isabella was born in 1837, the twins in 1838, John Abdy Stephenson in 1839, myself in 1840. There is every reason to suppose that my mother's constitution at this time was inadequate to the strain of child-birth, and that she transmitted a neurotic temperament to certain of her children.

At night I used to hear phantasmal noises, which blended terrifically with the caterwauling of cats upon the roof. I often lay awake for hours with my fingers in my ears.

I fancied there was a corpse in a coffin under my bed, and I used to wake up thinking it had risen, and was going to throw a sheet over me.

Lights seemed to move about the room if I opened my eyes in the dark. I feared them; but I was forced to stare and follow them about, until I either sank back hypnotised, or rushed from the bed, and sat in my nightshirt on the staircase. Yet I did not dread the dark so much as the light of a rush-candle burning in a perforated cylinder of japanned metal, which cast hideous patterns on the roof and walls of the nursery.

When I slept, I was frequently visited with the

following nightmare. I dreamed that we were all seated in our well-lit drawing-room, when the door opened of itself, just enough to admit a little finger. The finger, disconnected from any hand, crept slowly into the room, and moved about through the air, crooking its joints and beckoning. No one saw it but myself. What was the horror that would happen if it should touch me or any other person present, I never discovered, for I always woke before the catastrophe occurred.

My father, thinking, I suppose, that I needed to be looked after, took me to sleep with him in his own bed. He added to my terrors by talking in his sleep. I remember one especially grim night, when I woke up and saw a man seated by the bed, and conversing with my father earnestly in a low voice about some case of fever. I did not miss a word, though all that I can now recall of the conversation related to the swollen blackness of the patient's tongue.

In some way or another, perhaps by listening to the dismal sermons of the Blind Asylum, I developed a morbid sense of sin, and screamed at night about imaginary acts of disobedience. My aunt or my father, hearing me sob and cry, left their chairs in the drawing-room, and tried to reassure me. I can see him on one occasion entering the bedroom with a yellow pamphlet in his hand—a number of "Vanity Fair," which began to come out in January 1847.

I was persuaded that the devil lived near the doormat, in a dark corner of the passage by my father's bedroom. I thought that he appeared to me there under the shape of a black shadow, scurrying about upon the ground, with the faintest indication of a swiftly whirling tail.

When the cholera was raging in the year 1848, I heard so much about it that I fell into a chronic state of hysterical fear. Some one had told me of the blessings which attend ejaculatory prayers. So I kept perpetually mumbling, "O God, save me from the cholera." This superstitious habit clung to me for years. I believe that it obstructed the growth of sound ideas upon religion; but I cannot say that I was ever sincerely pious, or ever realised the language about God I heard and parroted.

Burglars entered my father's house in Berkeley Square one evening while a dinner-party was going forward. They carried off considerable booty from my aunt's and sisters' wardrobe and trinket-boxes. It appeared that they had worked their way through the attic-windows from an adjacent house, which was empty at the time. We could see the marks of their dirty clumsy hands upon the staircase-wall next morning. I then made the mental reflection that people who were afraid of robbers could never have seen visions or dreamed nightmares. These men did not affect my imagination disagreeably. So far as I thought about them at all, I sympathised with their audacity, and felt my curiosity

aroused.   Neither then nor afterwards did I fear
anything so much as my own self.   What that contained was a terror to me.   Things of flesh and
blood, brutal and murderous as they might be,
could always be taken by the hand and fraternised
with.   They were men, and from men I did not
shrink.   I always felt a man might be my comrade.
Dreams and visions exercised a far more potent
spell.   Nigh to them lay madness and utter impotence of self-control.

These childish terrors, of which I have written
thus much, were stimulated by the talk of our head-
nurse, Sarah Jones, a superstitious country woman.
She was not exactly kind in her ways with us, and
used to get drunk at times.   Then she would behave strangely, and threaten us children.   I lived
in fear of her.   Sarah's theory of discipline may be
illustrated by the following anecdote.   We were
passing some weeks of the summer at an old inn
on King's Weston Down—a very delightful place
for children, with a swing suspended from the bough
of a huge elm-tree, breezy downs where mushrooms
grew and blackberries were plentiful, a farm-yard,
an old park hard by, and shady copses of arbutus
and juniper to wander in.   Indoors the furniture
was deficient; I found it difficult to fall asleep in
a stiff arm-chair, covered with black horse-hair, and
prolonged, I do not know how, into a make-shift
for a bedstead.   Sarah sat beside me working in
the evening light, prodding the pillow and the

mattress at intervals with her needle, under the impression that she could frighten me into slumber.

A very superior being to Sarah Jones was Mrs. Leaker, head-nurse in the family of my cousins the Nashes. She had much to do with fortifying and ennobling my sense of the supernatural. Mrs. Leaker had been born and bred in a Devonshire village on the sea-coast. She claimed gipsy-blood, and belonged to a family of smugglers, so at least she told us. Her physiognomy and complexion, and the legends with which her head was stored, accorded with this account of her ancestry. She was a great reader of good literature, and had the plays of Shakespeare and the history of our old English wars by heart. Sitting round the nursery fire, we used to make her tell us stories; it was easy then to pass from Shakespeare and the landing of Monmouth in the West, to earlier traditions of the country-side—haunted churches, whose windows burned at night before a tempest; East Indiamen from Bristol firing distress guns in the offing; the parson leaving his pulpit, and the seamen stealing off to join the wreckers; the avenue to the old hall, up which a phantom lord rode in his chariot drawn by six black horses, holding his head upon his knee; the yeoman belated on Dartmoor, following a white rabbit, which disappeared when he arrived at home and found his only daughter dead in bed there; the wild carousings of smugglers in their caves, and murderous conflicts with coast-guards-men ; the wicked gentlemen who sat up days and nights at play, deep to their knees in scattered cards, losing fortunes, and sallying forth to exchange shots upon a Sunday morning. Ghosts naturally took a large place in these legends. But Mrs. Leaker had a special partiality for presentiments and warnings. She knew the dream of Lord Camelford before his duel, and the clasp of the fiery hand upon Lady Tyrone's wrist, and the bird which fluttered against the window of Lord Lyttelton at Hagley. Tales like these she related in the twilight with intense conviction of their truth, and with a highly artistic sense for the value of vagueness.

Our earliest memories of words, poems, works of art, have great value in our psychical development. They indicate decisive points in the growth of personality. The first English poem which impressed me deeply was Shakespeare's "Venus and Adonis." I read it before I was ten years old. It gave form, ideality, and beauty to my visions. I may mention some other literature which took hold on my imagination. We had a book of old ballads in two volumes, illustrated by Maclise and other draughtsmen. The pictures to "Glenfinlas," and "Eve of St. John," and "Kempion," made me feel uncomfortable, but I think that Marley's Ghost in one of Dickens' Christmas tales bit deeper. The most impressive books of all were not illustrated. These were a series of articles on spectral illusions in "Chambers's Miscellany," and a translation of a German collection of murder stories by some name like Feuerbach. It is certain that I ought not to have had access to these scientific or semi-scientific sources. They worked potently and injuriously on my brain, but books abounded in our house, and I was naturally drawn to literature. I used even to examine the Atlases of Pathological Anatomy in my father's cupboards, and to regard the skeletons of man and beast with awful joy.

The family consisted of my father, my aunt, Miss Mary Ann Sykes, and my three sisters, Edith, Mary Isabella, and Charlotte. I cannot recollect any bond of friendship between me and my sisters, though we all lived together in amity. One touch of sympathy drew me closer to Maribella than the others. When I began to learn arithmetic I could not understand the simplest sums. She noticed me crying over a sum in long division, and with great gentleness and kindness helped me through the task.

We used to go to children's parties together. On these occasions, I was reputed to have brought some confusion on my elder sisters. Once, when I thought I was being neglected at table, I pointed to a cake, and said, "I never ask, but I points." At another party, impatient of waiting for supper, I asked the mistress of the house, "Lady, when are you going to help?"

My grandmother, Sykes, played a considerable

part in our young lives. She was a handsome old lady with strongly marked features, and a great air of blood and breeding. This contrasted strangely with her material and social surroundings. She had become a Plymouth Sister, and held the most innocent amenities of life for sinful. Her house in Cornwallis Crescent, or the Lower Crescent, had nothing in it to rejoice the eye, except flowers, to which she was devoted. Yet it never impressed me with a sense of squalor. The perfume of pot-pourri in a blue china bowl, and of Tonquin beans exhaling from drawers and work-baskets, gave distinction to the rooms, and the old lady's stately person rendered it impossible to regard any of her possessions as beneath the dignity of a gentlewoman. Nevertheless, all objects of taste and luxury, all that delights the sense, had been carefully weeded out of the grim, bare dwelling. And what company my grandmother kept! It was a motley crew of preachers and missionaries, tradespeople and cripples—the women dressed in rusty bombazine and drab gingham—the men attired in greasy black suits, with dingy white neckties—all gifted with a sanctimonious snuffle, all blessed by nature with shiny foreheads and clammy hands, all avid for buttered toast and muffins, all fawning on the well-connected gentlewoman, whose wealth, though moderate, possessed considerable attractions, and was freely drawn upon.

I often went to stay with my grandmother when

circumstances, generally some infectious ailment in our nursery, made it desirable that I should be away from home. So I had plenty of opportunities for studying these strange people, and appreciating the marvellous figure which that formidable old lady, aristocratic to the backbone and terribly ill-tempered, cut among them.

Heavy teas, like those described by Dickens, were of frequent occurrence, after which the Chadband of the evening discoursed at a considerable length. Then followed prayers, in the course of which a particularly repulsive pharmaceutical chemist from Broad Mead uplifted his nasal voice in petitions to the Almighty, which too often, alas, degenerated into glorifications of the Plymouth sect at Bristol, and objurgations on the perversity of other religious bodies. My grandmother came in for her due share of fulsome flattery, under the attributes of Deborah and Dorcas. My father was compared to Naaman, who refused to bathe in Jordan— Jordan being Bethesda, or the meeting-house of the Plymouth Brethren.

Sometimes I was taken to Bethesda, a doleful place, which brought no healing to my soul, but seemed to me a pool of stagnant pietism, and turbid middle-class Philistinism. This chapel did not, however, afflict me so grievously as the Blind Asylum. Partly, perhaps, because I knew it less, and it always had a kind of novelty. Partly because nothing which my grandmother touched was wholly commonplace or sordid. I think, too, that I was even then capable of appreciating the ardent faith and powerful intellect of George Müller, who preached there, and who founded the celebrated Orphanage at Horfield, near Bristol.

My grandmother naturally made a strong point of family prayers. She delighted in the Lamentations of Jeremiah, the minatory chapters of the prophets, and the Apocalypse. In a deep, sonorous voice, starting with a groan and rising to a quaver, she used to chant forth those lugubrious verses, which began or ended with " Thus saith the Lord." I remember hearing nothing of the Gospel, or the love of Christ for the whole human race, either in her readings from Scripture or in the extempore prayers which followed. She concentrated her attention on the message to the chosen people, with a tacit assumption that all who lived outside the Plymouth fold were children of wrath.

She had one redeeming quality of great price. That was her love of flowers. The public garden of the Lower Crescent flourished under her assiduous care ; and the small plot therein which was her own particular property abounded with old-fashioned plants—grape hyacinths and double primroses, auriculas and polyanthuses and oxlips, pyrus japonicus and ribes and gum cistus, with its papery stained petals, heavy-scented jessamine, and burly cabbage-roses.

My grandmother was a thorough Abdy, subject

to chronic insomnia, and irritable to the highest
degree. She lived alone with two servants, in a
tolerably large four-storeyed house. She slept upon
the second floor, and no one was allowed to inhabit
the third. When I was there I occupied a bedroom
next the drawing-room, on the first floor. There
was no living creature except a cat and cockroaches
in the house below me. Between me and the servants slept the imposing old lady in her solitude,
and the whole habitation during the long night hours
resounded to my fancy with the doleful litany of
" Thus saith the Lord : Woe, woe to the ungodly."
It may be imagined how prolific of nightmares No.
14 Lower Crescent was for me.

Some of my father's relatives were settled in
Bristol, Clifton, and the neighbourhood. I will now
narrate what seems to me at all noteworthy regarding my paternal kith. They were excellent folk,
distinguished by the virtues of the backbone of the
English nation—the great middle-class. They also
shared its faults—faults inseparable from a Nonconformist ancestry of several generations, complicated
by ineradicable family pride. How this pride had
formed itself, I am incapable of saying. They knew
little about what is really interesting in their gene-
alogy. A tradition survived of ancient gentry, sacrificed to a religious and political creed. They were
proud of being members of a family which had
relinquished the world and dedicated all its energies
during two centuries to the maintenance of an ideal.

How narrow the ideal was, and how inconsistent with the progress of modern thought it had become, they did not stop to consider.

My father was a *rara avis* in this family. They looked upon him with suspicion, modified by respect and admiration. Intellectually he had joined the ranks of progress, and belonged to the age of widening thought. Morally he held with them, and exemplified in his own life what was best and noblest in the family tradition. To keep himself unspotted by the world, to admit no transaction with base motives, to live purely and act uprightly, to follow honour, to postpone mundane and selfish interests to duty, to deal mercifully, sympathetically, tenderly, justly with his brother men, to be unsparing in condemnation of rebellious evil, painstaking and long-suffering with struggling good, these were the principles which ruled his conduct. He transfigured in himself the inheritance he had derived from six generations of Puritan ancestors, and he retained something of their rigidity. But he also felt the influence of the age in which he lived. He was open at all pores to culture, to art, to archæology, to science, to literature. In a large and liberal sense, he yielded his spirit up to beauty, and imbibed the well-springs of modern philosophy. Judged by the narrow standard of his kindred, he was unsound on doctrine, dangerously allied with the revolutionary forces of the century. They not unnaturally regarded him as a bird of different feather from themselves;

and, while they looked up to him as the mainstay of their fortunes, the most eminent example of the vigour of their race, they felt a certain aloofness from this eagle born in the hencoop.

A son cannot speak adequately about his father. There is a certain impiety in formulating sentences about the author of our being and the moulder of our character; though I cannot express the truth of what I feel, it is possible for me to state the mature opinion that my father typified an exceptionally interesting moment of English evolution. He had abandoned the narrow standpoint of Nonconformist or Evangelical orthodoxy, but he retained what was ethically valuable in the religious tradition. He opened his mind to every influence of knowledge and of culture. He relinquished nothing which affected character and principle. In this way he formed a link between the past and the future, attaining to an almost perfect harmony of conservative and liberal ideas. I, the product of a younger period, regard his attitude with reverent admiration. I have been unable to preserve the equilibrium which he maintained, and which appears to me the flower of human virtue. He helped to liberate my spirit, and, starting from the point which he reached, I have been carried further, not so wisely, not to a result so mellow, so morally and æsthetically beautiful. We dare not regret the inevitable, we are impotent to strive with fate. What I am, is what I had to be. But these reflections do not prevent me from recording the conviction that my father was a man of plastically noble character—plastic in the sense ascribed by Hegel to that word—all functions of his nature meeting in a well-strung symphony which made the powerful yet kindly-tempered personality he had.

His constitution favoured him, perhaps. The serious obligations of his life, the duty of working for his family, helped him. And it must not be forgotten that his self-emancipation from the narrowing conditions of his earlier environment, absorbed a large part of his energy. This is no deduction from his merit. It only serves to show, how natural bias and circumstance contributed to make him the fine specimen of English manhood, in the second half of the nineteenth century, which he became.

How I, the son of such a father, came to be what I am, is a problem I must leave to Francis Galton and the students of heredity. Of my propensities, of my sensibilities, of my audacities, he had no share. They were inborn in me.

Two of his near relatives had helped to form my father's character; these were his own father and his great-uncle, Dr. John Addington, a courtly and stately old gentleman, who lived at Ashley Court on the northern side of Bristol. It was mainly by Dr. Addington's advice that my father settled in that city. Dr. Addington belonged to the small school of advanced thinkers, who formed themselves in England on the type of the French philosophers and Hume and Hartley. He boasted of having been present at the Bastille dinner. He was a friend of Rammohoun Roy. He corresponded with the leading Liberals in politics, religion, and philosophy. His carriage, conversation, and deportment combined aristocratic hauteur with the sarcastic wit and frankness of expression which characterised professed freethinkers at the beginning of the nineteenth century. This was remarkable in the case of a man whose father was a non-juror and Nonconformist minister, who claimed kinship with Lord Sidmouth, and who had acquired a moderate fortune by the practice of medicine in London. He had no children ; and after his decease this branch of the Addington family was represented by my father.

The gradual emergence from narrow intellectual conditions in a Puritan pedigree is always interesting. We see the process going forward in the case of Quakers, and of Dissenters who have acquired importance at the present time. The annals of my own family furnish an excellent example. When I broke up our home on Clifton Hill in 1881, I deliberately burned the correspondence of five generations—that is to say, the letters of my grandfather and of his immediate ancestors through four descents. I had two good reasons at the time for doing this. One was that I did not know where to deposit these bulky documents, some of which contained matters too personal for publication or for transference to any public library. The other was that the perusal of them left a deeply painful impression on my mind. The intense pre-occupation with so-called spiritual interests; the suffocating atmosphere of a narrow sect resembling that of a close parlour; the grim, stern dealing with young souls not properly convinced of sin; the unnatural admixture of this other-worldliness with mundane marrying and giving in marriage and professional affairs, caught me by the throat and throttled me. I could not bear to think that my own kith and kin, the men and women who had made me, lived in this haunted chamber, from which "eternity's sunrise," the flooding radiance of Nature's light, seemed ruthlessly excluded. So I committed an act of vandalism, whereof I am now half-repentant and half-proud. No doubt those documents, carefully sifted by successive members of the family from other papers of less moment in their eyes, epitomised the spiritual archives of a race who scorned their ancient or decaying gentry, and who boasted—I remember the phrase in one of those letters—that they had been "renowned for their piety through two centuries." This, by the way, was written by the head of the family about 1830 to one of its younger members, who innocently asked for information about such insignificant trifles as Sir Richard Fitz-Simon, K.G., temp. Edward III., and the quartering of Mainwaring. He was

told that seats and crowns in the heavenly Jerusalem had far more value, and were far more
difficult to win, than coronets or garters bestowed
by kings, or than arms inscribed upon the heralds'
books by Clarencieux. An undoubted truth. The
man who penned those sentences of scornful rebuke
displayed no ignoble pride. Yet he was proud and
stubborn to the backbone in his unworldliness;
and if I have any grit in me, I owe it to this
proud humility of my forefathers.

This brings me to speak of my grandfather,
John Symonds of Oxford, who was the first to
react against the hereditary narrowness of the
family creed. Remaining a Dissenter, he became
in mature life what may best be described as a
Christian Stoic. He was a good Latin scholar,
and wrote voluminous diaries and meditations in
the style of Seneca. Not an elastic or optimistic
nature—on the contrary, rigid and circumscribed,
depressed by a melancholy temperament and by
the gloom of Calvinism, which assumed in him
the form of philosophical fatalism. This compara-
tive disengagement from sectarian doctrine, combined with the study of the classics and of English
thought—from Bacon through Locke to Hume and
Adam Smith—formed a type of character well
calculated to start my father upon his own path of
emancipation. A severe uncompromising sense of
duty, a grim incapability of any transactions with
the world, marked my grandfather out as the lineal

and loyal descendant of his Puritan ancestors. These moral qualities were transmitted to my father. In my father they became transfigured and spiritualised. The advanced ground reached by my father was the soil in which I grew up. These three generations of men—my grandfather, my father, and myself—correspond to the succession of Æschylus, Sophocles, and Euripides, to the transition from early pointed Gothic, through Decorated, to Flamboyant architecture. *Medio tutissimus ibis.* The middle term of such series is always superior to the first, and vastly superior to the third. How immeasurably superior my father was to me—as a man, as a character, as a social being, as a mind— I feel, but I cannot express.

My grandfather left Oxford and came to live with his daughter, Mrs. James Nash, at Cossington Villa, Clifton. He soon proposed to teach me Latin. I began to learn this language before I was five years old, and can remember declining some Latin nouns to my father on my fifth birthday. It was rather a long walk for a little boy from Berkeley Square to Cossington Villa, which stood in its own garden not far from Buckingham Chapel.

The grammar used for instructing me in Latin was, so far as I can remember, one by Arnold. When we came to the doctrine of the potential and subjunctive moods, I could not comprehend the rules, and refused to learn them by rote. Considering that I was an extremely docile and timid child, this argued an extraordinary amount of intellectual repugnance.

My grandfather declared that he would not teach me any more; I was incorrigibly stupid or obstinate. I had to write an apologetical letter, which I remember doing with mighty solemnity and sense of importance, propped up on cushions at a big high table. On these conditions he took me back as a dull but repentant pupil.

The difficulty of grasping abstract statements made learning very irksome to me. Some branches of knowledge I wholly failed to acquire. Among these was arithmetic. I could not do the sums, because the rules, which were never properly explained, oppressed me with a nightmare sense of unreality. Even when I got hold enough upon them to apply them, I was sceptical about the result. The whole process seemed to me like a piece of jugglery, which offended my intelligence. Euclid, on the other hand, offered no obstacles. Geometry gave me pleasure by its definite objectivity, clear chains of reasoning, and direct appeal to the senses. I could remember the figures, and work a theme or problem out with ease. I always learned best through the eyes, and I am convinced that a tutor who discerned this bias in me for the concrete could have taught me anything in mathematics.

As time went on, I used to take country walks with my grandfather and cousins. What he told me then—the names of plants, and the Latin words for things we saw—I have never forgotten.

During our excursions on the Downs, nature began to influence my imagination in a peculiar way. When the light of evening was falling, or when we found ourselves in some secluded corner, with a prospect toward the Bristol Channel and the Welsh hills, I passed from the sense of a tangible present into a dream. This was a very definite phase of experience, approaching hypnotism in its character. I partly dreaded the subjugation of my conscious will, and partly looked forward to it with a thrill of exquisite anticipation. I learned to recognise the symptoms of this on-coming mood. But I could not induce it by an act of volition. It needed some specific touch of the external world upon my sensibility.

I am not sure whether this was the rudimentary stage of another form of self-absorption, which afterwards, for many years, recurred at intervals, giving me more of serious disturbance than of pleasure when it came. That was a kind of trance. Suddenly, at church, or in company, or when I was reading, and always, I think, when my muscles were at rest, I felt the approach of the mood. Irresistibly it took possession of my mind and will, lasted what seemed an eternity, and disappeared in a series of rapid sensations, which resembled the awakening from anæsthetic influence. One reason why I disliked this kind of trance was that I could not describe it to myself. I cannot even now find words to render it intelligible, though it is probable that many readers of these pages will recognise the state in question. It consisted in a gradual but swiftly progressive obliteration of space, time, sensation, and the multitudinous factors of experience which seem to qualify what we are pleased to call ourself. In proportion, as these conditions of ordinary consciousness were substracted, the sense of an underlying or essential consciousness acquired intensity. At last nothing remained but a pure, absolute, abstract self. The universe became without form and void of content. But self persisted, formidable in its vivid keenness, feeling the most poignant doubt about reality, ready, as it seemed, to find existence break as breaks a bubble round about it. And what then? The apprehension of a coming dissolution, the grim conviction that this state was the last state of the conscious self, the sense that I had followed the last thread of being to the verge of the abyss, and had arrived at demonstration of eternal Maya or illusion, stirred or seemed to stir me up again. The return to ordinary conditions of sentient existence began by my first recovering the power of touch, and then by the gradual though rapid influx of familiar impressions and diurnal interests. At last I felt myself once more a human being; and though the riddle of what is meant by life remained unsolved, I was thankful for this return from the abyss—this deliverance from so awful an initiation into the mysteries of scepticism.

This trance recurred with diminishing frequency until I reached the age of twenty-eight. Though I have felt its approaches often, I have not experienced it fully now for many years. It served to impress upon my growing nature the phantasmal unreality of all the circumstances which contribute to a merely phenomenal consciousness. Often have I asked myself with anguish, on waking from that formless state of denuded, keenly sentient being, which is the unreality?—the trance of fiery, vacant, apprehensive sceptical self from which I issue, or these surrounding phenomena and habits which veil that inner self and build a self of flesh-and-blood conventionality? Again, are men the factors of some dream, the dream-like unsubstantiality of which they comprehend at such eventful moments? What would happen if the final stage of the trance were reached?—if, after the abduction of phenomenal conditions beyond recovery, the denuded sense of self should pass away in a paroxysm of doubt? Would that be death and entire annihilation? Would it be absorption into the real life beyond phenomena? Could another garment of sensitive experience clothe again that germ of self which recognised the unsubstantiality of all that seemed to make it human?

It is obvious that I am straining the resources of language at my disposal in the effort to adumbrate the exact nature of this trance. I find it impossible, however, to render an adequate account of the initiation. Nor can I properly describe the permanent effect produced upon my mind by the contrast between this exceptional condition of my consciousness and the daily experiences — physical, moral, intellectual, emotional, practical—with which I compared it. Like other psychical states, it lies beyond the province of language.

When I first read Pindar, his exclamation—

ἐπάμεροι· τὶ δέ τις; τὶ δ'οὔ τις; σκιᾶς ὄναρ ἄνθρωπος;

"Things of a day. What is a man? What is a man not?
A dream about a shadow is man"—

awoke in me reverberating echoes. This was for me no casual poet's question, no figure of rhetoric let fall to point the moral of man's fleeting day on earth. The lyric cry pierced to the very core and marrow of my soul.

When I was eight years old, my father sent me to a tutor, the Rev. William Knight. This gentleman kept a school. His house in Buckingham Villas (now part of the Pembroke Road) was at least a mile from Berkeley Square. I used to perform the journey, going and coming, four times in a working day. The institution was probably not worse than the majority of private schools. How bad it was I dare not say. Mr. Knight had little to do with the teaching. The boys—several of them sons of Somersetshire gentlemen, others like me, day scholars—did pretty much as they liked. Bullying of a peculiarly offensive sort took place there. But I am bound to say that I was neither bullied nor contaminated in my morals. I think that Mr. Knight, owing special obligations to my father, insisted on my being treated with more consideration than the other pupils.

It was rather a *via dolorosa* from Berkeley Square to Buckingham Villas. The road led through a street of poor people, among whom I became interested in a family of mulattoes, the children of a negro sailor and a Bristol woman. A narrow alley led to the Roman Catholic Church, then half finished; and this alley was always adorned on both sides with obscene or blasphemous *graffiti*. Emerging at the top, I passed through some dismal, decaying terraces and villas, and then took a straight line along decent dwelling-houses, with a great field on the right hand, until I eventually arrived at the school. The whole line of march recurs to my mind's eye; but I am characteristically oblivious of the names of places.

Just before I reached Buckingham Villas there was a tall house on the right, cresting the rising slope, and looking down upon the large field I have mentioned. I think it was also called Buckingham something. There was a grating in the basement floor of this house, which gave light to a cellar of some sort. I fancied that a magician lived in the semi-subterranean apartment. I used to see him squatting by a fire upon the floor, raking up embers, and stirring ingredients in a caldron. He became a positive reality to my imagination; but I never attempted to converse with him, and did not feel sure whether he was a wizard or an alchemist. The alternative puzzled me.

About this figment of my fancy I spoke freely at home, and proposed to take my sisters to watch the magician at work. My aunt, however, looked seriously on the matter, and requested me not to tell lies. The same thing happened when I arrived one evening in a state of considerable excitement at home, and declared that I had been attacked by robbers on the way. The artlessness of my narration must have proved its worthlessness. I was soundly scolded. Yet neither the magician nor the robber are less real to my memory than most of the people who surrounded me at that time. It was right to treat me harshly about such waking dreams. I learned in this way to distinguish what we call true from what we call false.

To my father I owe a debt of gratitude for his sympathetic treatment of quite a different occurrence. I sold my Latin Dictionary to a comrade called Emerson for sixpence. When I was asked at home where I had lost it, I said that I did not know. Stings of conscience made me speedily confess the truth, and I did so with no little trepidation to my father in his library. He spoke gently and wisely on the topic, pointing out that lies were not only wrong but ignoble. What he then said touched my sense of honour, and struck my intelligence. I was thenceforward scrupulous about telling the exact truth.

The occurrences I have recently related seem to me important in the development of my character. They saved me from becoming a visionary, to which I was too prone by temperament. They forced me to draw a sharp line of distinction between what happened in my dreaming self and what impinged upon my senses from outside. They revealed the all-importance of veracity—the duty and the practical utility of standing on a common ground of fact with average men and women in affairs of life. In other words, I became capable of discriminating between fancies and things, and I learned to abhor and scorn mendacity.

CHAPTER II

BOYHOOD

Change to Clifton Hill House.—Home life.—Evening readings.—
Clifton described.—Its effect upon his growth.—Early educa-
tion.—At his tutor's.—Learns Greek.—Composes English verses.
—The legend of Apollo.—Boyish games.—Illness.—Sent to Tor-
quay.—Fishing for sea-weed.—His governess, Mdlle. Girard.—
Sleep-walking.—Recurrent dreams.—Early perceptions of beauty.
—Greek statuary and picture-books. — Landscape. — Love of
Nature.—Mr. Vigor's portrait.—Sensitiveness.—His psychical
condition.—Mdlle. Girard's account of him.

UP[1] to this point I have recorded memories of my
life before the age of ten, admitting only those
which can be referred by some clear local indication
to that period. I now pass from childhood to the
first period of boyhood. The transition is defined
by the change of residence from 7 Berkeley Square
to Clifton Hill House.

This stage, which extended from June 1851 until
May 1854, was one of greatly increased happiness.
My health improved. We were nearer the country,
and our new house satisfied my sense of what is
beautiful. I had a pony and began to ride. This
I enjoyed, though I did not become a good horseman, mainly, I think, because I was allowed to go

out riding alone before I had been trained by a groom.

My youngest sister Charlotte and I became great friends, and we both profited by the companionship of her governess, Mdlle. Sophie Girard, of whom I shall have more to say. We three formed a little coterie within the household.

Hitherto, so far as people were concerned, my inner life had been almost a blank.

It is a great misfortune for a boy to lose his mother so early as I did; and my father was so busy in his profession that he had very little time to bestow on me. Yet even in my childhood his strong and noble character, his sense of honour and duty, and his untiring energy impressed me. The drives I took with him were not thrown away. In the evenings also, when he had a spare hour, he used to read to us, choosing ballads, portions of Scott's poems, passages from Hood's "Miss Kilmansegg," stories from Hans Andersen, adapted to our intelligence. These readings stimulated my literary instincts.

So far as my father was concerned, I grew up in an atmosphere of moral tension, and came to regard work as the imperative duty imposed on human beings.

It was a great day for all of us when my father announced, on one June morning, that he had bought Clifton Hill House, and drove us in his carriage to visit our future home.

This house had been built by a Bristol merchant
named Paul Fisher. It carries on its garden front
the date 1747, together with the coat of Fisher em-
paling what other arms I know not.   Paul Fisher
himself sleeps in Clifton churchyard, and the vestibule to what is now the parish church contains his
defrauded and neglected monument.

At the time when this substantial piece of early
Georgian architecture was erected Clifton still remained a country village.   Paul Fisher's habitation
had no rivals in antiquity but the Church House and
the Manor House, none in stateliness except the
fine suburban villa of the Goldney family.   At this
period—a period anterior to "Humphrey Clinker"
and "Evelina," novels which have made the Hot
Wells of Clifton famous in literature—Bristol merchants had begun to plant a few rare mansions
in the immediate neighbourhood of the city, while
the overflow of Bath fashion crowded the incommo-
dious lodgings which nestled beneath St. Vincent's
rock upon the sheltered banks of Avon.

In those days Clifton must have been beautiful
and wild indeed.   The few houses of the gentry
clustered around the humble village church—not
that ugly building which now perpetuates the bad
taste of the incipient Gothic revival, the dismal
piety of the Simeon trustees—but a rustic West
of England chapel, with narrow windows and
low sloping roof.   Grass-fields spread around this
church, open to clear heavens and pure breezes

from the Bristol Channel. The meadows merged
in heathy downs, stretching along the Avon at the
height of some three hundred feet above the water,
until the land again broke into copse and pasture,
sweeping with gentle crests and undulations to the
estuary of the Severn.

At a considerable distance below the village slept
the great city, which next to London was still at
that epoch the most important town in England.
Bristol stands at the junction of the rivers Frome
and Avon, which from this point flow together
through a winding defile of high limestone cliffs to
the Severn. Sea-waters from the Channel washed
its walls, and tided merchant vessels to the quays of
antique commerce. They brought with them the
sugar and the spices, the tobacco and rare timber of
Virginia and the Indies, to be stored in the ware-
houses of the city wharves. When Paul Fisher
gazed from the windows of his new-built mansion
over an expanse of verdure, he saw the streets
and squares of the red-roofed town threaded with
glittering water-ways, along which lay ocean-going
ships, their tall masts vying with the spires and
towers of clustered churches. St. Mary de Redclyffe's broken spire, the square tower of the Cathedral (that old Abbey Church of the Augustine
monks, enriched by Barons of Berkeley Castle), the
sharp shaft of St. Nicholas, the slender column of
St. Stephen, surveyed from the altitude of Clifton
Hill, were all embedded in groves of limes and

elms and masts with pennons waving from the top.

Clifton Hill House, at the present day, turns a grim grey frontage to the road. It is a ponderous square mansion, built for perpetuity, with walls three feet in thickness, faced with smooth Bath stone. But, passing to the southern side, one still enjoys the wonderful prospect which I have described. Time has done much to spoil the landscape. Mean dwellings have clustered round the base of Brandon Hill, and crept along the slopes of Clifton. The city has extended on the further side towards Bed-minster. Factory chimneys, with their filth and smoke, have saddened the simple beauty of the town and dulled the brightness of its air. But the grand features of Nature remain. The rolling line of hills from Lansdown over Bath, through Dundry with its solitary church-tower to Ashton guarding the gorge of Avon, presents a free and noble space for cloud shadows, a splendid scene for the display of sunrise. The water from the Severn still daily floods the river-beds of Frome and Avon ; and the ships still come to roost, like ocean-birds, beside the ancient churches. Moreover, the trees which Paul Fisher planted in his pleasaunce have grown to a great height, so that a sea of many-coloured foliage waves beneath the windows of his dwelling-house.

On that eventful June morning, I entered the solemn front door, traversed the echoing hall, vaulted and floored with solid stone, and emerged upon the garden at the further end. An Italian double flight of balustraded steps, largely designed, gives access to the gravelled terrace whieh separates the house from the lawn. For us it was like passing from the prose of fact into the poetry of fairyland.

The garden, laid out by Paul Fisher in 1747, had not been altered in any important particular, except that a large piece of it was cut away at the bottom to build a row of houses called Bellevue Terrace. Four great tulip-trees, covered with golden blossoms, met our eyes at four points of vantage in the scheme. Between them, on either hand, rose two gigantic copper-beeches, richly contrasted with the bright green of the tulip-trees. Eight majestic elms, four on each side, guarded the terrace. They dated from an older period than the foundation of the dwelling-house. The grove, which clustered round the central grass-plot, was further diversified by ilexes and mulberry trees, wych-elms and pear trees, a fragile ailanthus and a feathery acacia, with cypresses from the black boughs of which the clambering roses fell in showers. Sycamores, beeches, and walnuts formed a leafy background to these choicer growths, and masked the ugly frontage of Bellevue.

Two ponds, quaintly enclosed with wired railings, interrupted at proper intervals the slope of soft green turf. Each had a fountain in its midst, the one shaped like a classic urn, the other a Cupid

seated on a dolphin and blowing a conch. When
the gardener made the water rise for us from those
fountains, it flashed in the sunlight, tinkled on the
leaves and cups of floating lilies, and disturbed the
dragon-flies and gold fish from their sleepy ways.
Birds were singing, as they only sing in old town
gardens, a chorus of blackbirds, thrushes and
finches. Rooks cawed from the elms above. The
whole scene was ennobled by a feeling of respect,
of merciful abstention from superfluous meddling.
When Paul Fisher planned his pleasure ground he
meant it, according to the taste of that period, to be
artificial, and yet to vie with Nature. Now Nature
had asserted her own sway, retaining through that
century of wayward growth something which still
owed its charm to artifice.

Although I am speaking of my home, and must
of necessity be partial, I do not think I violate
the truth when I say, that this garden possessed
a special grace and air of breeding, which lent
distinction to the dignified but rather stolid house
above. It was old enough to have felt "the unimaginable touch of time," and yet not old or
neglected enough to have fallen into decay. Left
alone, it had gained a character of wildness, and
yet kind touches had been given which preserved
it from squalor. Wealthy folk had always inhabited
the mansion, and their taste respected the peculiar
beauty of the place. Afterwards, at New College
and St. John's, among the Oxford College gardens,

I recognised the same charm. But the distinctive feature of the Clifton Hill garden was that the ground fell rapidly away from the terrace and the house, so that the windows above enjoyed a vast prospect across its undulating roof of verdure to the towered city, the glimpses of the Avon, the sea-going ships, and, far away beyond all that, to the hills of Bath and the long stretch of Dundry. It was a remarkable home for a dreamy town-bred boy of ten to be transported into.

On that eventful morning, the air hung heavy with a scent of hidden musk. The broad flower-beds upon the terrace and along the walls were a tangle of old-fashioned herbs in bloom—mulberry-coloured scabius, love-in-idleness, love-in-a-mist, love-lies-bleeding, devil-in-a-bush, holly-hocks, carnations, creeping-jenny, damask and cabbage, and York and Lancaster roses. The mingled perfume of musk and rose pervades my memory when I think of that day; and when I come by accident upon the scent of musk in distant places, I am again transported to the fairyland of boyhood. The throat-notes of thrush and blackbird, the music of tinkling fountains, the drowsy rhythm of hammers struck on timber in the city dockyards, blend in my recollection with pure strong slumberous summer sunlight and rich colours.

There was much in the mansion itself which satisfied my craving for architectural solidity and stateliness. The pediment of stone above our front-door in Berkeley Square had, as I have already mentioned, consoled my childish senses. The style of that detail was here expanded through the whole substantial edifice. The rusticated work upon the spacious massive basements, the balustraded stair-cases descending to the terrace, the huge balls of Bath stone placed at proper intervals upon the lower line of office-buildings, the well-proportioned if too lofty rooms, the dignified waste of useful space in the long passages; all these characteristics of the Georgian manner gave satisfaction to my instinct of what is liberal in art, though of course they could not feed my fancy. I did not then reflect how gloomy that square house might be, how prosaic the inspiration of its builder was, how like prisons the upper rooms with their high windows are, and how melancholy the vast prospect over city, sky, and stretching hills would afterwards appear to me in moods of weariness.

Then there were stables with hay-lofts, and a paved yard, where my father generally kept eight horses; a summer house, upon the wall of which vines clambered and nectarines ripened; a kitchen-garden full of strawberries and currant-bushes, apricots and plums and peaches. The top of the house itself formed a capital playground for us children. A rambling attic, which we called the loft, stretched away into mysterious recesses and dark corners. In some of these obscure chambers cisterns were hidden, which supplied the house with rain water;

from the narrow windows of others we could clamber
out upon the roof, the sloping gables of which were
covered with solid lead, and fenced about with broad
slabs of rough clean chiselled stone. From this
height the eye swept spaces of the starry heavens at
night; by day town, tower, and hill, wood, field,
and river lay bathed in light, and flecked with
shadows of the clouds.

The transition from Berkeley Square to Clifton
Hill House contributed greatly, I am sure, to make
me what I am. I cannot, of course, say what I
should have become had we remained in our old
home; but I am certain that the new one formed
my character and taste at a period when youth is
most susceptible. My latent æsthetic sensibilities
were immediately and powerfully stimulated.

Some years after the time of which I am writing, I brought a Balliol friend to stay with me at
Clifton. On taking leave at the end of the visit, he
remarked, " I understand you now, and know what
it is that made you what you are." He was right, I
believe. Places exercise commanding influence in
the development of certain natures. Mine is one of
them, and Clifton, with the house we lived in, had a
magic of its own. Thirty-nine years have elapsed
since I first went to live at Clifton Hill. The place
has changed to such an extent that any one who
knows it now might be excused for thinking I am
rhapsodising. He must bear in mind, however,
that there were few buildings then between the

parish church and Durdham Downs. The suburb
which has grown up round the College was a tract
of fields, at the end of which lay the Zoological
Gardens. Pembroke Road formed part of a narrow
footway between quickset hedges, bearing the
agreeable title of Gallows Lane. The Tyburn of
old Bristol occupied a plot of ground at the head
of it toward the downs. Coal-smoke had not contaminated the air to any appreciable extent. The
sea and river-fogs of November were fleecy-white.
No ironworks defaced the vale of Ashton. The
thousands of middle-class houses, which now stretch
from Clifton Church to Redland, and which are
crawling on from Redland to Westbury, were then
represented by two or three straggling terraces, by
here and there a villa enclosed in its own crofts
and gardens, by the long line of miscellaneous
dwellings called Whiteladies Road, which extended
from the top of Park Street to the sign of the
Black Boy, and there abruptly stopped before the
silence and the solitude of the windy down. The
downs too were wild, heathy, and covered in the
spring with flowers; not, as now, a kind of suburban
park, but a real wilderness, a pleasure-ground for
the romantic soul.

My tutor, the Rev. William Knight, gave up
his school, and came to live at no great distance
from our house. He occupied a dreary abode in
Wetherell Place; the outer walls rough-cast and
painted a dull lilac; standing in a stuffy plot of

shrubbery between a blank wall to the front and a tall row of houses to the back. How any reasonable human being could in Clifton—the very essence of which place was poetry in some form or another—whether of the ancient town beside it, or of the free nature on its northern borders—have selected to abide in Wetherell Place, that region of shabby-genteel prose and stifling dulness, I am not prepared to say. Probably there were economical reasons, and social inducements, together with conveniences of contiguity to the Blind Asylum and St. Michael's Church, which determined Mr. Knight in his choice.

Mr. Knight could not be called an ideal tutor. He was sluggish, and had no sympathy for boys. Yet he was a sound scholar of the old type, and essentially a gentleman. He let me browse, much as I liked, about the pastures of innocuous Greek and Latin literature. He taught me to write Latin verses with facility. If I did not acquire elegance, that was the defect of my own faculty for style. I think he might have grounded me better in grammar than he did; and it would have been an incalculable advantage to me if he had been able to direct my keen, though latent, enthusiasm for books. In this respect, I owe him one only debt of gratitude. We were reading the sixth book of the Æneid. He noticed what a deep hold the description of Elysium took on my imagination, and lent me Warburton's " Divine Legation of Moses." A chapter in that book about the Mysteries opened dim and shadowy vistas for my dreaming thoughts. I cannot remember any other instance of my tutor's touching the real spring of thirst for knowledge in my nature. For the rest, he took care that I should understand the Odes of Horace and be capable of reproducing their various metres. This gave me a certain advantage when I came to Harrow.

With Mr. Knight I read a large part of the Iliad. When we came to the last books I found a passage which made me weep bitterly. It was the description of Hermes, going to meet Priam, disguised as a mortal:

βῆ δ'ἰέναι κούρῳ αἰσυμνητῆρι ἐοικὼς,
πρῶτον ὑπηνήτῃ, τοῦ περ χαριερτάτη ἥβη.

The Greek in me awoke to that simple, and yet so splendid vision of young manhood, "In the first budding of the down on lip and chin, when youth is at her loveliest." The phrase had all Greek sculpture in it, and drew my tears forth. I had none to spare for Priam prostrate at the feet of his son's murderer; none for Andromache bidding a last farewell to Hector of the waving plumes. These personages touched my heart, and thrilled a tragic chord. But the disguised Hermes, in his prime and bloom of beauty, unlocked some deeper fountains of eternal longing in my soul.

Somewhat later, I found another line which im-

THE·TERRACE·CLIFTON·HILL·HOUSE·

pressed me powerfully, and unsealed hidden wells of different emotion. It was in the Hippolytus of Euripides:

ἡ γλῶσσ᾽ ὀμώμοχ᾽ ἡ δὲ φρὴν ἀνώμοτος.

The sense of casuistry and criticism leapt into being at that touch. I foresaw, in that moment, how pros and cons of moral conduct would have to be debated, how every thesis seeks antithesis and resolution in the mental sphere.

These were but vague awakenings of my essential self. For the most part, I remained inactive, impotent, somnambulistic, touching life at no edged point, very slowly defining the silhouette of my eventual personality.

Walking to and fro between Clifton Hill and Wetherell Place, I used to tell myself long classic stories, and to improvise nonsense verses on interminable themes. The vehicle I used was chiefly blank verse or trochaics. I delighted my sense of rhythm with the current of murmured sound. The subject I chose for these peripatetic rhapsodies was the episode of young Apollo, in his sojourn among mortals, as the hind of King Admetus. What befell him there, I expanded into nebulous epics of suffering and love, and sorrow-dimmed deity involved with human sympathies. I declaimed the verse *sotto voce* as I walked. But now I can recall no incidents in the long poem, which, like a river, flowed daily, and might for ever have flowed on.

The kernel of my inspiration was that radiant figure of the young Apollo, doomed to pass his time with shepherds, serving them, and loving them. A luminous haze of yearning emotion surrounded the god. His divine beauty penetrated my soul and marrow. I stretched out my arms to him in worship. It was I alone who knew him to be Olympian, and I loved him because he was a hind who went about the stables milking cows. I was, in fact, reading myself into this fable of Apollo, and quite unconsciously, as I perceive now, my day-dreams assumed an objective and idealised form. Indeed, this legend of the discovered Phœbus casts vivid light upon my dumbly growing nature.

It is singular that a boy should have selected any legend so dim and subtle for treatment in the way I have described. But, what is far more curious, it seems that I was led by an unerring instinct to choose a myth foreshadowing my peculiar temperament and distant future. I have lived to realise that obscure vision of my boyhood. Man loves man, and Nature; the pulse of human life, the contact with the genial earth are the real things. Art must ever be but a shadow for truly puissant individualities. In this way I have grown to think and feel. And just for this reason, my boyish pre-occupation with the legend of Apollo in the stables of Admetus has psychological significance. It shows how early and instinctively I apprehended the truth, by the light of which I still live, that a disguised god, communing with mortals, loving mortals and beloved by them, is more beautiful, more desirable, more enviable, than the same god uplifted on the snow-wreaths of Olympus, or the twin peaks of muse-haunted Parnassus.

Rightly or wrongly, the principles involved in that boyish vision of Phœbus, the divine spirit serving and loving in plain ways of pastoral toil, have ended by fashioning my course. It has become my object to assimilate culture to the simplest things in man's life, and to assume from human sympathy of the crudest kind fuel and fire for the vivifying of ideas. By means of this philosophy I have been enabled to revive from mortal sickness, and what is perhaps more, to apprehend the religious doctrine of democracy, the equality and homogeneity of human beings, the divinity enclosed in all. It was not, therefore, by accident, I think, that the prolonged daydream of Apollo in exile haunted me during my somnambulistic boyhood. Temperaments of my stamp come to themselves by broodings upon fancies which prefigure the destiny in store for them, and are in fact the symbols of their soul.

I took little pleasure in athletic sports of any kind. To ramble over the downs and through the woods was enough for me. I hated the exertion, rivalry, and noise of games. Want of muscular vigour and timidity combined to make me solitary. Yet

I could run well, and jump standing the height of my own shoulders.   I liked riding also, but was neither a bold nor expert horseman.

What I most enjoyed was leading a band of four boys, my cousins, in wild scrambles over Durdham Downs, and on the rocks that overhung the Avon. We played at defending and attacking castles, which were located upon points of vantage in the gully near the sea-walls and the steep descent of cliff beneath St. Vincent's rock.   No harm came of these adventures, although we defied each other to deeds of daring in places where a fall would have been perilous exceedingly.   Tired out and panting with this kind of exercise, I used to fling myself upon some grassy ledge among the lady's-bed-straw and blue hare-bells, watching the ships coming floating down the Avon or the jackdaws chattering in their ivy-curtained crannies.

For everything which I took up, whether study or amusement, I showed a languid dilettante interest, pursuing it without energy or perseverance. Thus I played with an electrical machine and microscope, collected flowers and dried them, caught butterflies and pinned them upon corks; but I was far too dreamy and impatient to acquire any solid knowledge of natural science.   I crammed my memory with the names of infusorial animalcules, sea-weeds, wild-flowers—a great many of which still lie in the lumber-room of my brain. I got to know the aspects of such things, and

enjoyed the places where I went to find my specimens. But of animal or vegetable physiology I
learned nothing. One reason was, perhaps, that
I had no one to teach me and no attractive text-
books. The real secret of my inefficiency lay,
however, in want of will and liking for accurate
study. I was a weakling in mind and body, only
half awake.

Early in the winter of one year I fell ill of
chronic diarrhœa. To this I had been subject at
intervals from my earliest infancy; and now I
poisoned myself by drinking some cheap efferves-
cing mixtures. My father sent me to stay with
friends at Torquay. They lived in a little cottage
with a front garden full of sweet-smelling violets,
fuchsias, and shrub veronicas in bloom. I date a
considerable mental progress from this visit. There
I learned the beauty of the sea—low tides and
pools upon the shore of Torbay. Dr. Tetley used
to drive me about the country in his carriage; and
a diminutive naturalist was very kind to me. He
took me with him out upon the reefs to gather sea-
weeds. I made a huge collection of such things.

Even now I can remember the solemnity with
which my friend exclaimed, when I hauled some
spidery black weed out of a pool, " I do believe
that you have captured Gigantea Taedii." All
through the remainder of the winter and spring,
after I returned to Clifton, hampers sent by a Torbay
fisherman used to arrive stuffed with the wrack of

the shore.   Charlotte, Mdlle. Sophie Girard and
I, divided the slimy mass into three equal por-
tions, floated our booty in three separate tubs, and
fished with eager fingers for Delesseria Sanguinea,
Padina Pavonia, or a fine specimen of Plocaria
Coccinea.

It was on my return from this visit to Torquay,
that I first set eyes on Mdlle. Girard.   She had
arrived in my absence to be my sisters' governess.
They came back from a walk while I was standing
in the hall, between the dining-room and drawing-
room doors.   Her bright face, rosy with the freshness
of the open air, her laughing eyes and abundance of
glossy yellow hair made a very pleasant impression
on me.   I felt at once that she would be a great
addition to our home circle ; and this in truth she
was, far more than I could then imagine.   She
taught me German ; the little German I know I
owe entirely to her.   She had a gift for teaching,
and was the first person from whom I consciously
learned anything whatsoever.

About this time I began to walk in my sleep.   It
seemed to me that a corpse lay beside me in the
bed.   To escape from it, I got up and roamed
about the house ; but there were corpses standing
in the doorways as I hurried through the long dark
corridors.   One night I wandered into the loft, and
was walking straight into an open cistern which
collected the rain-water from the roof, when I felt
the hands of a great angel with outspread wings laid

upon my shoulders. For a moment I woke up, and saw the moonlight glinting on the water through some cranny. Then I fell asleep again, and returned unconsciously to bed. Next morning my shins and thighs were badly bruised, and the footman, who slept in the loft, had a mysterious tale to tell, of a white being who had moved about the furniture and boxes. It appears that the stupid fellow had allowed himself actually to be shoved by me, bed and all, from the door through which I passed into the remote corner where the cistern lay.

After this occurrence, my father had me tied into bed by one of my ankles every night. When the corpse came to expel me, I floundered on the floor until I woke and crept back shivering between the sheets. This Spartan discipline effectually cured me of sleep-walking. A recurrent dream of quite a new sort now visited my slumbers. It was the beautiful face of a young man, with large blue eyes and waving yellow hair, which emitted a halo of misty light. He bent down gazing earnestly till he touched me. Then I woke and beheld the aureole fading away into darkness.

Much might be written about the self-revealing influence of dreams and the growth of the inner man in sleep. The vision of ideal beauty, thus presented to me in slumber, symbolised spontaneous yearnings deeply seated in my nature, and prepared me to receive many impressions of art and literature.

A photograph of the Praxitelean Cupid— ·

> That most perfect of antiques
> They call the Genius of the Vatican,
> Which seems too beauteous to endure itself
> In this mixed world—

taught me to feel the secret of Greek sculpture. I used to pore for hours together over the divine loveliness, while my father read poetry aloud to us in the evenings. He did not quite approve, and asked me why I would not choose some other statue, a nymph or Hebe. Following the impressions made by Shakespeare's Adonis and the Homeric Hermes, blending with the dream I have described, and harmonising with my myth of Phœbus in the sheepcotes, this photograph strengthened the ideal I was gradually forming of adolescent beauty. It prepared me to receive the Apoxyomenos and Marlowe's Leander, the young men of Plato, and much besides. I was certainly a rather singular boy. But I suppose, if other people wrote down the history of their mental growth with the same frankness and patience, I should not stand alone.

What I really wanted at this period was some honest youth for comrade. My equals repelled me. As it was, I lived into emotion through the brooding imagination, and nothing is more dangerous, more unhealthy than this.

I was very fond of picture-books, and drew a great deal from Raphael, Flaxman, and Retzsch.

Our house was well stocked with engravings, photographs, copies of Italian pictures and illustrated works upon Greek sculpture ; Lasinio's Campo Santo of Pisa, Sir William Hamilton's vases, the Museo Borbonico, and the two large folios issued by the Dilettante Society were among my chief favourites. But I carried my habitual indolence and irresolution into these studies. I had no artistic originality, and would not take the trouble to learn to draw well. We went to an art-school just then established in Bristol. The hexagons, cubes, patterns they gave me to copy filled me with repugnance.

It is probable that the abundance of art material at home was not an unmixed good. It certainly familiarised me with a large variety of masterpieces, and taught me to discriminate styles. But when I came to study critically, my mind was stocked with a mass of immature associations and imperfect memories. The sharp impression made on me by Botticelli, Tintoretto, Signorelli, Mantegna, Bellini, Luini, and Gaudenzio Ferrari, during my earliest Italian journeys, may be ascribed to the fact that their works were almost entirely unrepresented in my father's library. We had one piece of Signorelli's, by the way. It was Macpherson's photograph of the Fulminati at Orvieto. It had come by accident, I think, and nobody knew what it represented or who had painted it. I used to brood over the forcible, spasmodic vigour of this tragic group—feeling it quite different, far more penetrative, than anything in Raphael or Michael Angelo. Yet, Duppa's large studies from the Last Judgment in the Sistine were well known to me. Toschi's admirable engravings of Correggio's frescoes at Parma, which were sent to us at intervals by Colnaghi, as they appeared, taught me to appreciate the melodic suavity of design. I always connected them with the airs from Mozart's Masses which my sister Edith used to play.

My sensibility to natural beauty meanwhile expanded. The immersion in the mystery of landscape, which I have already described, yielded to more conscious pleasure and a quicker sympathy. Yet I grew but slowly, and disengaged myself with difficulty from the narcotism of my mental faculties.

When the family was gone to bed, I spent hours alone in my bedroom at the north-east angle of the house, watching the clouds and mists of autumn drifting and recomposing their flying forms around the moon, high up above the city lamps.

I woke at dawn to see the sunrise flood the valley, touch the steeples of the town, shimmer upon the water where ships lay, and glance along the stirless tree-tops of the garden, green in dewy depths below me.

One morning in particular I can remember. On the preceding evening we had picked autumn crocuses in the fields by Westbury. The flowers were placed in a great bowl outside my bedroom door. The sunrise woke me, and I opened the door to look again upon them. A broad, red ray of light fell full upon their lilac chalices, intensifying and translating into glowing amethyst each petal.

Winter sunrise provided pageants of more fiery splendour. From the dark rim of Dundry Hill, behind which the sun was journeying, striving to emerge, there shot to the clear sapphire zenith shafts of rosy flame, painting the bars of clouds with living fire, and enamelling the floating mists, which slowly changed and shifted across liquid spaces of orange, daffodil, and beryl.

Lightning, in thunderstorms of summer nights, made the wide world beneath me visible by flashes; deluged the hissing rain with palpitating whiteness; brought into metallic clearness leaf by leaf of the intensely verdant trees; restored a momentary scarlet to the geraniums and verbenas in the flowerbeds.

The evening-star, liquid, dilated, in pure skyspaces above the churchyard gate, or tangled in the distant trees of Ashton, drew my soul out with longings such as melodies of Mozart excite.

Once there was a comet, a thin rod of amber white, drowned in the saffron of the sunset, which slowly sank, and disappeared into the western hills beyond the channel.

Mellow mists above the Avon in October, veiling

the russet woods; the masts of great ships slowly moving, scarcely visible through pearly vapour; glimpses of sea-gulls following the barques from their far ocean-journeys; knee-deep wanderings in Leigh Woods' bracken; climbings of the grey S. Vincent's Rocks in search of flowers, where the jackdaws flew frightened from their holes as I came near them; the panoply of silver bloom with which the thorns on Clifton Downs arrayed themselves in May; the ripe horse-chestnuts found in drifts of rustling leaves in autumn;—it is enough to rapidly note such things, which bred in me the sense of natural beauty and the love of colour.

After my recovery from the illness alluded to above, an amateur artist, Mr. Vigor, painted the portrait of me in oil, which now hangs in the dining-room of Sidbury Manor. I used to sit for this picture in his studio, which was a north room of a house in the Royal York Crescent. The likeness was reckoned very good. It shows me to have been a slight boy, with abundance of brown hair, soft brown eyes, delicate hands, and a dreamy expression.

I am sure that I was not personally vain. Inside the family I was twitted so unmercifully with my mealy complexion, snub nose, and broad mouth, that I almost shrank from sight, and felt grateful to people who did not treat me with merited contempt. "O Johnnie, you look as yellow as a lemon this morning." "There you go, with your mouth stretching from ear to ear." These were

some of the amenities, not unkindly meant, and
only expressive of a real concern about my weakly
constitution, which developed in me a morbid and
unamiable self-consciousness.   I had no power of
reacting vigorously, and did not set my back up
or assert myself.   But I nourished a secret resent-
ment, and proud obstinate aloofness.

Physical weakness depressed me.   I had more
nervous vitality than muscular robustness, a small
share of bodily pluck, and no combativeness.   Naturally shy and timid through sensitiveness, though
by no means morally a coward, I sought to be left
alone, convinced that I could interest nobody.

But I developed some disagreeable qualities akin
to vanity.   Being told us that our name was "so
common," the sound of it became odious to my ears.
We were also reminded, and I think rightly, that
the ease in which we lived, the number of servants
who waited on us, the carriages and horses, the large
house and its profuse objects of interest and beauty,
the dinner-parties we gave, and the crowds of distinguished people who visited our home, were all
contingent on my father's professional success.
Doctors, it was added, have no rank in society.
This was very true, and it argued something un-
generous in my nature that I did not accept the
fact cheerfully.

[It should be borne in mind, however, that this
retrospect was written late in Symonds' life, when

many years of internal struggle and physical suffering had thrown a shadow over the past. The picture requires modification, and this it will presently receive from the correspondence of Mdlle. Girard, and, to some extent, from Symonds' own schoolboy letters written from Harrow. Meantime the autobiography has to be followed.]

I[1] soon perceived that my father's character, ability, and many-sided culture separated him from the ordinary run of medical men. He was sought after on his own rare merits by men and women of birth, position, political and social importance. The friend of John Sterling, Frederick Maurice, Myers of Keswick, Lord Lansdowne, Hallam, Jowett, Lord Monteagle, Principal Forbes, Lord Aberdare, Lady Dufferin, Dean Elliot, Sir Edward Strachey, Dr. Carpenter, Dr. Prichard, Sir Montagu Macmurdo, and scores of others I could mention, was an exceptional physician, and his only son enjoyed exceptional advantages in the society of such people.

This did not, however, compensate to my own cross-grained consciousness for the patent facts of my personal drawbacks. I was a physically insignificant boy, with an ill-sounding name, and nothing to rely on in the circumstances of my family. Instead of expanding in the social environment around me, I felt myself at a disadvantage, and early gained the notion that I must work for

[1] Autobiography.

my own place in the world—in fact, that I should
have no place till I had made one for myself. The
result was that, instead of being flattered, I almost
resented the attentions paid me as my father's son,
and was too stupid to perceive how honourable, as
well as valuable, they might be, if I received them
with a modest frankness. I regarded them as acts
of charitable condescension. Thus I passed into
an attitude of haughty shyness, which had nothing
respectable in it, except a sort of self-reliant, world-
defiant pride, a resolution to effectuate myself, and
to win what I wanted by my exertions.

The inborn repugnance to sordid things, which I
have already described as one of my main characteristics, now expressed itself in a morbid sense of
my physical ugliness, common patronymic, undis-
tinguished status, and mental ineffectiveness. I did
not envy the possessors of beauty, strength, birth,
rank, or genius ; but I vowed to raise myself, somehow or other, to eminence of some sort. How this
was to be done, when there were so many difficulties
in the way, I did not see. Without exactly despair-
ing, I felt permanently discouraged.

My ambition took no vulgar form. I felt no
desire for wealth, no mere wish to cut a figure in
society. But I thirsted with intolerable thirst for
eminence, for recognition as a personality. At the
same time I had no self-confidence, no belief in my
intellectual powers. I was only buoyed up by an
undefined instinct that there was stuff in me. Mean-

while, all I could do was to bide my time, and see how things would go, possessing my soul in silence, and wrapping a cloak of reserve about my internal hopes and aims.

The state which I have just described began to define itself during the first period of boyhood. But it grew and strengthened with the following years. It was highly characteristic of my temperament that, powerfully as I felt these cravings, they did not take a very distinct form, and did not stimulate me to any marked activity.

The depressing conviction of my own unattractiveness and inefficiency saved me perhaps from some evil. If I had been a little vainer, I might have become presumptuous, or vulgarly ambitious. I might perhaps, too, have fallen into moral difficulties. As it was, this conviction kept me aloof from companions, and hedged me round with the security of isolation.

The result of my habitual reserve was, that I now dissembled my deepest feelings, and only revealed those sentiments which I knew would pass muster. Without meaning to do so, I came to act a part, and no one knew what was going on inside me. A boy wants a mother at such periods of uneasy fermentation. I was ready enough in writing to communicate such portions of my experience as I chose to exhibit—impenetrably reserved in the depth of myself, rhetorically candid on the surface. My father, not unnaturally, misunderstood this complication.

He afterwards told me that he sent me with un-
doubting confidence to Harrow, because he had no
conception that I was either emotional or passionate.
The unconscious dissimulation I habitually prac-
tised blinded him to the truth. Feeling that I was
growing and must grow in solitude to an end I
could not foresee, which no one could help me to
shape, and which I was myself impotent to determine, I allowed an outer self of commonplace cheerfulness and easy-going pliability to settle like a crust
upon my inner and real character.

Nothing is more difficult than to analyse such
psychological conditions without attributing too
much deliberation and consciousness to what was
mainly a process of spontaneous development. Con-
genital qualities and external circumstance acted
together to determine a mental duality—or shall we
call it a duplicity?—of which I became aware when
it had taken hold upon my nature.

On my twelfth birthday I went up as usual to
kiss my father. He said gravely, "Shake hands;
you are growing too old for kissing." I felt rather
ashamed of having offered what my twelfth birthday rendered unseemly, and took a step upon the
path toward isolation. But there was something
savage in me which accepted the remark with
approval. Henceforth I shrank from the exposure
of emotion, except upon paper, in letters, and in
studied language.

I have drawn a somewhat disagreeable picture of

my early boyhood. It is very probable that I am, to some extent, imparting to this period qualities which were really developed by my intense hatred for life at Harrow. I was bound to do so, because it presents itself under these aspects very vividly to my mind, and because I find that the recollection is confirmed by a poem called "Theodore," which I wrote at Malvern in the autumn of 1862, when the facts of that period were still fresh in my memory.

Still it must not be imagined that I was a moody, discontented, miserable boy. I had high spirits enough, and knew how to make myself agreeable in congenial society. I was talkative, easily interested, ready to find amusement in all sorts of petty things, so long as these were not school-games, and involved no sort of physical competition. The inner growth was so much more important to myself, and still remains so, that I have failed to communicate a proper notion of the whole. Indeed, no one can get outside himself and see what he appears. He only knows himself inside, and knows that aspect only in part.

One thing is certain. I acquired a passionate affection for my home and Clifton, which included my family, although I think I cared for them chiefly as forming parts of the delightful environment.

I believe that Mdlle. Girard would correct the impression I have conveyed through my sincere desire to record the truth of my internal nature;

and at my request she has written the following account of what she remembers of the first year of her life at Clifton.

"MY DEAR JOHNNIE,—I will endeavour to tell you what you ask, and if I fail, it is not from want of remembering but from general stupidity. Those early Clifton days stand in their minutest details before me. I came to you in '53, when I suppose you were twelve. We became friends at once over a bundle of seaweeds you had brought back. You were fond of imparting knowledge, and I was glad to learn, so I very soon became your devoted slave like the rest of the household. We all vied in doing what you would like, and it was a pleasure, a natural instinct, I may say.

"Your temper was perfect, so it was not fear that compelled us to submit to your rule. When you were with us, you never showed the least sign of the despondency that troubled you as soon as you were away from home. You were always joyous and bright, fond of teasing us in the manner of boys, and very fond of sitting on other people and cutting them to pieces. It was the besetting sin of us all, but certainly you were the leader and were merciless to a set of frumps (your name for them), which before each party Charlotte, you, and I were ordered to amuse, while Edith and Maribella devoted themselves to a more select company. When the decisive moment came, no one could have been more suave and fascinating than you were, and the frumps, one and all, adored you and had a happy evening.

"The acquirement of any kind of knowledge seemed equally easy to you, and was pursued until conquered. Natural history and poetry were then your favourite studies, and we never took our walks abroad without either Chaucer or Southey. I speak of quite the earliest days of our acquaintance, when I scarcely knew enough English to understand everything you read to me. How well I remember sitting by the pond at the Zoological Gardens, and your reading Thalaba and the curse of Kehama to me, while Charlotte, who certainly had no liking for the divine Muse then, fed the swans and ran about.

"In those days you liked women's society, and abominated boys. Woe to us if we dared, in order to tease you, express admiration or liking for one of your friends. It was not to be tolerated a moment, nor was it ever meant in earnest, for you certainly were the most delightful, intelligent, cheerful, and amusing companion. Your activity of mind and body were wonderful, and as I was never so happy as when climbing a tree or a precipitous rock, we got on admirably.

"I must not forget to mention that you dearly loved arguing, and that on Sunday evenings when we had tea instead of dinner, and recited a poem to Miss Sykes afterwards, you never missed the opportunity of having a religious argument, and almost reduced her to tears with your inflexible logic. We all thought you must become a barrister, and you actually promised me a handsome Mausoleum when you became Lord Chancellor.

"I do not remember your writing poetry or stories then. Many years after, when we had 'The Constellation,'[1] you wrote of course.

"These impressions relate to the time before you went to Harrow. I can still feel the desolation and the void your absence made. You went off bravely enough the first time, but the second you cried and we cried, and there seemed no pleasure in the house. How dull the schoolroom was until the holidays.

"Now, I hope, you will gather some notion of what you were then. I could go on for a long time in the same strain. Don't you really remember what you were like in the least?"

[1] A magazine compiled by the members of Clifton Hill House.

CHAPTER III

BOYHOOD

(continued)

WHEN [1] I left home for Harrow in the spring of 1854—it was the month of May—I had acquired a somewhat curious personality. Weakness and strength, stoicism and sensibility, frigidity and tenderness, ignorance of the world, and stubborn resistance to external influences were strangely blent in my raw nature. The main thing which sustained me was a sense of self, imperious, antagonistic, unmalleable. But what that self was, and why it kept aloof, I did not know.

My aunt and my sister Edith left me at the King's Head. They drove back to London. I walked down alone to my tutor's house. This was the house of the Rev. Robert Knight, son of my Clifton tutor, and curate to the Vicar of Harrow.

[1] Autobiography.

He took, so far as I remember, three boys as lodgers : a son of Abel Smith, the banker, a young Wingfield, and myself. We slept in one room.

I felt that my heart would break as I scrunched the muddy gravel, beneath the boughs of budding trees, down to the house. But I said to my heart : " I have to be made a man here." This was the one thought uppermost.

Sometimes, when I was alone in bed, I cried— thinking of Clifton. I remember one night when I felt sure that I had been at home, and stood in twilight at the end of the bedroom corridor, looking through elm-branches into the grey south-western skies ; I did not doubt that my spirit could somnam- bulistically travel from the place I hated to the place I loved.

But this made no impression on my daily con- duct. I accepted life at Harrow as a discipline to be gone through. It was not what I wanted. But being prescribed, it had its utility. Thus from the commencement of my schooling I assumed an at- titude of resistance and abeyance. Unutterably stupid this, perhaps. Yet it could not have been otherwise. Such was my nature.

I had never been thrown so entirely upon my own resources before. The situation accentuated that double existence, which I have described, and which was becoming habitual. Internally, as a creature of dreams, of self-concentrated wilfulness, of moral force sustained by obstinate but undeveloped individuality, I was in advance of my new comrades. Externally, compared with them, I was a baby—destitute of experience, incapable of asserting myself, physically feeble, timid, shrinking from contact.

The imperious, unmalleable, uncompromising egotism, which I felt unformed within me, kept me up. I did not realise whither I was going. I felt that my course, though it collided with that of my schoolfellows, was bound to be different from theirs. To stand aloof, to preserve the inner self inviolate, to await its evolution was my dominant instinct. I cannot imagine a more helpless and more stiff-necked, a more unsympathetic and more unlovable boy than I was.

To make the situation worse, I had no escapement from self, no really healthful enlargement of nature at Harrow. I shrank from games of every sort, being constitutionally unfit for violent exercise, and disliking competition. I had no inclination for cricket, football, racquets, and I even disliked fencing. My muscular build was slight. I could not throw a ball or a stone like other boys. And, oddly enough, I could not learn to whistle like them. And yet I was by no means effeminate. My father, judging rightly or wrongly of my physical capacity, took measures for having me excused from playing either cricket or football. I was placed too high in the school for fagging. In this way I did not come into salutary contact with my schoolfellows. It would assuredly have been far better for me had I been cast more freely upon their society. My dislike for games had more to do with a dreamy and self-involved temperament than with absolute physical weakness. I could jump standing to the height of just below my own chin, and could run with the swiftest. Fagging again would have brought me into practical relations with the elder boys, and have rubbed off some of my fastidious reserve.

Intellectually, in like manner, I did not prosper. I got a remove from one form into the next above it every term, and always at the head of the new detachment. But none of my form-masters took hold upon my mind or woke me up. I was a very imperfect scholar when I left Harrow in 1858; and though I competed for the prizes—Latin and Greek verse, English Essay and Poem—I invariably failed. Such mark as I made was due to general ability and punctuality in work.

The spring for which my whole nature craved did not come to me at Harrow. My tutor—to whose house, called "Monkey's," I went at the end of my first year—used to write in his reports that I was "deficient in vigour, both of body and mind." I do not think he was mistaken. Want of physical and cerebral energy showed itself in a series of depressing ailments. I slept uneasily, and dreamed painfully. Repulsive weaknesses—tedious colds, which lasted the whole winter—

lowered my stamina, and painfully augmented my
sense of personal squalor.   I grew continually more
and more shy, lost my power of utterance, and
cut a miserable figure in form.   I contracted the
habit of stammering.   This became so serious that
Vaughan left off putting me on to read and con-
strue Greek.   The Monitors had to recite poems
on Speech Day, which were previously rehearsed
before the school.   On one occasion I chose
Raleigh's " Lie " for my piece.   At the rehearsal
I got through the first stanza, well or ill.   Then
my mind became a blank ; and after a couple
of minutes' deadly silence, I had to sit down dis-
comfited.

My external self, in these many ways, was being
perpetually snubbed, and crushed, and mortified.
Yet the inner self hardened after a dumb, blind
fashion.   I kept repeating, " Wait, wait.   I will, I
shall, I must."   What I was to wait for, what I was
destined to become, I did not ask.   But I never
really doubted my capacity to be something.   In a
vague way I compared myself to the ugly duckling of Andersen's tale.

Life at Harrow was not only uncongenial to my
tastes and temperament.   It was clearly unwholesome.   Living little in the open air, poring stupidly
and mechanically over books, shut up for hours in
badly ventilated schoolrooms and my own close
study, I dwindled physically.   A liberal use of
nerve-tonics, quinine, and strychnine, prescribed by

my father, may have been a palliative; but these drugs did not reach the root of the evil, and they developed other evils which I afterwards discovered.

It is no wonder that I came to be regarded as an uncomradely, unclubbable boy by my companions. Yet I won their moral respect. The following little incident will show what I mean. One day the mathematical master accused me before the form of cribbing, or copying from my neighbour's papers. I simply declared that I had not cribbed. He punished me with 500 lines. I accepted the punishment in silence. Thereupon some of the other boys cried loudly, "Shame," and those who were sitting near me said I was a fool to bear it.

In like manner, though I was neither intellectually brilliant nor athletic, I acquired a considerable influence in my house, of which I was the head for nearly two years. I maintained discipline, and on one occasion I remember caning two big hulking fellows in the Shells for bullying. When I left Harrow the boys at "Monkey's" subscribed to present me with a testimonial. It was Muir's "History of Greek Literature," handsomely bound, which my successor, Currey, handed to me with a speech of kindly congratulation.

My tutor, I think, made a great mistake in not consulting me with regard to the management of the house. According to the Rugby system, which Vaughan applied with certain modifications at Harrow, important duties devolved upon the

Sixth Form, and Monitors were theoretically held responsible for the behaviour of their juniors. Yet I cannot remember any act of personal friendliness or sympathy on my tutor's part towards myself. He never asked me to breakfast or to walk with him ; never invited me to talk with him in the evenings ; never consulted me about the conduct of the lower boys, or explained his own wishes with regard to discipline. I daresay he did not feel the want of my assistance, for he was very well served by his house-tutor, the Rev. John Smith. But he missed an opportunity of discharging his duty toward the ostensible head of his house with kindness, and through me of making his authority felt.

A sign that Harrow did not suit me in any way was the sentiment, approaching to aversion, which I felt for the fat clay soil and pasture landscape of the country round it. During long summer days, the slumberous monotony of grass-land, hedge-rows, buzzing flies and sultry heat, oppressed me. I could not react against the genius of the place, and kept contrasting it with Clifton's rocks and woods and downy turf.

Sordid details, inseparable from a boy's school life in a cheaply built modern house, revolted my taste—the bare and dirty rough-cast corridors, the ill-drained latrines, the stuffy studies with wired windows, the cheerless refectory. But these things, I reflected, were only part of life's open-road, along which one had to trudge for one's affairs—not worse, not more significant to the indwelling soul of man, than the *via dolorosa* from Berkeley Square to Buckingham Villas had been.

The uncongeniality of Harrow life and landscape made my holidays at Clifton very charming by contrast. There were long walks and talks with Charlotte and Sophie Girard, rides on the downs or toward the Bristol Channel, drives with my father through the Somersetshire lanes, discussions about poems and pictures, ramblings in the city streets, prowlings around the shelves of musty bookshops, musings in the Cathedral and St. Mary Redclyffe, dreamy saunterings in the alleys of our garden, lonely hours upon the housetop with that wide and varied scene outspread beneath me, dinner parties, and the company of cultured men and women.

All this, as I have said, contrasted only too sweetly with Harrow and the realities of school existence. In justice to myself, I think I ought to say that, although I always returned to Harrow unwillingly, I did so with the sense that Clifton was a Capua, and Harrow the camp, where I had to brace myself by discipline.

Meanwhile, I formed the habit of idealising Clifton, with results which the history of my aftergrowth made apparent. More and more it became for me the haunt of powerful emotions, the stage on which my inner self would have to play its part.

It would be absurd to pretend that I formed no

friendships at Harrow. In order to complete the picture of my life there I must devote some paragraphs to sketching them.

The Rev. John Smith takes the first place. To his generous sympathy, manly and wise, at a period when I sorely needed sympathetic handling, I ascribe the only pure good of my Harrow training. Doubtless, not I alone, but hundred of boys who came within the influence of that true Christian gentleman, whether they are now alive or sleeping in their graves upon all quarters of the habitable globe, would deliver the same testimony. It is possible, however, that I enjoyed a double portion of his kindly interest; for he had recently settled at Harrow, as form-master and house-tutor to " Monkey's," at the time when I was cast adrift upon school life. He took notice of me, and must have felt my special needs. Without making any demonstrations of friendship he so arranged that a peculiarly delightful comradeship should spring up between us. We took long walks together through the fields. It was our custom on these walks to repeat alternate passages from Shelley, Tennyson, and Keats, which we had previously learned by heart. In this way I absorbed a stupendous amount of good English verse. The house where his dear old mother dwelt at Pinner was frequently the goal of our excursions. Here we rested, after spouting the Skylark or the Palace of Art, the Two Voices and the Ode to the Nightingale, during our early morning or late

evening passage over dewy fields and high-built stiles.
There was always a cold veal-and-ham pie to be eaten
with voracious appetite, strawberry-jam to follow, and
an excellent brew of tea with thick country cream.
Gradually I learned much about the history of this
pure-hearted friend, the deep humility of his strong,
patient nature, the calm and mellow touch of his religious philosophy upon feverish things of human life.

Gustavus Bosanquet comes next. He joined the
school in the same term as I did; and though I
left him behind in our progress through the forms,
we remained firm friends until the last. His parents,
or rather his mother, had trained him in narrow
Evangelical principles. These did not sit quite
easily upon the boy. A strong religious bias formed
the hard-pan of his nature. Yet, in his own way,
he felt the riddle of the universe. His exuberant
affectionateness, indomitable humour, and generous
devotion to a few friends raised him in the moral
sphere high above the ranks of mere intelligence.
Down to this day, I owe him a deep debt of gratitude
for the love he gave me, for the loyalty with which
he sustained me in my hours of self-abasement, and
for the homely cheerfulness of his familiar conversation. We chummed together, cooked sausages
together, played childish pranks, and called each
other by ridiculous nicknames, living a little life
of comradeship secluded from the daily round of
lessons and school-business. Gustavus had his feet
more firmly fixed upon the common ground of

experience than I had. He saw the comic side of things, and this was very helpful to me. With him I was able to laugh and joke about incidents which angered or depressed my solitary nature. In return I gave him something from my ideality. Our fraternal love was very precious during my school life; and if I were asked who was my bosom friend at Harrow, I should reply, "Gustavus Bosanquet."

There was another boy at "Monkey's," with whom Bosanquet and I had much to do. He possessed what neither Bosanquet nor I could boast of—the insect-like devotion to a creed. This was Ritualism, then in its green infancy. Half laughing at him and ourselves, we followed him to compline, donned surplices and tossed censers, arrayed altars in our studies, spent spare cash on bits of execrable painted glass to dull our dingy windows, and illuminated crucifixes with gold dust and vermilion.

In the company of these and other friends I was confirmed. Confirmation ought, if it means anything, to exercise a decisive influence over the religious life of the individual—to make a new epoch in his spiritual progress. To some extent it did so with me. The preparation for the Sacrament worked like a ploughshare on the sub-soil of my piety. It turned up nothing valuable; but it stimulated my æsthetical and emotional ardour. I now inclined to the farcical ritualism of ——, handling pseudo-sacred vessels in a night-gown surplice before a pseudo-altar. I laid myself open to

W.... ...

J. A. SYMONDS - HARROW.

enthusiasms of the shrine and sanctuary. In a dim way I felt God more. But I did not learn to fling the arms of soul in faith upon the cross of Christ. That was not in me. And it would be unfair to expect from any sacrament of the Church that it should work a miracle on catechumens.

[This period of Symonds' Harrow life may well be illustrated by extracts from his letters to his sister Charlotte, afterwards Mrs. Green, written during the years 1856–1858]:—

"I[1] should scarcely have hoped to survive to write to you. The weather is melting. Never—not even last August — have I felt so oppressed. I very nearly fainted in Church, and was on the point of going out, but got better by resolutely thinking of something else.

"It has been a tiring day. I have heard three sermons. Do you not think that four services, three sermons and one school, are too much in this hot weather?

"I find Edith's Italian Bible so nice. I take it to church and read the lessons with it, and prepare my Greek Test. by it, so that I pick up a good many words and phrases in an easy and ungrammary way.

"Would you ask papa whether he has the two last volumes of Arnold's 'Thucydides'? He gave me the first to take, but I think it was the only

[1] To his sister Charlotte. Harrow, May 17, 1856.

volume he had.   We are going to read it soon,
and I thought if he could pick up the other two
it would be less expensive than my getting a whole
new edition, which I should be obliged to do.

" I have had a new cover and cushion made for
my chair.   It is much fatter and more comfortable
than the old one, which used to lump up all in a
heap.   I find it pleasant to work in while it is so
hot.   I think the nights are the worst part, where
you fry and then go and be stewed for breakfast
by a morning sun which beats in.   I never, however, saw this place looking so pretty before.   The
leaves are full sized, but of the most delicate green,
while the sky is cloudless and the atmosphere perfectly clear, so that we see every speck on the
plain from Sydenham to the far-off Surrey hills,
with Windsor, Hampstead, and Elstree.   Is it not
unusual to be so hot now?   I have divested myself
of all the clothes I can.   It reminds me of that
splendid summer of '51 when we first came to
Clifton Hill.   Do you remember the garden then?
It had a smell of musk and roses and thick dew
which it never has had since.   It used to be a
miniature garden of the Hesperides, where those
Buddleia bosses were the golden apples.   There
was not even the sleepy dragon to spoil our
pleasure."

[The Mr. John Smith, who is so warmly eulogised
in the " Autobiography," is frequently referred to

in the letters. It is clear that his was the personality from which Symonds gained most during his Harrow days. The walks and talks with this friend are always recorded with enjoyment].

"Yesterday[1] I had a delightful expedition. I started with Mr. Smith at half-past two from the station, and went by rail to Watford, where we got out and walked to Cassiobury, a place of Lord Essex. There are some splendid avenues and parks filled with deer there. We stayed in the park about two hours, and then walked on through woods and valleys until we came to the most exquisite beech avenue I ever saw. It was narrow, but very long, and the trees were planted so closely that they grew straight for some way without leaves, and then met at the top, making an exquisite cathedral aisle.

"I read to Mr. Smith a Latin Alcaic poem on Cato. He seemed dissatisfied. My composition has gone off two-thirds since I was with Mr. —— Mr. Smith asked Mr. Westcott about a poem on the Rhine. His answer was, 'It is the work of a tired mind.' I am extremely vexed at this, for I know that he means a want of energy, freshness, and raciness, which I once had, but have now entirely lost. I shall soon send papa this same Cato. It is two hundred lines, and I wrote it in about two hours. It was certainly too fast. I am

---

[1] To his sister Charlotte. Harrow, June 1, 1857.

now just looking through it, and by care I think I might make it better."

[Symonds, even as early as these Harrow days, began to show that natural gift for descriptive writing which has made him the delightful companion of so many travellers. His weekly budgets to his sister, written on Sundays, with an important postscript added usually on Monday, are full of charming and often of amusing details, for which he possessed a keen eye. Here is an elaborate description of the Confirmation at Harrow :]—

"We[1] shall have a very tiring day to-day. First there is the early service before breakfast. Then the Confirmation lecture. Then the morning service and sermon. Then, after dinner, school. Then the evening and Confirmation services, and then the Bishop's address.

"*Monday morning.* — Now I must tell you all about the Confirmation. At school several notices were fulminated in Dr. V.'s obscurest style—highly calculated to confound and disorder all the arrangements and to bamboozle the clearest and most intelligent mind. One thing, however, appeared, that we were to have the evening service at half-past eight, and the Confirmation after. So, after school I set out for a walk with a friend of mine ; we got into a discussion and found ourselves nearly at Pinner, above two miles off. There we heard the

[1] To his sister Charlotte. Harrow, June 14, 1857.

far-off tinkling of a bell. I looked at my watch,
and finding it was half-past four, conjectured that
it was nothing. After talking and sitting for half-
an-hour more, another bell was heard. This time
we set off, and tore over ploughed fields, hedges,
ditches, and arrived at Harrow, hot and miserable,
at 5.15, to hear that the Confirmation service was
to take place at 5.30. I had a mash of confused
notices in my head, but found myself all right in
the chapel at last. Then a dead pause. Every one
was assembled as it seemed. But the Bishop was
not there. Every moment fresh boys came drop-
ping in from their walks. The bell was ringing like
a tocsin. The organ played a melancholy air, and
everybody was in suspense. At last all the can-
didates for confirmation were collected, and the
Bishop, preceded by Dr. V., and followed by a
chaplain, walked in and ascended the pulpit, and
commenced the proceedings by an address. He
looks taller and younger than I expected. His face
is quite colourless now, and marked with deeper
lines than I ever saw in anybody else. There was
a kind of fixed, inflexible determination in him.
His voice was very changeable, sometimes deep
and harsh, at others soft and musical. In his
address he dwelt upon the sorrows of the world, so
surely to be suffered by all, the vows by which we
were bound, the condemnation of those who took
them lightly, and then, changing his tone, talked of
the blessings of the service. After the laying on of

hands, he gave a second short address on the Lord's Sacrament, standing with his cap in his hand in front of the communion rails. We went up six by six. Both addresses were extempore. After the service he and his chaplain departed, and we had the evening service. He had been preaching before the Queen in the morning, and had been invited suddenly in the afternoon to dine with her at eight, so he posted down here at once, and the boys had thus to be collected by these bells from over the country."

[Although Symonds in certain moods, perhaps the most permanent moods, represents himself as shrinking with dislike from all school games, the following passages show that he took his part in them, and not without a dash of pleasure :]—

"I[1] have been down this afternoon to football with the school. The game was the Fifth Form against the School. I found out the meaning of certain terms I had not hitherto quite appreciated, such as that of a 'squash.' A squash is a large collection of boys, about twenty, with the football in the midst of them. They are all kicking it and each other in their endeavours to extricate the ball, and woe to the unlucky wight who falls. He is instantly trampled upon by every one. I, to-day, when in a squash, was suddenly propelled by one of the heaviest boys in the school. I rushed forward and

[1] To his sister Charlotte. Harrow, Oct. 3, 1857.

stood in a semi-upright position on another boy, whose thigh I was grinding and pounding with my heavy boots, until the ball was hurled out, and then every one came on the ground together. On the whole, there is not so much real danger as I expected, except from great boys dashing their weight against you, and using you as a battering-ram or wedge for entering the crushes. It is thus, I imagine, that most accidents occur. I think it a very healthy exercise in fine autumn weather like this, but doubt its good in colder and damper days. Altogether, I hope that I shall like it. I enclose some edicts, to give you an idea of my kind of power in the management of the republic. I sit here, like Hildebrand in the Vatican, and make my house tremble as he did Europe with his thunders."

[In a subsequent letter he records with obvious satisfaction that—

"Yesterday I played in a house match and distinguished myself. I was the first to get what is called a base; that is, to carry a ball, kicking it, into the enemy's goal in spite of the attempts of the adverse party to stop you."

[The round of schoolboy life,—reading in chapel for the first time, the Debating Society, hampers from home, lessons, Speech Day,—finds ample illustration in Symonds' letters; the details are observed and recorded with a precision which is remarkable in a lad of seventeen. Characteristically, Symonds says little about his achievements. It would be difficult to gather from his correspondence that he was rising rapidly through the school, and was about to reach the Sixth Form far before the usual date. Indeed, even thus early in life what he had not occupied his attention far more than what he had, and there is foreshadowed that marked feature of his maturer years, the ceaseless striving forwards towards something new, to some region not yet explored.]

"This evening [1] I had to read the first lesson, Proverbs xii. It was my first essay in the new chapel, and that, too, before a number of strangers and Harrow people. The reading-desk is a lectern. You stand one step above its base, and overlook the congregation. Your back is turned to the altar, the chancel, and all the people in it, so that you are between a double fire of eyes. I felt rather like a noisy reading-machine, and had very little appreciation of what I read. My fault was not that of false intonation, I am glad to say, but of too little strength of voice, which I hold to be no very great sign of bad performance in a new place, and one so inexperienced. I did not feel very nervous, only a coldness of the extremities, a want of sensibility, and a kind of mental estrangement. I am going on Tuesday to read with Mr. Smith in Pinner Church, and so get a little practice, and hope to come out

[1] To his sister Charlotte. Harrow, Nov. 15, 1857.

strong some day or other. I think this is a good practice. It gives confidence, and prepares for public speaking.

" I think I have never told you that I spoke in our debate on Tuesday last, on the subject of 'The Reality of Ghosts.' I defended them, and made my speech a definition of their (to me) real character, which I upholded by papa's story of Cromwell's ghost in his lecture on sleep and dreams. Although I worked up the subject, and showed the growing influence of that apparition on Cromwell's life, yet I am sorry to say that my audience were too sceptical. They derided me for unfounded assertions about females, and their influence on the fate of mighty nations."

" Thank [1] Edith very much for the parcel, which arrived quite safely on Friday. I can assure you we are doing justice to the tongue, and (cousin) James was invited last evening to partake of it. Also the biscuits were most delicious. Of course the frost is broken, now that I have my skates. It always does so, and yesterday I went down to football. It had been pouring, and was then mizzling with a sort of Scotch mist. The ground was in that condition that when the ball fell it gave a 'thud' into the water and mud, and spurted up little fountains of the same all round. It was really too much like pigs wallowing in the mire, and I thought of my favourite quotation from the 'Palace of Art' about

[1] To his sister Charlotte. Harrow, January 31, 1858.

'the swine that range on yonder plain,' which I used to recite with such hearty goodwill, before I joined in the same wallowing.

"This evening I have just done learning my Butler. He is the stupidest old creature ever seen, and I do not see why I should have all his ideas about the future state rammed down my throat, or be forced to profess (in school) those things and arguments conclusive and settled, which I do not at all see to be such. I think that such a book tends towards Calvinism or Atheism."

"Although[1] you will have a better account, I hope, of our Speech Day in the *Times*, I yet send you a little description of my own, with my own feelings. The day was glorious, but so hot that it was the greatest exertion to move. I kept quiet till twelve, and then, as the company began to arrive, went up and saw them going into Speech Room. Among the *distingués* present were the Bishops of Oxford, St. David's, and Jamaica. Lord J. Russell, Lord Palmerston, Sir W. W. of Kars, Mme. Goldschmidt, and several other titles not worth recording. I then moved off and helped to join a double line from the school to the chapel, through which the visitors had to pass. The heat was awful. As soon as the visitors had passed, and got seated in the wooden amphitheatre, prepared for them to see the laying of the foundation stone of the new aisle, the whole school rushed down

[1] To his sister Charlotte. Harrow, June 28, 1858.

together over a set of sloping terraces that lead to
the new buildings. We were then cooped up in
a small space and crushed, and, what was worse,
glared upon by the sun to a dreadful extent. The
ceremony was very interesting. Dr. V. read first
a form of prayer for the occasion, and then a list of
those Harrovians who had fallen in the war. Sir
W. W. then mortared the stone and patted it, after
which he made a speech. It was very nice, but too
hesitating to sound well, and besides that I was
nearly touching him. Lord Palmerston then made
a speech of much the same character, but with
greater fluency and style. His speaking disappointed me, since it consisted of a series of commonplaces disposed of in short barks; perhaps this
unfavourable impression was owing to my near
position and uncomfortable feelings. There was
immense cheering for the celebrities. We then
returned to Mr. R.'s *déjeûner*."

[In his autobiography Symonds minimises both
his athletic and his intellectual achievement at
Harrow. He did not like the place; it did not
suit his health, and he did not feel that he was
spiritually growing there. This conviction remained
throughout life, and was frequently expressed. But
as we have seen that his place in school games was
probably higher than he would acknowledge, so his
record of intellectual honours was far in advance
of anything which his letters or reminiscences would

lead us to suppose ; for example, that rare distinction the medal, "ob studia uno tenore feliciter peracta," which he was the first to win, is not mentioned once. An exceptionally brilliant boy he certainly was not, but one of his masters, Mr. Coker Adams, recorded of him that he was always a good and very painstaking pupil, far above the average, though not expected to acquire that distinction which he subsequently achieved.

The truth is that Symonds, like many boys of imaginative and intellectual temperament, was more concerned with his own fancies, thoughts, feelings, than with the main current of school life about him.]

At[1] this period of my boyhood, I dreamed a great deal of my time away, and wrote a vast amount of idiotic verses. During the night-time I was visited by terrible and splendid visions, far superior to my poetry. In the long slow evolution of myself, it appears that the state of dreamful subconscious energy was always superior to the state of active intelligent volition. In a sense different from Charles Lamb's, I was a dream-child, incapable of emerging into actuality, containing potential germs of personality which it required decades to develop.

In this respect I was probably by no means singular. The situation might be summed up in one sentence : I was a slow-growing lad. The memory

[1] Autobiography.

of my experience at Harrow, of my non-emergence, of my intense hidden life, of my inferiority in achievement, has made me infinitely tender towards young men in whom I recognised the same qualities of tardy laborious growth.

[The autobiography of the Harrow period is not copious. It closes upon the following incident :]—

We[1] were reading Plato's Apology in the Sixth Form. I bought Cary's crib, and took it with me to London on an *exeat* in March. My hostess, a Mrs. Bain, who lived in Regent's Park, treated me to a comedy one evening at the Haymarket. I forget what the play was. When we returned from the play, I went to bed and began to read my Cary's Plato. It so happened that I stumbled on the "Phædrus." I read on and on, till I reached the end. Then I began the "Symposium;" and the sun was shining, on the shrubs outside the ground-floor in which I slept, before I shut the book up.

I have related these insignificant details, because that night was one of the most important nights of my life; and when anything of great gravity has happened to me, I have always retained a firm recollection of trifling facts which formed its context.

Here in the "Phædrus" and the "Symposium"—in the "Myth of the Soul," I discovered the revelation I had been waiting for, the consecration of a

[1] Autobiography.

long-cherished idealism.   It was just as though the voice of my own soul spoke to me through Plato. Harrow vanished into unreality.   I had touched solid ground.   Here was the poetry, the philosophy of my own enthusiasm, expressed with all the magic of unrivalled style.

The study of Plato proved decisive for my future. Coming at the moment when it did, it delivered me to a large extent from the torpid cynicism of my Harrow life, and controlled my thoughts for many years.

[It also begat a mood of dreaming which coalesced with the powerful though vague impression of beauty awakened by his Clifton home, and grew to be what Symonds himself in his later diaries calls his *Seelensehnsucht*, a "Cliftonian state of yearning." This mood became localised at Clifton, centred in the Cathedral, and invariably returned whenever he came back to his home from Oxford term-time, from Welsh or Yorkshire reading parties, from tours in Italy, Belgium, Switzerland, or France.]

CHAPTER IV

YOUTH

MARCH[1] came to an end, and brought this eventful term to its conclusion. In April I went to

---

[1] Autobiography.

Clifton for the Easter holidays. The change from Harrow to my home always tranquillised and re-freshed me. It renewed that sense of dignity, repose, and beauty in existence, which was ab-solutely necessary to my spiritual being.

This time I felt the change more strangely than usual. Clifton did not offer the same simple satis-faction as before. The recent quickening of my intellect, the revelation I had found in Plato, re-moved me almost suddenly away from boyhood. I was on the verge of attaining to a man's self-consciousness. My ritualistic pranks at Harrow had had this much of reality in them that they indicated a natural susceptibility to the æsthetic side of religion. I felt a real affection, a natural reve-rence, for grey Gothic churches. The painted glass and heraldries in this cathedral, Crusaders cross-legged on their tombs, carved wood work and high-built organ lofts, the monuments to folk long dead, over all the choiring voices, touched me to the quick at a thousand sensitive points.

At this period of my youth I devoured Greek literature, and fed upon the reproductions of Greek plastic art, with which my father's library was stored. Plato took the first place in my studies. I dwelt upon the opening pages of the "Charmides" and "Lysis." I compared these with the "Clouds" of Aristophanes, and the dialogues of Lucian and Plutarch. I explored Theognis and the anthology, learned Theocritus by heart, tasted fragments of

Anacreon, and Ibycus, and Pindar. I did not reflect upon the incongruity between this impulse to absorb the genius of the Greeks, and the other impulse which drew me toward mediævalism. The Confessions of St. Augustine lay side by side upon my table with a copy of the Phædrus.

This confusion of ideas was grotesque enough; and gradually it introduced a discord into my life. Yet, it marked a period of vigorous development. If the modern man is destined to absorb and to appropriate the diverse strains which make him what he is, some such fermentation cannot be avoided. He emerges from it with a mind determined in this way or that, and retains a vital perception of things that differ, grounded in his personal experience.

My mental and moral evolution proceeded now upon a path which had no contact with the prescribed systems of education. I lived in and for myself. Masters, and school, and methods of acquiring knowledge lay outside me, to be used or neglected as I judged best. I passed my last term at Harrow between that April and the ensuing August in supreme indifference; and looked forward to the university without ambition.

In the summer vacation, before I went up to Oxford, I made a tour through Scotland. There were the Forbeses at Pitlochry, Dalrymple at New-hailes, Jamieson on the Gair Loch, the Forrests at Edinburgh, to be visited.

[Some report of this visit was sent to his family at Clifton in the following terms :]—

"We[1] have been to Roslin and are come back, and I am sitting in my room. It is late and I am tired, therefore I shall not write much. We have had a charming day. We set off at a quarter to one and got by train to Hawthornden. Mr. and Mrs. J. Fergusson have a place on one of the sides of the glen at Hawthornden, looking straight over to the Castle and Chapel of Roslin. There we lunched. The woods are private property, and cover the whole sides of that deep and narrow ravine through which the Esk flows. Roslin stands at the head, Hawthornden at the foot of the glen, each built upon a most precipitous rock, and commanding a splendid view up their own parts of the ravine. The path was very steep and went straight down to the Esk, which we crossed by a bridge, whence a most splendid view of Hawthornden is to be got. You look up to an immense red cliff on which stands this old and irregular Castle. The walls go sheer down to the precipice and end in rocks beside the water. On each side the trees rise thick and green to a great height, broken occasionally by bits of cliff and caves. Every sort of the rarest ferns grow in these woods. Some of them I picked. These were Dryopteris, Thegopteris, several kinds of Cystopteris Dilatata,

---

[1] To Miss Sykes. Newhailes, 1858.

Lady Fern, and many others I forget, all growing as thick and rank as the commonest Filix Mas in Leigh Woods. From the bridge we began to ascend, and walked in a slanting direction by the water to Roslin. As we passed along, we had Wallace's and Bruce's caves pointed out to us, though I confess I could not see them, for they were high up on the other side and shaded with trees. However, I hardly ever remember a more charming walk. Roslin Chapel both exceeded and fell beneath my expectations. The architecture is so late and debased that one cannot be enthusiastic about it, but then its ornamentation and situation surpass anything I had ever seen. I could not have conceived such an immense variety and minuteness of tracery. Each arch and column is different; one part of the roof, spangled with goodly stone stars, pleased me as much as any of the decorations. I mounted on a horrid swinging ladder to the top, which was being repaired. Having arrived there with some dizziness, I found myself the centre of attraction to a nest of bees who inhabit one of the pinnacles. The great height, the swing of the ladder and the attacks of the bees (who did not, however, sting me) almost made me lose my balance, and I beat a speedy retreat. However, I secured some ferns from the very top for Mdlle. G. Exquisite maiden's hair grew on the roof inside in festoons. It was a fatiguing day, and a long walk. But I found it very pleasant. We were such a

merry party, and made so much fun. All the
Misses F. are very nice girls, but quite the most
amusing is called 'Hetty' (for Henriette). She is
a perfect Hetty, always laughing and making some
joke or other. I am so sorry to go to-morrow.
They, too, had not expected so early a departure,
but I must not waste time, and it is better to go
ere people get tired of you. Good night. Best
love to papa and all."

[The Trossachs, seen in a great rain-storm, call
forth an observation upon grand scenery, "It makes
me melancholy to look at it. I do not know why,
but fine scenery has that effect on me. It seems
to elevate and at the same time to depreciate one's
estimate of self." In Edinburgh Holyrood interested him, and he is sceptical about the portraits
of the Scottish kings; he adds maliciously, "I am
sure that tons of hay might be mown off the streets
of Edinburgh." The return journey was made by
way of Carlisle and Manchester, where Symonds
saw the first great loan collection of old masters.

The close of the year 1858 brought the important
change from school to college. He was not yet
eighteen; he had already been some time in the
Sixth; Harrow had little more to give him; he
himself was anxious to leave, and both his father
and Dr. Vaughan concurred. Symonds entered
Balliol as a Commoner, and tried, though unsuc-
cessfully, for a scholarship in November of his first

term. He records his early impressions of Oxford life as follows :]—

My[1] first feeling upon coming up to Balliol in the autumn of 1858 was one of relief. The greater freedom of university as compared with school life, both as regards the employment of time and the choice of studies, suited my temperament. I was not one of those boys who, after hugely enjoying their career at Eton or Harrow, leave their hearts to some extent behind them. Nor, again, was I abandoning that prestige and flattering sense of self-importance which a popular head of the school resigns when he enters the ranks of freshmen in a first-rate college. I, on the contrary, had everything to gain and nothing to lose by the change.

Cambridge absorbed the majority of the Harrovians who went up to the universities. Consequently I was but poorly furnished with school friends. I began to make friends with freshmen—Urquhart, Duncan (afterwards Lord Camperdown), Stephens (a nephew of the Lord Chancellor Hatherley), Malcolm (now a partner in Coutts's bank), Cecil Bosanquet (the brother of Gustavus), Cholmley Puller and Wright (two scholars of Balliol), Lyulph Stanley, and others whose names I find recorded in my diaries of that date. During my first term I also became acquainted with Edwin Palmer, Robinson Ellis, and Professor John Conington. These elder

[1] Autobiography.

men introduced me to their several sets. I came thus early in my career to know people of distinction like Goldwin Smith, Charles Parker, Charles Pearson, Arthur Stanley, Albert Dicey, T. H. Green, Mark Pattison, Francis Otter, A. O. Rutson.

[As at Harrow so now at Oxford, Symonds' sister was still his chief correspondent.   To her he sent frequent accounts of his rapidly expanding interests in life, his friends, his studies, his social surroundings.]

" I [1] think you must have been expecting to hear from me lately, but I have been very busy the end of this week.   Indeed, I have only once heard from home, and had intended to warn you that letters overweighted will in future be opened and returned to the writers.   Very often the Sunday letters I get from home are too heavy.

" This last week I have been seeing a great deal of Mr. Conington ; he is so kind as to look after my composition, and still urges me to try for a scholarship at Corpus.   Of course papa's dislike to my doing that, and also my own liking for Balliol, prevent me at present from so doing.   I now know well several men in college — Jamieson, Brodrick, Malcolm, Jefferson, Campion and I are perpetually together, and I should lose a great deal of them were I to change to C. C.   They are all Eton men, and very gentlemanly, quiet companions,

[1] To his sister Charlotte. Balliol, February 1859.

though not at all reading men. For this reason
I see less of them than Jamieson. That is to say,
I cannot be about with them in the mornings, &c.

"On the whole, I find it difficult to know what
to do about acquaintances here. One has either to
keep up a great number, or lose several that one
would like to have, as well as Brodrick and Company, who, on the other hand, are distracting from
their non-reading turn. At Harrow I existed almost
without associates till very late, and now I begin
to despise myself, because I find how much I care
to have them, and how much sacrifice this care is
likely to produce. However, I suppose things
settle themselves down, and we are shaped by
destiny and circumstance in the choice of friends
as in other things."

" I [1] am writing to you in Puller's room on one of
the most lovely mornings we have yet had. The
sun is quite warm, and every trace of snow, 'even
to the last faint streak,' has disappeared, and I am
beginning to think that I shall like the incoming
of summer. You, I believe, sympathise with me
about the decided superiority of winter over every
other part of the year ; yet I think it is the winter
of December and the early parts of January that I
like. When the days grow longer and no warmer,
and one has a disagreeable uncertainty of light
about six o'clock—no firelight dusk before dinner,
e.g.—is the time that plagues me most, for I anti-

[1] To his sister Charlotte (1859?).

cipate that gradual rising of things, buds, and leaves, and flowers, and then a sultry pause, and then fruits and corn, and then yellow leaves, and all that before the rest of winter comes again. It is the sense of flux and progress that makes a prospect from spring to winter so dreary; and I always connect it in my mind with that interminable Harrow Summer Term, and its all-pervading 'buzziness' of heat.

"Do you think you could find out from Mrs. B—— where and when Mr. Congreve preaches, and whether he does preach regularly? Puller is very anxious to hear him, and wants me to go with him some day to London for that purpose. As the risk of my conversion to Positivism is extremely small, I should not mind it."

.   .   .   .

The [1] association with Conington was almost wholly good. It is true that I sat up till midnight with him nearly every evening, drinking cup after cup of strong tea in his private lodgings above Cooper's shop near University. This excited and fatigued my nerves. But his conversation was in itself a liberal education for a youth of pronounced literary tastes.

My studies advanced so badly that I was plucked for Smalls in the spring of 1859. The examiner, D. B—— of Exeter, made me conjugate the Greek εἰμί "to be," and εἶμι "to go," tense by tense. This was perhaps rather severe upon any candidate for

[1] Autobiography.

his *testamur* in Responsions. The examination, however, was meant to search our knowledge of the rudiments; and nobody can deny that an accurate knowledge of the Greek auxiliary verbs is a rudimentary requisite of scholarship. I failed to fulfil the condition, and deserved to be plucked. The test selected by Mr. D. B—— discovered the weakest point in my panoply, and paralysed a mind which, however quick and sympathetic, was never very self-controlled or ready at a pinch. To confuse me with the multiplication table would have been equally easy.

I did not greatly mind this rebuff. I had been gathering fritillaries in Magdalen meadows all the afternoon, and enjoying the sunset from the top of Magdalen Tower. The memory of that pleasant May-day is fresher now than my recollection of the disagreeable news that I was "plucked." But I greatly disliked having to go down to Clifton and tell my father that I had been "ploughed in Smalls for Greek Grammar." Fortunately, before the end of June, I had been elected, together with Charles Elton, to an open Exhibition at Balliol. My father's wounded feelings were soon soothed by quite sufficient academical successes; and my own sense of duty in study was sharpened by the salutary snub inflicted on my not too stubborn vanity.

[At the end of the summer term of 1859, Symonds, T. H. Green, Rutson and Cholmley Puller went

with Conington on a reading party to Whitby.
They engaged a lodging-house kept by a woman
called Storm, whom Conington christened λαῖλαψ.
Symonds was deeply impressed by the sternness of
the place, "the village churchyard" (he writes in
the autobiography), "full of monuments erected
to captains and sailors of the name of Storm,
many of whom had perished as whalers and fishers
on the northern seas. The church itself, an old-
fashioned edifice, built on the cliff's brow, with
galleries in which the choir droned out hymns and
anthems to the accompaniment of a stringed and
brass band. It affected my imagination with the
feeling of generations of shipwrecked seamen, as
though it had been itself a hulk stranded up there,
and redolent of marine reminiscences."

The letters and diaries of the next year, 1860,
show a marked advance in firmness of tone. It is
quite clear that Symonds was growing rapidly, that
his spirit was expanding in the Oxford atmosphere,
that he keenly enjoyed its intellectual attractiveness
in the society of able and distinguished men, its
æsthetic charm in the antique splendour of its
college services.]

"This morning,[1] when I went to fetch a book
in Conington's room, there was a great assembly
of distinguished people. I found him seated with
Monro, a Cambridge man, and Henry Smith, who

---

[1] To his sister Charlotte, February 5, 1860.

is the greatest universal genius Oxford has, and Currey, and a Lord Strangford, who has just returned from Constantinople full of the forgeries of Simonides. Whilst we were thus assembled, a Marlborough master, called Bright, son of a Dr. Bright, came in, and shortly after Goldwin Smith, bringing his lecture, which I am about to send to papa. This completed the gallery of celebrities. Their conversation was very interesting. G. S. speaks like a book, and delivered most sententious dicta on many subjects, chiefly political.

" I have to go off as fast as I can, chapel having intervened, to dine at Pembroke."

" Yesterday [1] I had a very intellectual breakfast: Conington, Rutson, Green, Tollemache, Dicey, Lyulph Stanley, and Puller. I find these breakfasts formidable things; for there is a succession of meats, all of which I have to dispense, to change plates, and keep people going with fresh forks and knives, &c. It is not the custom for any scout to be in attendance, so that the host has to do all menial offices. You would be amused to see these intellectual men begin with fried soles and sauces, proceed to a cutlet, then taste a few sausages or some savoury omelette, and finish up with buttered cake or toast and marmalade. Up to the sweet finale coffee is the beverage; and tea, coming when hunger has abated, prolongs breakfast *ad infinitum*.

" I went for a ride yesterday afternoon with Rutson,

---

[1] To his sister Charlotte, March 11, 1860.

not feeling very well. We were taken in the most furious snowstorm I ever was in ; there was a strong wind driving, and the snow came into our eyes and mouth, and down our necks and up our arms. It was at its height when we were on Port Meadow ; floods were out, and what with half-frozen bogs and sheets of water, and the inability to see anything on account of this snow, our chances of return-ing undrowned or with whole horses were slight. We did, however, succeed in piloting ourselves to Wolvercote, and thence spurred home in miserable plight. It was vexatious ; for when one does in-dulge in a ride, one expects to get pleasure and good by it.

"I have been reading some of Kingsley's 'Mis-cellanies,' and have been utterly disgusted with one on Shelley and Byron ; he makes the most odious preferences for manly over sentimental vices, and preaches on poor Shelley as full text and type of the latter. Besides the injustice and the repulsive-ness of the matter, one felt insulted by the man's loose writing. These Essays seem to have got together somehow, but to have followed no distinct plan—maybe to have been jotted down in the saddle by some cover. Such slap-dash writing is not un-pleasant in other Essays, where he talks of sport and rural delights, but it jars on my taste when used as the vehicle of such wholesale and unfounded criticisms on poets like Shelley, and on the age that reads him."

"I[1] have just come from taking composition to Jowett, who talked to me about my Moderations. He gave me hope, blowing a trumpet-blast of determination. Such a man was never found, so great to inspire confidence and to rouse to efforts. Other people may prate for hours, and set the pros and cons before you, yet never stir your lethargy. By a single word, with no argument but a slight appeal to the natural powers of most men, and a plea for work as work, he makes one feel that to be successful is the only thing short of dishonour.

"It is good to hear a man of such broad and unprejudiced views: Conington is the reverse, great in his own way, but the way narrow. Conington is stationary: he has cut out his notions, and will obstinately keep to them.

"Jowett says that my only thought till Mods. must be my work. I shall therefore not bring home with me any of my genealogical apparatus; the rules I laid down for reading must be steadily adhered to, and herein help me; all byways of literature must be carefully eschewed, hard.

"Such are the resolutions roused by Jowett's trumpet, how long to last?"

[The letters from which the preceding extracts have been gathered make it quite clear that Symonds thoroughly enjoyed the epistolary form of expres-

---

[1] To his sister Charlotte, March 16, 1860.

sion. Witness to this fact would be borne by those hundreds of correspondents with whom he came into epistolary contact during his later years. Talking and letter-writing were, indeed, the forms of intellectual exercise which yielded him most delight. Even as early as January 1858, while he was still at Harrow, he had professed himself "a great lover of old letters," and upon letter-writing in general he now puts out his views to his sister Charlotte as follows :]—

"I [1] wish you would pay more attention to the writing of letters. I am not the proper person to read you a sermon upon this subject, because I do not think that the specimens I send you are at all what letters should be. Yet I labour under the disadvantage of writing to a mixed audience. You have only me to talk to, and, moreover, being a lady, are perhaps more bound to write good letters. I think you should consider more to whom you are writing, in each instance, and try to say something suitable to the tastes, &c., of the individual. It is quite a mistake to suppose that one ever needs subject-matter in writing a letter. I think those are most interesting which detail least of daily affairs, but, taking one occurrence as a kind of text, go on and discourse upon collateral points of interest. The younger Pliny, who was one of the most graceful of all letter-writers, recommends a

[1] To his sister Charlotte, May 27, 1860.

friend to be careful not to write journals in letters.
I daresay you think this contradictory of my craving
after news; it does sound so, but yet much news
may be conveyed without formal statement, the
more so if you are careful to select such news as
will be especially interesting to your correspondent.
Letters might be raised into an intellectual exercise;
and, if you took to view them in that light, I do not
think that an hour or so spent upon one would be
any waste. You ought to be looking out sharp now
for any mental fillip or stimulus. I think you are
very much like myself in possessing a generally listless and inactive intellect, and one which requires
constant goading and keeping up to the mark. I
only hope that by lying in wait for it perpetually,
and keeping it in exercise, it may eventually become
less flaccid than it is at present. On the other hand,
I doubt whether inherent weakness can be era-
dicated by any exercise. I always fancy that want
of concentration and feebleness of comprehension are the result of some softness and nerve-
lessness in the texture of my brain; so much has
this idea sometimes possessed me that I have
wished to become a physiologist for the mere
purpose of studying the conditions of the brain
and endeavouring to connect them with mental
energies, &c.

"I should not be babbling so much were it not
Sunday. This afternoon I hope to hear 'The
Heavens are Telling' at Magdalen. That chorus is

the grandest interpretation of 'light' that has ever been conceived. Its restless radiation, the full broad centre of sound from which those brilliant undulations are continually darting forth, the bounding flux and reflux of its changes—all this seems perfectly to represent the vital energy and ceaseless motion of light, as coming from the sun, or in the cycles of the planets. In Beethoven's great Hallelujah we have the gradual development of infant worlds, but in Haydn's Chorus the whole universe has just been set in ceaseless motion by the first utterance, 'Let there be light.' By the way, do you know how clergymen invariably proceed to 'And there *was* light'? This should certainly be read, 'And there was—Light.'"

"I[1] ought not to be writing just now, for last Sunday I did nothing to the Gospels. Yet I cannot help scribbling a little to tell ·you of a charming ride I had on Friday with Rutson. It was a delicious summer day; we started at half-past four, riding along Port Meadow, and through fields that still skirted the river, with Wytham Woods upon our left. By this route we got about seven miles of uninterrupted grass land, covered with cowslips and burning marigolds. The fields seemed quite deserted, and we saw nothing but pheasants or partridges running from their cover, with now and then a plover making melancholy human cries. So, soon we came to Bablock Hythe,

[1] To his sister Charlotte, May 6, 1860,

a place celebrated in Matthew Arnold's 'Scholar Gypsy,' a solitary house guarding a ferry; here we crossed in a broad horse boat, and rode on to Stanton Harcourt. I had often wished to see the graves of the Harcourts in this church, the room where Pope is said to have lived, and the great medieval kitchen, still black with smoke. The first thing, however, was to get some dinner for ourselves, and stabling for our horses. We found a little inn, but alas! found neither stablemen nor dinner. There were two stalls for horses in a shed, one empty, the other filled with straw. Rutson's horse was honoured with the empty stall; I took a pitchfork, and dispossessed the straw from the other for my beast. Having taken off bridles and saddles we foraged for hay and corn, which at last we found; and so returned to the inn kitchen, tired and dusty. Soon, however, we discovered that it provided less accommodation for man than the stables for beast; a loaf of bread was its only eatable. Food for contemplation there was plenty in the churchyard, and its splendid yew. The church itself is beautiful—a much restored specimen of pure Early English. Some of the Harcourt tombs are most elaborate—one especially of ancient painted stone tabernacle-work. Others were flat, with knights and ladies all in rows—their dress and armour, shields and crests and helmets, gorgeously emblazoned. Everywhere hung coronets, with the Harcourt peacock drooping his long tail behind the helmet; the arms of Harcourt and of Byron shone conspicuous. They give the most gorgeous combinations of colour that heraldry can boast— gold and crimson, silver and crimson, in alternate bars and bends.

"As we returned, Bablock Hythe was even calmer and more beautiful than it had been before. The perfect sunset reflection on the one hand, the moon on the other, as we crossed the Weir, seemed to fill even our steeds with calm and poetry. They went more gently. We reached Oxford a little before ten. I was very tired and exhausted. The only eatable to satiate my hunger (before a visit for composition to Jowett at a quarter-past ten) was buttered toast and coffee. On this somewhat bilious diet I buoyed myself up to discuss my own Iambics.

"I enjoyed the expedition exceedingly; it made me long more and more that I had some friend of my own age at Clifton. Had I my own way, I would willingly transport about three of my Oxford friends, and place one in the Crescent and another in Cornwallis Grove; that so I might have companions for long walks, or that often-con-templated moonlight expedition to Leigh Woods. The latter I must accomplish in the summer.

"Mind, what I say about wishing for Oxford friends at Clifton, does in no way diminish the full perfection of home. I need some attendant in those places only, where my dear sister cannot go. As it is, if I had my choice between the two, I would rather live at home, with solitude and cherub contemplation, when I walk about, than stay at Oxford with fifty devoted friends."

"I[1] have been amused just now by the visit of a very High Church acquaintance of mine, who came in redolent of incense. He had been to a friend's rooms, who is of the same persuasion, and found him at service. 'Accordingly,' said he, 'I vested myself in my sky-blue cassock, then I put on a white chasuble with gold border; after that the stole and maniple; and, lastly, the beretta. Thus attired, we went through the service.' To think of the absurdity of these men. He went on to describe how he had a 'triptych' with ruby-glass doors, containing an ivory crucifix on an ebony stand, and how his incense cost seven shillings the pound, and how he had clothed a Welsh choir with 'due vestments' as an Easter offering, and how his cousin the Abbot had made seven proselytes to the 'true faith.' I had thought the Tractarian humbug had died, and given way to philosophical cant of infidelity; but it seems that the very dregs and offscourings of Oxford youth still rock themselves upon this nonsense. . . ."

"This[2] morning I went to hear Stanley preach the Assizes sermon: the judges' procession and trumpets burst upon me for the first time, but the

---

[1] To his sister Charlotte, June 3, 1860.
[2] To the same, 1860.

clangour of the latter was inferior to my expectations, and decidedly surpassed by Stanley's brazen bidding prayer.   There is a great charm to me in hearing that gradual dissection of the Universal Church : it becomes sublime at the ' seminaries of sound learning,' 'and herein Oxford,' with the long roll of Christ Church benefactors—kings and cardinals, archbishops and noblemen.   Stanley has an unusually long list, for he prays likewise for University and for Balliol—for ' John de Balliol and Dervorguilla his wife,' as well as for ' Thomas à Becket, Archbishop of Canterbury, for Henry the Eighth, for Thomas Wolsey, Cardinal and Archbishop of York, for the Lord Clarendon,' for knights innumerable, and doctors of divinity without limit.   Such enumerations come sweeping by with pall and sceptre, and remind one of the line of Banquo's kings—our only ideas of them being phantoms of our own creation.

" I am so tired and so lamentably dismal about my work for Moderations, that I do not know what will become of me.   I forget everything that I read and have read, and am now unable even to read with understanding, so that I am beginning to dread that my Mods. will have to be put off till the autumn."

In[1] the summer term of 1860 I won the Newdigate Prize for an English poem on the Escorial.   It was recited in the Theatre on June 20th.   Conington, who did not believe (and very rightly, perhaps, did not

[1] Autobiography.

believe) in my gift as a poet, was curiously perplexed by this occurrence. He had twice competed for the Newdigate without success. Gifted with an extraordinary memory, he declaimed to me, on one interminable evening, his two unsuccessful poems, together with the two which won the prizes—four Newdigates in all, two inedited and two in print. It was a colossal occasion, called forth by the unexpected good luck of my littleness. When I came to recite my poem in the rostrum, Matthew Arnold, then our Professor of Poetry, informed me very kindly, and in the spirit of sound criticism, that he had voted for me, not because of my stylistic qualities, but because I intellectually grasped the subject, and used its motives better and more rationally than my competitors. This sincere expression of a distinctive judgment was very helpful to me. It gave me insight into my own faculty, and preserved me from self-delusion as to its extent.

[Apropos to this success Symonds wrote to his friend Mr. Stephens, "I am reduced to the last stage of self-loathing by being lauded for what I cannot help despising. Yet I succumb, and suffer people to read 'The Escorial' as if it were a new idyll with which Tennyson might electrify the world. Some people imagine that it is a final classical first : they have to be undeceived."

In the same term Symonds obtained a first-class

in Moderations, and so was immediately started
upon his work for the final schools in Litteræ
Humaniores—philosophy, logic, history.

For the summer vacation Conington formed a
reading party, which included Symonds and Green.
They went to live in a farmhouse upon the Lake
of Coniston, facing the shore which Ruskin has
since made famous. Thence Symonds writes to
Mr. Stephens :—"Green is coaching me in Plato.
He does it well, for he knows an immense deal
about the Platonic and Aristotelian philosophy, as
well as about modern systems. On the other hand,
because he is a very original thinker, he does not
express himself quite as clearly and fluently as such
beginners as myself would like. The spirit of
Plato's philosophy is surprising to me, who had
never conceived to what an extent Christianity had
been anticipated by Socrates. But it is the constant
search for the Real over the Seeming, for Truth as
Truth, which strikes me with such new light."
Here then, from the study of Plato, we find
Symonds imbibing for the first time that passion
for the absolute, that dislike of the relative which
controlled his intellectual growth, and to which we
shall find him recurring again and again in his
maturer speculations upon Life and Conduct.

To Mr. Stephens he sent this further account of
his work : " My reading may be divided into three
sections, 'deep,' 'middling,' and 'shallow.' In the
'deep' department the 'Phædrus' and the 'Phædo,'

and perhaps Theocritus, Bion, and Moschus. My 'middling' studies have been chiefly in Swiss history. Germany in the eleventh and twelfth centuries was as tangled as the gordian knot, and, in modern phraseology, I am minded to 'cut' the whole thing. My 'shallow' reading has fallen much on music. Besides 'Consuelo,' I have been interested in a strange novel of Miss Disraeli's. It is called 'Charles Anchester;' it is a romantic history of Mendelssohn, Hullah, and many eminent modern performers. I daresay you have read the Shelley memorials. It seems impossible that anything new can be said about him. 'Requiescat in pace.' Let us hope they won't go on stirring up his bones."]

A [1] trifling incident occurred at Coniston, when on this reading party with Conington, which I shall relate, because it is more powerfully imprinted on my memory than all the other details of those weeks. I had been talking to S—— upon a grey stone wall tufted with *cystopteris* and *ruta muraria*, the ordinary fern-grown sort of wall which divides fields in the Lake District. When twilight fell he went off to his lodging and his loves. I returned to the little room in the farm-house, where I pursued my studies. There I sat and read. Conington and Green were conversing in the paved kitchen, used by us as a dining-room, and perhaps they were not conscious of my presence. There was only a door

[1] Autobiography.

between the two chambers. Conington said—
"Barnes will not get his First." (They called me
Barnes then, and I liked the name, because they
chose it.) "No," said Green, "I do not think he
has any chance of doing so." Then they proceeded
to speak about my æsthetical and literary qualities,
and the languor of my temperament. I scraped my
feet upon the floor and stirred the table I was sitting
at. Their conversation dropped, but the sting of
it remained in me; and though I cared little enough
for first classes, I then and there resolved that I
would win the best first of my year.

This kind of grit in me has to be notified. Nothing
roused it so much as a seeming slight, exciting my
rebellious manhood. It was the same spur, as when
my Harrow tutor wrote home of me, "wanting in
vigour both of body and mind;" and Conington once
more, in the course of a long Clifton walk, remarked
upon my "languor," and Jowett told me I had "no
iron to rely upon," and F—— M—— said, I had
"worked myself out in premature culture," and an
M.P. at Mr. North's indulgently complimented me
on "writing for the magazines." All these excellent
people meant little by what they said, and assuredly
forgot soon what fell so lightly from their lips.
But they stimulated my latent force by rousing
antagonism.

The autumn of this year, 1860, before I returned
to Balliol, was spent in a Belgian tour with Charles
Cave, my sister Edith his wife, and my sister Char-

lotte, and upon the top of this, a rapid scamper with my father through Berlin, Prague, Vienna, Salzburg, Munich. The diary of these travels I possess, and it shows how hard I worked at art and nature.

[The diary opens thus: "I am going to begin a diary again in order to record my doings. Last time I kept a journal was between Jan. 17 and Sept. 25 of 1858. I have it still, and love it as a record of many happy days. The pleasure I have taken in it since ought to have made me more regular in noting down the daily occurrences and feelings of these years. Yet I think there needs unity of subject to keep up the interest of a journal. I must hope that our travels will supply one." The book is an extraordinary record of activity and absorption. Everything is studied, noted, compared, recorded to the full; nothing is omitted; a headache which prevented Symonds from being fully alive to the treasures of the Antwerp Museum, is bitterly resented. Music, Architecture, and Italian pictures are the main subjects of his descriptions and reflections; and through all runs a note of keen enjoyment, which was characteristic of his nature when ill-health or overwork did not interfere. So careful, so accurate was his habit that this journal, covering 233 pages of a small note-book, is indexed at the end with a list of hotels, churches, public buildings, pictures, and notes of expenditure. The diary, so diligently

kept, seems to have confirmed a natural tendency
to this form of self-expression. On Thursday,
October 11, 1860, or two days after the close of
his travel-records, he began a series which was
virtually never laid aside till the day before his
death. The diary of October 11 opens thus: "It
is rather adventurous to begin keeping a journal,
after so many failures, and without the unity of
subject which I thought so necessary to make the
trouble endurable. Yet, as I consider a diary
useful as a mechanical memory, and interesting
personally for the future, I shall attempt to keep
one. The custom of writing when abroad will
make it easier to do so here, and my 'unity of
subject' must be esoteric. The journey was decidedly historical and exoteric. This I will try to
make more a record of what passes in myself and
my more private concerns. Herein, however, let
me determine to avoid any essay-writing on these
pages. One journal begun at Oxford failed thus.
Also, let me not strive too conscientiously after
recording conversations. This bad habit made
another too tedious for continuance."

Symonds had come back from his tour fully prepared to test his beloved Bristol by the famous cities
and buildings which he had just visited. "On entering the Cathedral," he writes, "and seeing its beautiful
bare aisles, I felt the whole superiority of English
architecture over Belgian, and even over German.
The massive mullions and exquisite tracery of the

windows, the grand roofing with its clustered spandrils and lacy boss-work, the harmony of the parts
produced by greater length, the purity of the bay-
arches and their moulded columns—all combine
to exalt Bristol Cathedral over any I have seen
abroad;" and he adds, what is obviously true at
this time of his life: "'Cœlum non animum
mutant qui trans mare currunt.' I tested the
view from the roof of the muniment room at St.
Mary's, Redclyffe, and remain convinced of its
superiority over Ghent or Bruges." He enlarges
on the same topic to Mr. Stephens, in a letter
which is overflowing with affection for his home,
for Clifton and Bristol. "It gives me more pleasure to sit in Bristol Cathedral than in the duomo
at Milan, though the latter's transept aisles could
hold the former, roof and tower and all. When
you come to us I shall make you understand why
the peculiar intricacies of arch and groined vaults
—subtle as a Mass in D by Beethoven—have more
influence over me than the bare illimitable space
of gorgeous foreign churches. I cannot understand
why some people think size necessary to magnifi-
cence. Quality alone affects me; I am ludicrously
ignorant of quantity."

The winter term of 1860 at Oxford which followed
this journey was one of very great strain, both mental
and emotional. The diary, with its constant records
of breakfasts, luncheons, dinners, abundantly prove
that he was sought for socially. The inner circle

of his friends—Conington, Palmer, Puller, Ollivant, Vickers, Green, Stephens — absorb an immense amount of his time and energy. He sits with them till late at night, or rather early in the morning, discussing such feverish subjects as "The Universe," or "Moral Conduct," or "Mesmerism," or "Love," with the result that entries like the following become frequent : "I am feeling very ill—my memory weak—my head heavy—my limbs dragging—my whole being low." And no wonder. Intellectually two men, Conington and Jowett, were working him very hard ; emotionally, his friends were wearing him out, while the conduct of one of them brought him face to face with a problem of morals which was no longer abstract, but concrete, the solution of which compelled him to define his own views, and precipitated all his earlier speculations in the region of the affections.

It was at this period that the influence of Mr. Jowett began to make itself markedly felt. As Symonds had already taken a first in Moderations and was reading for the final schools, he naturally came more directly under the notice and the tuition of the Professor of Greek. He attended lectures on the Republic, of which he says little, and wrote frequent essays to be read to his lecturer. Of these he says much. The figure of Mr. Jowett runs all through the diary of this period; with his brief, weighty, pregnant remarks, and his touches of kindliness where he thought that his trenchant criticism had wounded a sensitive nature. "I took an essay on 'Historical Evidence' to Jowett. I had spent pains upon it, and was pleased on the whole with his reception of it, though he chid me for ornaments and mannerisms of style." There is more about this essay a little further on. "After dinner the Essay Society in my rooms. Green, Rutson, Puller, Bryce present. Dicey came in after I had read my essay on 'Historical Evidence.' I felt its poverty as I read, and still more so when we discussed. Perhaps this, and the cold way with which Conington received some translations I had done my best by, makes me feel so mentally inferior as I do to-night. I look round me and find nothing in which I excel. It is desire for many things and appreciation of some. Yet those who care for such powers less and have them more, are strong and happy. What is it? and where is comfort? Oh, not here—yet if not here, then where? Do I know anything beyond this 'here' and this 'myself'? In neither of them can I find consolation, and I do not feel that there is aught beyond. Perhaps I feel there is, but I know nothing; and what I feel is more a dread than a hope."

"After lunch to hear Mat. Arnold on Translating Homer. A good lecture, and full of impudence." "Walk with Conington to Bagley Wood. Interesting talk about religious doubts, with special reference to A——'s. I thought all doubt led up to the great doubt about God." "Tait and I met

at eight to read essay on the Eleatics to Jowett.
Tait read first, while Jowett gave me tea. Jowett
was pleased with his essay. Then I read mine,
which was elaborate. He interrupted me several
times to talk, but at the end seemed pleased: he
said, 'That is very good, Mr. Symonds, a good
essay;' nor did he make any strictures on the style
or mannerism, with the exception of the use of
'Generally' in opening the subject. . . . Then he
gave me a lecture on Hegel. He thinks him marvellous in metaphysical distinction, practical acumen,
and poetry. His theory, one in which the existence of a universal God is to be seen in all things
and thought. Distinct personalities are allowed by
this God to exist under and independent of Him.
This I had not understood from Hegel. The view
I had got of our being limited parcels of divinity,
destined to be resolved, he called Spinozism." The
next entry is: "I passed a very bad night, and am
feeling ill." That was on Nov. 10th, and six days
later came a telegram from his father, Dr. Symonds,
" Pray give up all study at once." The Master, Dr.
Jenkyns, was quite willing to assent to this pro-
posal, and to allow Symonds to go down, and Mr.
Jowett promised "to send me some of his lectures,
and offered a large book of them, clasped and
locked."

The strain of all this emotional and intellectual
life was indeed more than Symonds' delicate constitution could support. The only reliefs from the

besetting problems of conscience and the bewildering conundrums of philosophy were walks to Bagley Wood or Iffley, or in Magdalen walks— where the process was continued, not suspended— uncongenial gymnastics at Maclaren's, and music at Magdalen and New, which, though it soothed for the moment, really served to feed the emotional fires which were consuming him. On November 24th he went home.

But that which was wearing him out could not be escaped by a flight from Oxford. The process which was exhausting him was the formation of his own character; he carried all the elements of the ferment with him to his home. "In hopes of keeping 'mens sana in corpore sano,'" he says, "I have made these rules for home life:

"1. To walk to the Sea Walls, or at least that distance, every day.

"2. To attend no cathedral service except on Sundays and Christmas Day.

"3. To read (if I can) from 9.30 till 1, from 4.30 till 6, from 10 till 11.

"4. To go to bed at 11, rise at 7.30.

"5. To drink no strong tea or coffee, and take only one glass of sherry at dinner." But in spite of these excellent resolves, he did not grow stronger. "It is idle to record each of these languid days," he writes, "the reading in the morning, the stupid walk in the wet afternoon, and the dull evening."

On December 10th, term being over at Oxford,

Conington came to stay at Clifton Hill House.
"After lunch walk to Sea Mills, and round by
river. Conington told me that he had heard from
Halford Vaughan (who inspected the depositions
before Lord Eldon) that the judge could not have
acted otherwise, so immoral had Shelley's life been.
This tallies with what the Miss Shelleys said, that
the less people inquired into their brother's life the
better." A dinner party is recorded in which the
conversation turned on ghosts, magic, witchcraft,
spiritualism, and curious astronomical theories,
"which of course made Conington stonily silent.
He can talk of nothing but Oxford, books, and
some sorts of politics."

The life at Clifton was full and varied, had
Symonds' health been adequate to the enjoyment
of it, had his whole mind and all his feelings not
been already engaged and absorbed by the problems which Oxford life had brought to an acute
point. The walls of Clifton College were beginning
to rise, and young Symonds was taken to see the
plans of those buildings, with which he was subsequently so closely connected. Dr. Symonds' house
was always full of company, and that of the best.
But though these things are noted in the diary, the
record of ill health, "bad depressed headache,"
"painful reveries," "weary dreams," "weak and
melancholy," occupy the prominent place. He does
his best to enjoy: "I have spent my Christmastide
on the whole pleasantly. The cold clear weather,

the morning bells when dressing, the presents, the
service—all were cheery. But for this *Sehnsucht*
I should be happy." But this is followed by "Very
nervous at night. Went to Auntie and got some
Nepenthe, which did not do much good."

So this vacation came to an end with the following entry: "I go back to Oxford to-morrow,
and have just concluded my vacation's reading. Is
it satisfactory? Tolerably. I have analysed the
Republic, read two books of Thucydides, written
an essay for the Stanhope, and three essays on
Chatterton. Considering my state of health, morbid
condition of mind, and many interruptions, this is
good. I am very sorry to go away, even though I
have been so awfully dismal here."

The effort he was making to go the way he
thought right is made abundantly clear through all
the journal of this period. As he himself notes: "At
the beginning of last vacation I made rules, which
I kept pretty well. Read as much as I intended,
I could and might not. Go to bed as regularly, I
could not. But I did not drink beer at dinner, nor
did I ever go to a morning cathedral service, much
as I longed to. This term let me make some
rules.

"1. To go to bed at 11.

"2. To go to Maclaren's[1] when I can, and always
take some exercise.

"3. To read from 10 till 2, 5 till 5.30, 8 till 10.

[1] Gymnasium.

"4. To drink no beer in hall, but try and take some at lunch."

How full his intellectual life at Balliol really was may be illustrated by this account of a single day, taken from his diary :—

"*Sunday, Jan.* 27, 1861.—Breakfasted with L. Stanley, and had an amusing party. Met Owen— old Balliol man, returned from Bombay College— Wordsworth, Green, Jackson, Ford, Wright, White, Bethel. Talked about ' Essays and Reviews,' and the storm brewing for them : about Jowett's parent- age—Ford knows his mother and sister slightly, they live at Torquay—then of De Quincey, without some allusion to whom I hardly remember any in- tellectual Oxford breakfast go off: then about historic portraits—Wycliffe's at Balliol, Chaucer's from an old illumination, Dante's in the Arundel Society's publications. Sat on till 11.15. I went and wrote a long letter to papa about myself.

"Green came up to lunch, and we went to hear the Bishop[1] at St. Mary's. Full to overflowing. Preached from the text, ' For all that He did so many miracles, yet they believed not on Him.' I knew he would level at the Essayists, and, from the text, expected more than came. It was a general harangue against neglect of Revelation, considered in four lights—kinds, causes, consequences, cures thereof. The kinds were three, as resulting from pride of the world, pride of the flesh, pride of in-

[1] Wilberforce.

tellect. And each of these three kinds he treated
with regard to the three last divisions of his subject.
Therefore the Essayists only came in for the third
part of the abuse ; but he gave it them strong. His
peroration to the consequences was fine. He spoke
of men who, trusting to their own reason, thought
they could elevate themselves into a purer atmosphere, leave behind for the vulgar a belief in the
Crucified, and hold direct communion with the unapproachable God.

"More oratory than argument.

"Then to Magdalen. Service begins to-day.
'Praise the Lord, O Jerusalem,' Hayes. For
voluntary, 'Fallen is the foe.'

"After hall, read 'Alastor' through, and felt its
truth. How strange it is that the pictures it produced in my mind when I heard papa read it long
ago, and could not have understood it, are still vivid,
nor do I get beyond them. Query, would such
vivid pictures be suggested by a new poem now?

"Went out to see C. B., who was not at home.
Went to Holford B.'s room, and heard him play
Beethoven."

Such a day as this, begun in keen conversation
with the best of his contemporaries, carried on
through a powerful sermon by Wilberforce, and
ending with Shelley's "Alastor" and Beethoven, is
quite sufficient to account for the entry of the following date: "Very bad night. Unable to do anything in the morning." And the passages quoted

above do not record anything exceptional in the tenor of Symonds' Balliol career; his whole life was burning continually at this high emotional and intellectual altitude. He is keenly alive to all that is going on round him, and every event is recorded, often with a touch of humour in his impatience of dulness. "Breakfast with Jowett. Met a stupid man called S—— S——, who spoiled every effort at conversation by insisting on talking about Miss Eagle and ventriloquists."

About this time Symonds took to riding again. It was an exercise which always gave him pleasure, and from it he derived much benefit to his health. He writes to his aunt, Miss Sykes: "I am feeling the benefit of my rides; they take away the fanciful headaches and depression, making me more fresh, but, I fear, more idle. I get sleepy, and read less than I might; enough, perhaps, to be good for me." This is the record of his second outing: "Rode to Woodstock with R——, a short ride, and rather stupid, for he would talk about miracles and Jowett, and would not ride fast;" and this is followed by "Rode alone to Stowe Wood, Stanton St. John, Forest Hill. Stupid riding alone, both for man and beast."

It would seem that at this period Symonds was in the throes of an intense religious contention, which, under the influence of his philosophical studies for Greats, had assumed in him a highly intellectual form.

"Went to Communion, and found it seemed to do me good. Immediately after to hear the Bishop preach. Very fine sermon directed against doubt of portions of Revelation, as leading eventually to doubt of all Revelation—intellectual paralysis, moral weakness."

In the following letter to his sister, while regretting the decline of his pleasure in music, he tries to estimate the loss in the region of æsthetic enjoyment, which results from the admission of doubt :—

"None[1] of the musical services are much worth hearing, for Magdalen is not recommenced. After the inflexibility with which I avoided our week-day Cathedral service, I feel half inclined to make some such rule for Oxford. I must think about it, because, though it takes up time to go to Magdalen, still it is sometimes a great refreshment. I have lost, to my humiliation be it said, much of the pleasure I took in music. The enjoyment is less spontaneous and less suggestive. I analyse and try to enjoy more ; I have fewer ideas and less delight in hearing. A great many things must have combined to produce this result, but chiefly a less firm belief in the supernatural. Airy music and dark aisles inspire far deeper enthusiasm when the church is peopled with myriads of unseen angels. I believe that half of what may be called natural, emotional poetry comes from a belief of something in the Unseen. A tree is a tree, but when a Dryad

---

[1] To his sister Charlotte, January 20, 1861.

haunts it, it is something more.   So a star is a star
till one of Raphael's angels guides it, or its spirit
hovers over Hymenæus.   For the same reason we
feel that what Masson would call subjective descriptions of nature, are far higher than any gorgeous
word-painting.   The simple scene, 'when sundown
skirts the moor,' seen through the glass of Tennyson's melancholy doubt, is worth a whole landscape
of Thompson's nature-copying, simply because a
power, a spirit, has been put into the lonely heath,
and sinking sun, congenial with the poet's spirit."

Symonds' speculations upon religious subjects
were keenly stimulated by the sermons of Bishop
Wilberforce, and, as was habitual with him, in the
vigour of his intellectual sincerity, he carried those
speculations fast and far.

"The [1] Bishop preached a magnificent sermon
yesterday on 'doubting.' I have never heard anything from him so powerful : indeed, I think I have
never heard such a grand sermon from any one.
It was chiefly rhetorical—starting on the old pre-
mises of the Church's dogmas and the Bible.
From this premise his conclusions were unassail-
able.   However, it did not pretend to be argu-
mentative.   It was an impassioned warning to
young men, bidding them not let in the thin end
of the wedge of scepticism.   He told them that
the admission of doubts on subjects of pure criticism
and history would lead to metaphysical doubts, and

[1] To his sister Charlotte, February 4, 1861.

end in doubt of God. This seemed to me to be
the line of his argument, when stripped of its illustration. Therefore, the theory was that religion is
a thing of the heart, into which intellect may not
penetrate without blunting itself and killing the heart.

"I think he is right here. Many a man begins
by doubting the eternity of punishment; and then,
believing in his right to exercise private judgment, can find the doctrine of the Trinity nowhere
in the Bible. The habit of appealing to Reason
once gained, and strengthened and supplied with
food by philosophical studies, he comes to apply
the test of Reason to higher mysteries—that of
the Incarnation; that, finally, of the existence of a
God. Each step has been destructive—as it must
be, if men try to understand dogmas which their
powers pronounced unintelligible. For a time such
a man lives without God in the world. If he has
a weak moral instinct, bad training, a strong temptation, he may in this period give way to sin and
lead a life of careless crime. If he is earnest and
of moral purpose, he comes in the end 'to find a
higher faith his own.' He sees he cannot live
without God, and that Christianity is the most
satisfying human embodiment of this necessity of
God. All do not reach this higher faith; and
for this reason, I suppose, the Bishop wages
war against the beginning of even a healthy
scepticism."

It is remarkable that Symonds, while occupied

with the subject of dogmatic scepticism, should have turned his attention instinctively, for a time at least, to natural science, as though he divined that the battle-ground lay there.   He writes to his aunt :—

"Among my studies at present is a new one— that of brains.   I have been attending a course of Rollestone's lectures, and feel pretty competent to differentiate a monkey's from a man's 'cerebral hemisphere.'

"To-morrow I am to go and inspect one closely, and dissect a sheep's brain, and I intend to put many puzzling questions about the 'fissure of Silvius' and the 'Island of Reil.'   These two terms papa could explain better than I could at the present moment, for though I have heard plenty of metaphysical language about them, I do not quite understand their bearing on the great question of mind and matter.   I go to these lectures as preparatory to Ethnology, which seems to me a necessary vestibule to the sciences both of History and Philology.   Then I had a pet notion that a new psychology might be constructed on a purely anatomical and physiological basis, but Rollestone has upset that by assuring me that the more he studies the less connection he sees between the mind and the nerves."

.   .   .   .

"Jowett [1] I have not seen lately, except at lectures, and on those pleasant occasions when he gives tea

[1] To Mrs. Green, February 12, 1861.

and discusses essays with Tait and me. Tait last time was told that his essay was 'not quite good, had too much mannerism, and was gushing in part.' Having made these strictures, Jowett feared lest he had hurt Tait's tender feelings; so to compensate him, he rose from his chair, lifted the teapot very high, and sent a long amber stream of tea into a cup which he previously rinsed, after himself drinking from it, and exclaimed like Socrates—'Now I will give you some tea, oh my good friend.'"

The[1] Bishop's sermon is creating a great sensation. Few like it. R—— thought it repressive of that liberty of thought which the Protestant belief allows. But R—— on this showing would let every man have a little creed of his own, barring any of the great points, the Trinity and the Incarnation. He does not see how metaphysical doubts of God can arise from critical and historical questioning of the Canon. St. —— again misunderstood the Bishop. He thought the Bishop wished us to exercise intellect in examining the authority of the Church and of Revelation, and then receive all dogmas implicitly. Here are two objections to this view:

1st. If the Bishop said so, all we could test by intellect would be the validity of the canon. Then the question whether we could find the dogmas in Revelation would still remain.

2nd. The Bishop did not say this. He especially

<hr />

[1] Diary.

warned those "who received Revelation as a whole,
but began to doubt it in parts." In a word, he
opposed Luther's point of view. Here the Bishop
is no doubt repressive of the spirit of inquiry. But
he seemed to me to be so because he felt that even
an historical and critical doubt would lead to total
religious scepticism. This final state may not last
long, but it will eventuate either in "a higher faith,"
or in immorality. The alternative he felt, and
warned any from exposing themselves to the risk.
His moral was "Don't meddle with edged tools."
Moreover, he seemed to think the sceptical state
might continue. It may, but I pray it do not for
me. Non-recognition of a God and of any fixed point
weakens moral purpose, exposes one to temptation,
and may lead to a life of careless sinfulness. This
is the chief evil of a sceptical state. It also seems
to check the unity of Thought and Will, and certainly to impair the æsthetical enthusiasm." This
last sentence is of moment, for it shows how
Symonds imagined that religious doubts would
operate upon the two sides of his nature, the intellect
and the emotions. And in this context appears the
following entry : "I find I must make another rule
—not to talk of religious doubts. It is so exciting
to my mind that I am always exhausted by it."

But his rule of avoiding talk upon religious questions only drove the conflict inward upon himself. His health, indeed, did not improve under the
strain of speculation. He writes in his diary for

February 21st: "It is sad and strange this life of
ours. 'We lie on the knees of a mild mystery'
—as mild as the Egyptian goddess that holds the
naked child. Why should I say this, but that I
have had an evil night? The wind howled and
raged outside, peeling the scarred face of Balliol,
and blowing down one of our few trees. It is
strange what a sympathy and spirit this life of the
elements produces in one. I must needs be.rushing
out into the night to see the moon riding through
the torn clouds, and to hear the trees grinding one
against the other. After one of these nights, I
am βαρυγόνατος in soul and limb, my brain is hot,
and the *medulla oblongata* feverishly weak." He
was right in using this purely scientific expression,
for, as we shall see presently, a mischief was being
set up in the brain, which was to be the source of
trial and suffering for many years to come.

Symonds' sense of enjoyment, however, remained
very keen. The following notes of an *exeat* to
Sonning are full of life and interest :—" March 5,
1861—Met A. Pearson at Didcot, and went with
him to his uncle's (Hugh Pearson) at Sonning. We
drove from Reading, past Earley Court, through
Sonning walk till we came to the green gates of the
vicarage. H. Pearson welcomed us with 'Well, my
dear Albert,' and I felt as if I had known him all
my life. He first gave us luncheon, and we talked
about Jowett. He is so sorry about the 'Essays and
Reviews.' Says Jowett has never been the same

man since he missed his election to the mastership by one. He feels that in five years this book will be obscure, but Jowett will still be a marked man. Then we went out to see the church—a beautiful specimen of Restoration. Woodyear is the architect and Hardman has done the decoration in parts. Two windows by him, and all the brazen chandeliers, were very good. It is a late decorated building. From the carving of some bosses, and especially from a great arch over what may have been an Easter sepulchre, I think a French artist must have been at work. There is so much grace and profusion. The arch is filled with seated figures, like the figures at St. Ouen.

"Then we saw the churchyard, school, river, garden, and Hugh's house. It has a fine old panelled drawing-room. I was surprised with the immense amount he has done here. He has made the place. Besides restoring the church, he has built two others in the parish. He has made reading-rooms, and set up a rifle corps. Lastly, he has made his own house a paradise. He showed me a Tennyson in which Tennyson had written—

> ' Æennyson (attonitus)
> 14 Feb. . . 50 + 1.
> Sonning.'

It was one of the old editions with the ' Palace of Art' unaltered. One line in the ' Lady of Shalott,' 'and her smooth face sharpened slowly,' Tennyson said he had left out because it is so painfully an image of death. He (Tennyson) came to Sonning twice, once with Kingsley. Then he was in religious doubt, and made what H. P. thought a profound remark : ' The question of Christianity is a question of the Resurrection.' At dinner came Austin, the curate of Sonning, and Horn, the vicar of Earley. We had pleasant talk about Jenkyns and old Balliol days. They told some good stories of Tatham of Lincoln (who made the speech, ' I wish all the Jarman classics were at the bottom of the Jarman ocean '). Pearson said that when preaching once at St. Mary's on the text of the three witnesses, Tatham remarked that a MS. of St. John had existed once in Lincoln Library. The MS. had unfortunately been lost, and he added, ' When I last saw it my worthy friend the Bishop of Peterborough, whom I have now the honour to see opposite me, was with me.' About Jenkyns they told stories. Jenkyns had great tact in choosing the proper men for the college. He did not take them all of one sort, but mixed them—insisting on their gentlemanly behaviour. A man did ill in Latin prose. Jenkyns said, ' What can you expect from the son of a man who married his cook ? ' The Master once was thrown from his pony and lay in a ditch. An undergraduate hastened to his rescue, but he said, ' Stay, young man, stay—I think I see the Professor of Poetry coming, and he shall help me out.' "

Term came to an end, and soon after Symonds'
return to Clifton he started on March 25th for a
short tour with his aunt and sister to Amiens and
Paris. The diary of this journey is as fresh and
lively as ever. It is impossible to give more than
a faint indication of the immense variety of interests
and intellectual activity displayed by the young man.
Amiens Cathedral is visited from floor to roof;
triforium and clerestory galleries traversed at an
"aerial" height; nothing is omitted, for certainly
what the Symonds family visited, they visited
thoroughly; desire to learn and desire to enjoy
taking equal part in the direction of their journeys.
Then came Paris, and the Stabat Mater at the
Italian Opera. "Mario sang *Cujus animam*, and
his part of *Quando corpus*. He realised all I
ever heard of his voice—it is soft and pathetic,
but seemed to pierce and thrill more than a
soprano's. He gave *Cujus animam* with far
greater feeling than Giuglini. Giuglini has more
fluidity, more exquisite mellowness of voice, perhaps,
but there is not that mastery about him. The
soprani were Mesdames Bertrani and Battu. The
latter was young and pretty, and sang with great
effect. She had a French hard voice, which seemed
to rouse all the enthusiasm of the *vieux garçons*.
The chorus and orchestra were very good—the
performers (as far as I could see) really French."
Then comes a rhetorical De Quinceyan record of
the first impressions evoked by the Venus of Milo.

"As I stood and gazed, it terrified me to feel that she had worn that queen-like smile for nineteen centuries—that she had lain in the darkness of the earth, and still had smiled—that her arms had been broken in the crash of empires, and that still she had smiled—that she had seen the slow decay of years grind her fair breast and limbs, and yet had smiled—that now she rests as victoriously as when she gazed on shouting worshippers, and remains alone in majesty, unmoved by the adoration of thousands. Time has not destroyed her. She cannot die. Hers is the immortality of Thought. She lives for ever in the mind of her creator; she lives in the memory of all that once behold her. Were this red fool-fury of the Seine to rise again and shatter Paris, she would smile upon the tramp of armies; and though a *Carmagnole* of slaughter, led by Maenads, raged around her pedestal and crashed her to the ground, still would she smile and disclaim her murderers with eyes calm gazing forward."

This journey ended on April 6th; the party returning by Rouen, Havre, and Southampton. Symonds dreaded the resumption of his home and college life, with its speculations and introspections, which were overlaid, for a time, by what he called the "objectivity" of travel.

And, indeed, the old formulas begin again. "I have had a second bad night, and am feeling ill and nervous. Read in the morning about the Criminal Responsibility of Lunatics in the *Psychological*

Review, and some notes of papa's. I am going
to write about it for the Essay Society." Ill-health
and exciting speculations resume their ancient rôle
in his life. The day following the essay is completed,
so active and diligent was he in the execution of
any intellectual scheme. But he adds a reflection
which throws light upon his attitude towards the
practice of letters in his own particular case. " Had
I known more about the subject, I should have said
less and less quickly—perhaps not so well."

April 15*th*.—" Got up with the idea that I was
going to Oxford to-day. This did not make me
feel too lively—I hate a change." And his return
to Oxford did, in fact, renew all his old difficulties
as to conduct. The ill effects are seen at once
in such entries, as—" Three bad nights in succession have made me weak and nervous, and with
a pain in the trapezoid muscles." It must be borne
in mind, however, that these entries show what he
himself felt; how he struck the outside world is a
very different matter; as the following passages
sufficiently demonstrate. Dr. Symonds had just
received and forwarded to his son the following
letter from Dean Milman :—

" MY DEAR SIR,—I cannot refrain from expressing the pleasure which I received from reading your
son's prize poem. I have had much to do in my
day with such compositions, having adjudged them
for ten years of my life—a decade not, in that

respect, of unmingled enjoyment. But 'The Escorial'
seems to me to rank very highly among its class,
and the thought, feeling, and execution to promise
better things hereafter."

And soon after the Diary contains the following
note: "Conington has been hearing good things of
me from Bright at Marlborough. His brother, Balliol
Bright, has been talking enthusiastically about me
to him. As Conington says, he had got a very
exaggerated idea of me. The thing is, that I am
accustomed to talk to people I do not know, and
naturally show my best paces the first few times we
meet. But the fount dries up, and in time people
must see that one has a stock of conversation ready
to order, and power gained by long habit, of making
the most of what little one knows. Poor —— knew
little enough, yet marshalled it so well that people
thought him clever and well-informed."

At the close of this term Symonds joined his
father in London, and the two set off for what is
described as "an all-delightful tour" to Chamonix
and then to Lombardy; and as this was Symonds'
first visit to Switzerland and to Italy, with both of
which he was so closely connected in after life, his
diary becomes of great interest, and shall be quoted
at some length.

Macon, Sunday, June 16.—We left at five for
Geneva, where I now am. The journey from Am-
berieu to Belle Garde was extremely fine. It winds

through a pass cut by the Rhone, between Jura and some other mountains. The vine-clad slopes, grey rocks and bushy hills, were presented in every combination. After breaking fast we drove out to see Geneva. First we went to the cathedral, a small and symmetrical building of most interesting transition Romanesque. It has curious specimens of the use of round and pointed arch in combination, and borrows more from Roman models in the capitals than any I have seen. There is the pulpit, beneath whose sounding-board Calvin, Knox, and Beza preached. We sat in Calvin's chair. The church is perfectly bare, and Protestant. It was more injured in five weeks of French occupation, when 10,000 men garrisoned Geneva and made it a hospital, than in its three centuries of Protestantism. A little Roman Catholic glass is still left in the windows of the apse.

We had intended to go by steamer to Lausanne at two, but Sommerfeldt[1] never found out that they do not keep Paris time here, and we, depending on his, were late for the boat. However, we engaged a *voiturier* for to-morrow to take us to Chamonix. Immediately after dinner we were out again for a row on the lake. It was a glorious evening—the sun sinking below the western hills, and the lake as blue and clearer than the sky. Till now I never accredited "sapphire" and "crystalline" lakes; but now I did, when I saw the white pebbles at immeasurable depths beneath the surface. Geneva

[1] The courier.

is like Windermere as compared with the other lakes; it has the same expanse and gentle villa-studded shores, the same distant views of mountains and pleasant wooded banks.

Monday, June 17.—*Hotel de l' Union, Chamonix.* We started at seven this morning in a carriage and two horses. The journey has been one of uninterrupted beauty. The natural splendour of the country was heightened by the massy clouds which kept ever changing from peak to peak, altering the effect of light and shade, and making the distance clear and brilliant. I have met with all the Alpine peculiarities; multitudinous cascades, some thin as smoke, some foaming in strong falls; deep green lawns studded with trees along their park-like undu-lations; pines and crags and veins of snow. To call the fields a perfect green would be a libel, flowers of blue and red and yellow paint them; amethyst, ruby, and topaz set in chrysoprase. The wild flowers are innumerable, orchids, rhododendrons, columbines, saxifrage, salvias, vetches, pinks. We broke the journey at Bonneville, where we had breakfast. Up to this point the road was comparatively tame, though behind us rose the Jura, and in front the Alps were shadowy. But at Bonneville is the very port of the Mont Blanc Alps, and of this stands sentinel the great green Mole. From Bonneville to St. Martin, the valley of the Arve is narrow, one series of vast precipices cut by rivulets and pine-clad hills on either side. At St. Martin we first saw Mont Blanc, swathed in clouds, which slowly rose and left the monarch nearly bare. He did not seem quite so huge as I expected. The amphitheatre of mountains from the bridge over the Arve is splendid; especially that corner where stands the Aiguille de Varens. Here we learned that a bridge on the road to Chamonix had been swept away by a torrent, and that no carriages could pass. However, they telegraphed for carriages to meet us on the other side of the temporary plank bridge, and we set off, through avenues of apple-trees bordering gardens of wild flowers, beneath the park-like swellings of the hills, among whose walnut-bowered hollows slept innumerable chalets. Soon the ascent began, every turn discovering some great snowpeak or green mountain furrowed with the winter streams. At the bridge we found a one-mule carriage, and continued our journey, Mont Blanc growing on us momently. As we came into the Valley of Chamonix the highest peak was very clear, and all along the bold sharp crags swaddled in clouds, and glorified by the far setting sun, were gorgeous in their brilliancy and colours. We arrived at 7.30, and got two high rooms with a good view of the mountains.

Tuesday, June 18.—About nine, M. A. Balmat, Professor James Forbes's guide, to whom papa has an introduction, arrived. He is a pleasant, intelligent man, of about fifty, who, when he had read the Professor's letter, greeted us warmly. He no

longer acts as professional guide, but volunteered
to take us about for the sake of our friendship
with Mr. Forbes. Balmat is a curious instance of
a man refined by the society of great and philo-
sophic men. Having begun life as a guide, he is
now the respected friend and guest of Forbes,
Hooker, Murchison, and many others. Indeed, he
is intimate with all the savants of Europe. We
were surprised at the ease with which he spoke
to us, and to the commonest people. The same
bonhomie pervaded his address to both; but in the
one he never fell into familiarity, nor in the other
did he lose dignity. Having got alpenstocks, we
set off walking to the Glacier des Boissons, which
we crossed. I enjoyed picking my way among
the crevasses. The glare was just what I expected,
but it produced a curious effect of making the pine
hills seem quite black and sombre, adding to their
majesty. It is hard to estimate the height of these
mountains, and this is the one disappointing thing
about them. They do not displace as much sky
as the summer thunder-clouds, nor can we fancy
that two Ben Nevises might be piled one on the
top of the other below snow level (which is at the
foot of the Aiguilles). However, the higher you
get the more you can estimate the height above.
Mont Blanc is himself so far retired that he appears
small, while atmospheric differences, the want of
an Alpine standard, and the size of the pine trees
all tend to confuse English eyes, and lessen both

height and distance. Balmat told me just the contrary of himself. In Wales and Scotland he always made mistakes, thinking, with his Alpine standard, the heights and distances much greater. He allowed some time to ascend Arthur's Seat, and found himself immediately at the top of it. Under the noon-day sun, Mont Blanc, without a cloud except some filmy wreaths of nebulous smoke, was ineffably majestic—his robes of pine, and thrones of granite, and crowns of ice and snow. After lunching at a little wayside auberge on wine and bread and cheese, we walked home and lay down till dinner at five. At six Balmat fetched us with a two-mule char, and we drove to see the rise of the Arveiron, beneath the Mer de Glace. The air was cool; the sun had left the valley, though he flamed halfway upon the southern mountains. All the chain of Mont Blanc came out clear against the deep blue sky. Not a cloud was near it, and each needle sparkled in the sun point on point, up to the two silent domes of everlasting and untroubled snow.

Wednesday, June 19.—At eight this morning Balmat called for us with two mules, and took us to the Chapeau rock, which is on the other side of the Mer de Glace. Here we left our mules and began to walk. The road to Montanvert led us along the face of a shelving precipice, on the slope of which were cut steps and footholds. This pass is called the Mauvais Pas, and the precipice beneath is about 300 feet. A rope runs along the path,

by which people hold. Papa found it very giddy
and dared not look down, but my early experiences at Clifton have seasoned me to climbing,
and later on in the day Balmat praised me for my
agility. Leaving this precipice, the road wound
along the slope, until we came to a favourable
point for descending the moraine and taking to
the ice. There the footing is good and the air
deliciously cool. Every moment brings some new
excitement, either an ice cavern to see or a dangerous crevasse to leap, or some wonder of glacier
tables or glacier flowers to inspect. The glacier
tables are immense blocks of granite supported on
the hummocks of the ice. They invariably lean
to the south, where the sun has melted the ice
beneath them, so that it is easy to find the points
of the compass on a glacier. The flowers of the
glacier are arborescent congelations in the little
rivulets. We crossed the Mer de Glace and its
western moraine, and climbed up to the inn on
Montanvert, where we had lunch. Beneath us is
the frozen river gliding majestically among vast
pointed hills of rock, on whose summits sleep
eternal snows crowned with clouds. They rise on
either hand like vast armies guarding the realms
of Silence and of Frost. Few clouds were there
to impede the view, and the snow-wreaths burned
like silver beneath a scorching sun. Occasionally
we heard the roar of an avalanche down the cliffs,
or the breaking up of some great ice pyramid. I

longed for Charlotte, who would have enjoyed this glorious panorama of ice and precipice, though she would not have taken kindly to the Mauvais Pas and the crevasses.

Thursday, June 20.—I passed a bad night. When Balmat came at five to tell me it was a glorious morning, I felt better after breakfast—and truly it was a glorious morning. The sun was still between the Aiguilles de Dru and Le Moine, nor did his rays as yet interrupt the fresh repose of the atmosphere upon the glaciers. The sky was of a deep grey blue, without a cloud, and against it stood each peak and needle of the vast amphitheatre distinct. Our road lay to Tacul, a rock that juts upon the Mer de Glace, where the glaciers of the Géant and Lechaud join. From this point on the left lies the road to the Jardin, on the right to the pass of the Col de Géant. The whole of the Mer de Glace is a vast lake of ice, shut in by theatres and amphitheatres and vast recesses of untrodden rock—the home of eagles, chamois, and marmots, where men have never trod.

The air was clear and crisp, and the rain of last night was frozen on the surface of the glacier. The view became more sublime as we advanced, and when we were near Tacul, a scene of inconceivable splendour burst upon our view. Standing in the middle of the Mer de Glace we saw Tacul before us, and on either hand the gorges of the Jardin and the Col du Géant, deep in untrampled snow and blazing in the sunlight. The sky above was like melted sapphire, deep and clear and gorgeous, and against it stood the innumerable red pikes of the Moine, the Géant, the Flambeau, Charmoz and Dru. I now felt that I had seen the Alps. All my dreams were realised, nor could there be anything more sublime. A little more walking took us to the stone where Professor James Forbes passed many nights at the foot of Tacul, and near here, at the edge of a great snowfield, we had some lunch—bread and cheese, and curaçoa mixed with glacier streams.

Friday, June 21.—We set off this morning at seven for the Flégère. Papa and I rode mules— stupid beasts, that stopped at every bush and rivulet to eat and drink. Balmat was charming through the day. He is a perfect gentleman in manners and feeling, nor is there the least affectation or parvenuism about him. When I compare him with [some] specimens of English travellers, I blush for my countrymen. Here is a guide of Chamonix, the son of a guide (who would not allow him go to school or to learn the geology, for which he has always had a passion, for fear he might leave Chamonix), whose manners are better, sentiments more delicate, knowledge more extensive, views more enlightened, than most of these soi-disant gentlemen and educated men. It is a great pity that his father would not allow him to study when young, for he might have become one of the first geologists of Europe, such fine opportunities for discovery do these mountains

afford, and such an advantage his skill and intrepidity
have given him. Though a mountaineer he never
brags, and is always considerate for weaker brethren
like papa and me. I like very much to see him
walking before our mules with his green spectacles,
and old brown wideawake upon his grizzled hair,
nodding kindly to the old men and women, joking
with the guides, and smiling at the little children. He
is patriarch of the valley, and nothing can be done
without the advice of M. Balmat. After an ascent
of two hours we arrived at La Flégère, and saw
before us the whole Mont Blanc range. For the
first time we appreciated the height of the king
himself. Now he towered above all the peaks.
The names of most of the aiguilles and glaciers I
knew. Balmat told us the rest in order. The
Aiguille de Charmoz is still my favourite, guarding
the entrance to the Mer de Glace. Here papa read
"Come down, O maid," from the "Princess." It
was appropriate, for never were mountains better
described than in that idyll.

Arrived with threatening thunder, and an avalanche
from Aiguille de Blaitière at about two. Rested
till table-d'hôte at five. At half-past six Balmat
called to take us to his house, a nice chalet beneath
Mont Brevent, commanding a fine view of Mont
Blanc. Here he gave us coffee, with bread from his
own fields and cream and butter from his own cows.
He lives alone in the chalet with his sister—a fine,
tall woman, with a noble face worthy of the brave

Balmat stock. She is far superior to any woman I have yet seen near Chamonix, and though gaunt and hard with toil, has yet a simplicity and ease of manners that mark true good breeding, that is, good feeling. The room we sat in had two beds, and on the walls were portraits (Prof. Forbes' conspicuous), as well as three ugly R.C. coloured prints, kept for his sister's sake. He showed us his books, chiefly presents from great savants, and the various souvenirs he has received. The way in which he performed the part of host, without fuss, and without talking about the humility of his dwelling, put us at our ease. His cat and dog assisted at the feast. Then we walked back through his fields, and papa gave him a letter, written partly by him, partly by me, containing a ten-pound note, which he was to read after leaving us to-night. He mentioned the case of a cousin of his who had received some injury on the chest among the mountains, and papa asked him to bring him to see him, which he did while there was yet daylight. The young man (of about twenty-five) has Balmat blood, and shared the same respectful ease, good feeling, and delicacy which we had noticed in Auguste. I acted as interpreter to the medical questions and answers, but it was bungling work.

Saturday, June 22.—Up at five. At six, mounted mules for Martigny.

The whole day has been one of uninterrupted splendour, nor could I describe in detail the mag-

nificent view which we have seen. We took the
pass of the Tête Noire. Its beauty at first consists
in backward views of the Mont Blanc range. As
far as Argentière the whole valley of Chamonix is
in sight, but at that point the peaks are gradually
lost as the road winds among narrowing and descending mountains. The Aiguille de Charmoz
was the last I saw, and as Balmat bid me, I did not
say Good-bye but *Au revoir* to his cliffs. It was
six when we reached the Hotel Clerc at Martigny.
Balmat dined with us in a private salon. This
astonished Sommerfeldt, who has made friends with
Balmat, and sees him joking with the peasants on
the road. Indeed, it was necessary for Balmat's
comfort that we should have a private room. He
has not yet read our letter.

Monday, June 24.—At seven we left Brieg and
began the ascent of the Simplon. The clouds were
slowly drawing their length like dragons up the
hills, writhing through the gorges that dripped with
last night's rain. All the landscape was clear and
watery, and the valley of the Rhone, as we ascended,
looked exquisitely blue. For a long time we continued to see Brieg at intervals, but at last it was
lost in the involved valleys and barren precipices
by which we passed to Berisal. Between Berisal
and Simplon the finest view is that of the Bernese
Alps. They lay behind us, and their snow-capped
horns were seen through a vista of pine valleys.
The sun had nearly sucked up all the clouds upon

them, and the few that remained glided like pearls
along the silver snow, and shed soft shadows on the
grass beneath. It is a superb chain of mountains,
and continues visible for some miles of winding
ascent, till we reached the glaciers and the galleries
that keep off avalanches. At the extreme height of
7000 feet I found most lovely flowers—the larger
and smaller blue gentian, several pink primroses,
a very large white saxifrage, the Ranunculus glo-
bosus, and a sulphur-coloured anemone, of great
size and beauty, which gemmed the meadows; also
the little grey snow flower. Soon the descent
began, and at about one we came to Simplon—an
ugly village, in a dreary waste of hills, where we
had luncheon. The descent from Simplon was
grand in the extreme. It is one long divine pass
of granite walls, impending, towering, sloping,
polished, rifted, bare, tufted with pines, dry, seamed
with cataracts, now wide, now narrow, now sunny,
now black and gloomy—every change, in short, of
the wildest and most majestic cliff scenery presented in a long panorama of many miles. We
stopped at the Italian frontier for the Dogana,
which did not take long, in a little village perched
beneath some of the most overarching cliffs I have
ever seen, among the gigantic boulders that have
fallen from them. At about six we came into the
Italian valley, and our snow-accustomed eyes
were refreshed with vines and chestnuts in full
flower, and walnut trees—our torrent-deafened ears

with the soft Italian and strange patois of the people.

DOMO D'OSSOLA, *Tuesday, June* 25.—After breakfast we set out at seven for Baveno, on the Lago Maggiore. It was a beautiful morning, and the valley looked most richly coloured. Some great hills of purple stone set thick with trees quite came up to my ideas of Italian mountains. The road was lined with mulberry and walnut trees, and the usual magnificent Salvator Rosa Spanish chestnuts. The lake burst suddenly upon us, sleeping in its green expanse with all the summer on its shadowy hills. There is something peculiar in this Italian outline—a softness of sweep and a wooliness occasioned by the multitudinous trees that one recognises at once. We got very good rooms at the Belle Vue, looking on the lake, and soon after we set off to see Isola Bella, where the Borromeos have a palace. We got into one of the picturesque boats, covered with an awning of striped cotton, and were soon rowed across by two men. The opaque green of the water, which looked as if it could have been cut like chrysoprase, struck me greatly. The gardens which we saw first are full of rare plants and curious Louis Quatorze fountain work. What pleased me most was one terrace, looking on the lake, with great cypresses standing like sentinels beside the balustrades. Here I could fancy ladies or moonlight lovers. The house is a specimen of Italian villas—full of marbles and poor copies of pictures; tall, cold, gilded, and comfortless. It has hardly any furniture in it, but what there is is old, stately, and stiff-backed. On the walls are continually painted the armorials of the Borromeos, with their mocking motto, "Humilitas," blazoned for ever beneath coronets—not but what it suited the aspect of the sitting-rooms. The family occupy this palace four months in the year, and are always liberal in allowing strangers to visit it.

We returned and dined at two. Then we set out again, at half-past three, for the Lago d' Orta, in a carriage. We drove to Orta along the lake, which is a most beautiful sheet of deep blue water, placed among gently rising hills, like those of the English lakes. At the foot of the lake is a range of peaked hills, very grand, and surpassing any Cumbrian scenery, except, perhaps, Helvellyn from Ullswater. From Orta we crossed to the Isola di San Giulio, which stands covered with white houses, terraces, and bell-towers glassed on the blue lake. Here we saw an ancient Church of S. Giulio, in which was his body, clothed in full pontificals. By far the finest fresco in the church was a niche by one of Gaudenzio Ferrari's scholars, painted with St. George and St. Apollonia. Both were fully beautiful, and the exquisite youth of St. George, with his long yellow hair flowing over the breast-plate, was worthy to be copied by the Arundel Society. On our way home we saw innumerable fireflies. The sunset had been sombre, and it felt cold; but behind us was a clear green evening light with Hesper, and as we came near the lake it lightened over the eastern hills. The lightning increased and played upon the lake, revealing at intervals the line of mountains and a campanile in their dip. A great roof of clouds rose into the middle of the sky, and occasionally we heard very distant thunder, while the lake swelled with a sea noise. It was a fine scene, and became still finer when the moon slowly rose in a rift of sky between the hills and clouds, sullenly red, making a long tawny path upon the waves. I can hardly think it is the same lake which I saw this morning, basking in such blue summer mist and such ambrosial odours. The lightning still continues. But now the roof of clouds is broken into majestic masses, with ponderous round edges. Through these the summer lightning flashes about once a minute, like pulses of the sky. It reveals the most fantastic cloud-shapes, flickering at one time here, at another there, and again firing the whole horizon with one great illumination. Further to the south the moon shines with a steadfast light upon the water; her rays are greener and more powerful than in England, and they make a glory on the waves that keep chafing on the rocks and alder trees beneath us. It is truly a glorious scene, and if I had not already been too affected in describing it, I could go on—telling how the stars in chasms of the clouds shine with a lustre not their own, glittering like jewels—how the caves of heaven grow purple on the skirts of the lightning, full, as it were, with wells of starlight—how the moonbeams from behind a cloud are like the ladder in Rembrandt's dream of Jacob. I could fancy that yon pile of clouds was Sinai, and that so the Israelites saw God lighten from behind it. The flickering splendour of the one lurid region contrasts with the steadfast pearly lustre of the moonclad masses. It looks as if some competition were going on between the two glories, but the lightning is artificial and spasmodic in comparison with the moon.

BAVENO, *Wednesday, June* 26.—I had another bad night, which has left me very weak and depressed. The electrical state of the atmosphere must have something to do with it, for it thundered when I woke, and now at 12 o'clock a great storm is coming over us. We cannot leave for Lugano till 2.30. Meanwhile we rest.

To-morrow they open the cathedral. "O for the wings of a dove."

LUGANO, *Thursday, June* 27.—It was still wet, so we decided to go to Milan, and to start for Como, on our way there, at ten. After breakfast we went out again to see Luini's frescoes in the Church of the Angeli.

The cathedral at Como surprised me. It is a good-sized marble building of mixed Gothic and Palladian. Its façade contains some delicate sculpture, and the interior is liberal and broad. In its windows is fine Milan glass, a kind of imitation of

the Munich, of very brilliant colours and designs.
I wonder how it is that our English artists have
none of them this trick of glass.

To lunch.   Off at 4.20.   Reached Milan at
5.15.   I shall not describe my impressions of the
cathedral to-day.   Suffice it to say, that I was
immeasurably overpowered by the grandeur of the
interior.   It is well to have some buildings depre-
ciated.   Then they strike one.

Saturday, June 29.—I have not much to record
to-day when I open this new book, which Sommerfeldt got for me last night.   We left at 9.30 this morning for Como, where we spent the day.   It was a
beautiful morning, and this lured us, otherwise it
would have been hardly worth spending a whole
day there.   As it has turned out I do not think
it has repaid us.   I, however, take more pleasure
in the works of art than of nature, and in seeing
men moving than goats and cows.   In the train
was an Englishman, who delighted me because
·he so thoroughly came up to my theories about
physical science people.   The instant I set eyes
on him, I felt that such a pair of spectacles, cunning
cold grey eyes, sharp pale face, fresh light hair and
thin lips, with a generally intelligent but self-satis-
fied look and style of dress, in which greys and
drabs prevailed, could not but belong to some one
who had studied physical science exclusively; and
his enthusiastic geological remarks to papa, as well
as the cold way in which he received allusions to

Camelot and Tristram Shandy, confirmed my ideas
of him.

At Como we took a boat, and were rowed on
the water. Both papa and I were struck with
the strong resemblance this lake presents to the
Rhine. For beauty, as far as we could see, there
is nothing to choose between them, but that Como's
water is more intensely green, and that its banks
are dotted with white villas and red roofs instead
of grey castles. But I ought not to speak dis-
paragingly of Como, for I enjoyed its cool listless
air and sleepy sunlight very much, as I lay in the
boat, and heard papa read "The Lady of Shalott," and "Mariana in the South." I read
"Œnone," and then we returned to luncheon,
after which we drove to Camerlata, and so to
Milan. We had intended to shop after dinner,
but it is the Feast of St. Peter, and all but the
eating shops are closed. So we strolled into the
cathedral and then came back. We are disappointed at seeing so few pretty people. The
women are old-looking, sallow, and coarse-featured.
Yet with all this they are graceful when they
wear the pretty black lace mantilla and fan. The
men are better looking and of three types. The
first is a race of fair-complexioned gigantic soldiers,
chasseur and cavalry, a magnificently moulded set
of men. The second is a fair, pleasing, olive-
coloured, large-eyed kind of youth, "dissolutely
pale and femininely fair." The third is a regu-

larly Parisian, black-moustachioed, gross or withered abomination.

Milan is a most picturesque town.   Its streets are varied in architecture, and abound in balconies with hanging carnations, red cushions, and drapery. The people walk and sit about, ladies with fans and mantillas, lazzaroni on the church steps, old women selling fruit with dirty gorgeous handkerchiefs upon their heads.   The cathedral is the place for stalls of toys and fruit and books.

Sunday, June 30.—Breakfast at nine.   Off at ten to San Maurizio.   This church is also called Monastero Maggiore, from its having been an extremely rich foundation.   On the left hand wall of the chapel is a scene from the martyrdom of St. Catherine.   In the foreground she kneels bared for her execution.   Her hair falls about her, and her eyes are raised to heaven with their usual expression of piteous yet uncomplaining loneliness. Behind are the shattered wheels and slain soldiers, blasted by an angel, who leans with drawn sword from a fiery cloud.   On the right hand wall is the last scene of her martyrdom.   She is kneeling with her profile to the spectator, and her hands meekly joined.   A rich robe of brocade clothes her as befits a princess, and her face is more than queen-like in its sanctity of repose.   So extremely beautiful is this figure that one does not at once become conscious of the brawny ruffian who swings his body round, with clenched lips, to bring the drawn sword

with all its weight upon her neck. In the distance
are some soldiers looking on, and far away to the
left we see two angels in a mist of glory laying her
sleeping body in the tomb.

Monday, July 1.—Beautiful morning. Set off by
the 8.30 train for Arona. We passed Magenta on
our way, and were much entertained by the conversation of a spirituelle Italian lady. At Novara
we went up into the town, and from a high terraced
hill saw the immense amphitheatre of mountains
bounding the plain. They made a semicircle, rising
on either hand from shadowy blue hills, and gradually ascending with peaks of dazzling white to the
great mass of Monte Rosa, standing highest of them
all in the middle of the horizon. Such a view for
gorgeous colouring and overpowering beauty I have
never seen—not even at Salzburg. From our
terrace these mountains seemed impassable. They
rose like an army that had formed itself into a
crescent to defend Switzerland from Italian in-
vaders, and from every solid base of blue glittered
a spear of ice and snow. At Arona we took the
steamboat. The day was glorious, and we fully
enjoyed this lake. The finest point of view is got
opposite Baveno, looking up to the Simplon mountains. But the whole coast is lovely. Every turn
brought us to some red-tiled town, lying thick in
cypresses and chestnuts, or to a village perched
upon a hill, with its white fronts and slender campanile, or to a basking villa, with bright green window

blinds, and descending terraces to the water's edge set with oranges and oleanders. At the head of the lake a strong north-east wind blew from the mountains, and tossed the water into spray.

After dinner at Bellinzona came some musicians —two men, a woman, and a boy—violin, violoncello, and guitar—and played "Ah che la morte" with great spirit. I was touched, for just so did Consuelo and Joseph Haydn play their way through Germany. Papa gave them a franc, and I gave the little boy some cherries and a cake. Papa has gone to see one of the English ladies who is ill.

HOSPENTHAL, *Tuesday, July* 2.—Up to breakfast at seven. Started from Bellinzona at eight in a carriage, which is to take us to Fluelen for 150 fr. The ascent of the St. Gothard begins almost immediately after leaving Bellinzona, through a valley beautifully wooded with chestnuts and walnut-trees. The Ticino cuts it, and as you ascend the gorge becomes narrower and grander, guarded by steep cliffs and pines. A little before one o'clock, we stopped to luncheon at Faido. At Airolo it was a question whether we should pass the night; but as we arrived there about 3.30, we decided to go on to Hospenthal, a short way beyond the highest portion of the pass. So we had three horses put into the carriage, and began an ascent which, for ingenious and multiplied windings, exceeded anything upon the Simplon. Looking back, the valley, which had seemed so monotonous, presented a wide

and savage view, and to right and left came out
the snow peaks. But soon we left this valley, and
struck into another still more barren and desolate.
Such a furious wind swept from the glaciers that
we put on our greatcoats, and were glad to shiver
beneath two railway rugs. I shall never forget this
2nd of July for its alternations of heat and cold, and
for the curious experience of a sick headache under
the intensity of both. One advantage of being unwell in fine scenery is, that it frets the views into
your memory. We were now driving through snow-
wreaths, which, melted by day, were beginning to
freeze again at night. There was no vestige of
herbage, and the cold cruel cliffs rose impassable
before and all around us. Up them crept the road,
winding in and out upon itself, and giving the
appearance, with its strong walls, of a succession
of forts which we must storm and take. Our three
horses bore us bravely. Weary and piercingly cold
was this climb. Bastion frowned over bastion, and
Alp on Alp arose. The sun was lost to us, though
his light still sat upon the hills; and the strong
north wind was always blowing a ragged cloud from
the eyebrow of the mountains, which, as it spread
into the valley, dissolved and flew about in fleecy
foam. At the top of the pass we entered into this
cloud, and proceeded through a hideous region of
granite, sloppy snow, ice, and inky pools. Not a
vestige of anything more cheerful was there to
soothe the eyes. The cloud was all around us, and

through its rents we saw towering above us still more scornful crags. Here I got my ideas of mountains satisfied. Re-descent began, and we left the cloud, journeying now beneath his skirts through a valley rough with granite boulders.

We reached the Hotel de Meyerhof at Hospenthal about 7.30. The houses in the village are more picturesque than any I have seen in Switzerland. They are old and very large, and built on the Swiss cottage plan. But there is more variety and decoration about them. The wood is more carefully carved, and is arranged in curious patterns.

Wednesday, July 3.—I passed a very bad night, in the course of which I had this dream. I thought that papa and I were travelling, and were sleeping in adjoining rooms. We were in some hot country, and I had just come to the end of a night spent in great pain. Toward the morning I slept fairly, and when I woke the sun was shining hot upon my darkened room. For some reason or other papa had left his room, and I was alone. As I rose a horrid sense of impending evil oppressed me. I could hardly stand, and in great weakness I tottered to a chair that stood before a tall looking-glass. There I saw myself a hideous sight. My skin was leprous white, like parchment, and all shrivelled. From every pore burst a river of perspiration, and ran to my feet. My feet were cramped and blanched, and cockled up with pain. But the face was the most awful sight. It was all white—

the lips white and parted—the eyes pale, and presenting a perfectly flat surface. They were dilated, and shone with a cold blue eerie light. I heard a noise in papa's room, and knocked. He said, "Come in" in his usual tone, and I crept up to him. He was shaving and did not see me, till I roused him by touching him and saying slowly, "Papa." Then he turned round and looked intently at me and inquiringly. I shrieked, "Papa, don't you know me?" but even while I cried the vision of my own distorted features came across me, and filled me with my utter loneliness. At last he cried, "My son," and, burying his face in his hands, he added, "All in one night." In an ecstacy of deliverance I clasped his neck, and felt that now I need not go back into that twilight room with its bed and the mystery behind its curtains. But he went on in a hesitating voice, "My poor boy! what fiend—or demon?" I stopped the question with a yell. Something seemed to tear me, and I awoke struggling. Such was my dream—more horrible than it seems, for the terror of dreams bears no relation to the hideousness of their incidents, but to some hidden emotion.

We left at eight, and finished the St. Gothard in driving mist and rain. I am not certain whether I did not like it best so, for the grandeur half revealed left much to the imagination. Passing through Altdorf we came to Fluelen, on the lake Lucerne, and at 1.15 went on board the steamer.

The clouds were lifting, and we enjoyed a succession of beautiful views. This lake is incomparably finer than any I have seen. Maggiore is in quite a different style, and therefore shuns comparison; still I could not but feel how much more positive beauty, not to speak of grandeur, there is in the varied mountain forms, craggy precipices, snowy heights, and smooth green lawns of Lucerne.

[The Alps and Italy, reminiscences of his journey, were still in Symonds' mind, when, soon after reaching home, he makes the following entry :]—

Friday,[1] *August* 2.—Conington and I walked through Redland to the sea walls and home by the observatory. There we watched a great thundercloud, which for majesty of shape, size, and colour surpassed the Alps. Its change and progress was like a symphony. Far away, from west to north it stretched; above the channel the summits were of the pearliest white; domes and peaks, on which the sunlight rested; its middle was of light ethereal blue, like the base of Monte Rosa, but its feet were indigo, and a tawny fringe of angry red was driven mixed with mist and tempest all along the van. First it towered in simple beauty, transfigured with the sunlight that sat above it, pouring bands of glory down its chasms, and shooting in broad columns on the trees and rocks and downs—ever changing with the changing wind and scudding

[1] Diary.

fleecy sands, fleeces that ran before the armaments
of thunder. Soon this aspect altered ; more and
more of the blue sky was hidden as the masses
rose ; the cerulean blue was changed to deepest
purple, and the indigo to sullen black. The wind
swept furiously, the cloud came onward in a crescent,
the sun was darkened, and scarcely flamed upon the
topmost edges, and in a breath the gust of wind and
rain were dashed upon us. For a moment all was
dark and the landscape blurred, the vivid greens
and delicately pencilled outlines of the hills were
gone, the wind howled restlessly. But this again
changed. The cloud had broken with its own fury.
Like a squadron that rides upon the foeman's guns
and sweeps them off, and then returns scattered and
decimated to its camp, so this ponderous mass of
thunder-cloud was tattered, rent, and dissipated by
the fury of its onset—its domes were ragged, and
beneath its feet shone streaks of lurid sky, on which
the jagged tops of the firs and beeches trembled.
Now came the last movement of the symphony—all
the landscape was grey, but clear, and full of watery
sunlight. An exhaustion like that of a child fallen
asleep from crying seemed to hold the winds and
woods and distant plain. All was calm, but the
broken clouds went sailing on overhead, dizzy with
their own confusion, and, as it were, a ground
swell of its passion still rocked the upper air.
We turned and went homeward. In this symphony, or sonata, call it which you like, there

were three distinct movements—an adagio, an allegro, a presto, and a minuet. It should have been written in D flat, and no passage should have been free from agitation. But the first part should have most beauty. It should contain the germinal idea of the whole in a tremulous thought constantly recurring, and superinduced upon an air of calm majestic sublimity, which should be the basis of the movement. This agitation should gradually usurp the place of the calm air in the second movement. In the third it should reign supreme—all mere beauty should be lost in the tempestuous passion. In the last the calm air of the first movement should return, but shorn of any superfluous ornament, sad and melancholy, and often troubled by faint echoes of the central spasm.

[From Clifton, Symonds went on a reading party to North Wales. There had been a question as to whether he should join a party at Ilkley, in Yorkshire, or should go to Bangor. The advantages of having Mr. Rawlinson for a coach and Mr. Stephens for a companion settled the question in favour of North Wales, and the following are the notes of his stay there. He was far from well. The relaxing air of Bangor did not suit him, and he was oppressed by the prospect of the " Schools."]

Wednesday,[1] *August* 7. — Rose at 6.30, and

[1] Diary.

breakfast at seven. Ch. was down to see me off, so I said good-bye to her—dear, good, darling sister—and went off. How unselfish and thoughtful she is.

A long dreary day by Birmingham and Chester to Bangor. Drove to 11 Menai View Terrace. Mrs. Thomas can give us three rooms—one sitting-room on ground floor, a good double-bedded room above, and a tolerable bedroom.

Thursday, August 8.—Passed the morning in shopping and seeing Rawlinson. He has given us papers to do for him. Law came in about three; he has no rooms yet, but stays at the George.

Dined at three; then out to see the Tubular and Suspension Bridge. Through the former we saw two trains pass; clothed in thunder and with the breath of whirlwinds—one going in, the other coming out. It was a pleasant windy afternoon. Tea at seven.

Friday, August 9.—Went at nine after a second bad night to coach with R. He gave me a good lecture on the Indo-European nations, and the people of early Italy. We dined at three, and then went out a little into the town with Law. It was very wet, so we did no more than look for horses which we could not find. Bangor seems to be a damp relaxing place. I am in despair about Roman history. Livy seems, daily, more confused, and Arnold does not help him. My memory too is very weak.

Sunday, August 11.—Stephens and I walked round by Garth to cathedral. Came there at 11, found it began 11.30. Got a little well of a seat, and watched people come in—all like parrots, mean, unhealthy, hideous. Service atrocious—" *Venite,*" a sort of catch, in which all the voices tumbled in at the end one after another. No time or tune, or rhythm, or attempt at enunciation. A few monosyllables spit out viciously—all long words slurred over. Yet this choir sang, " The king shall rejoice," and " When the ear heard her." A good old blind Dean, with an earthquake-shaken face, enjoyed it all. Wet as usual—muggy, and depressing. Law and we dined at George table-d'hôte, such a skurry and bad waiting—English.

Stupid walk to Bridge. Read some Faust.

Tuesday, August 13.—A beautiful day. Stephens and I set out after dinner in a car, and were driven to the slate quarries at Penrhyn. Hence we set out walking up the pass to Capel Curig. This is a fine amphitheatre of hills ; the forms are bolder and more pyramidal than in Cumberland, the golden gorse, purple heather, and blue air tints, made a colouring that Maggiore did not surpass. Borradale, at the top of the Stye head and Langdale Pikes, perhaps are better, but I did not see them in such a flood of beautiful light. An exhilarating day.

Thursday, August 15.—Bad night. Fine afternoon. Stephens and I crossed to Anglesea, a nice blowing sail. Then we walked to Beaumaris,

along a road cut in the cliff with woods above us.
Penmaenmawr and the Aber hills clear in sunlight;
it was a beautiful scene. Beaumaris seems a
stupid little town, full of Manchester and Liver-
pool people, gross red-faced cormorants with keen
eyes and sensual lips, grown fat and cunning on
good living and sharp practice. The castle is a nice
grey building. These keeps have not been swept
away by the wars of the Roses and Common-
wealth as in England. Beaumaris, fair marsh,
must be a Norman name, and the people there
have not Welsh names, Delamere, Barker, &c.

Friday, August 16.—Stephens and I left Bangor
at 1.18 for Penmaenmawr. There we dined at
a neat, cheap inn. The day was glorious, and
soon after dinner we clambered up the mountain,
Penmaenmawr, from the seaside. The whole
face of the hill is quarried or cragset, full of
rolling stones or precipices. We worked up
first by a lateral path, then leaving that struck
up a ravine tufted with the most delicious thick,
springy ling, where we could lie full length on
beds of honeyed sweetness. Here we went lazily
pulling ourselves up by the long feathery branches
of the heather. This brought us to the foot of a
belt of aiguilles, which rose in a crown like the
Mont Blanc needles. Along the backbone of one
of these we clambered (here I found some white
ling), and sat astride upon its topmost peak. The
view beneath was fine—Anglesea on one side, and

the Great Orme's head, with English headlands beyond, and the blue sea between spread out below; on the right, a pleasant valley of green fields and trees dotted with white cottages, on the left the plain to Bangor, and the steep, stony sides of Penmaenmawr. From this point to the cairn at the summit was another scramble. There we drank an icy breeze, and ran down again over rocks to the golden furze, and the woods above the village. We were here in time to catch the 5.20 to Bangor.

Wednesday, August 21.—Slept very ill—a night of overtaxed brain, and constant weary dreams. I must begin some strychnine, I feel so low.

Stephens and I went to Carnarvon. We saw the Castle well—old, perfect, interesting. It had been our intention to drive to Llanberis, and walk back, but a return car we wanted to take kept us waiting, and finally did not come. We walked about two miles out, to a pretty stream, where I felt very depressed and ill. I cannot read to-day. Stephens is like a cart-horse, and I am very melancholy.

Thursday, August 22.—Quite wet all day long. So I have been melancholy, but, on the whole, feeling better than yesterday. I am reading Schœlcher's "Life of Handel"—full of matter, but ill written. These I wrote coming here :—

> Have pity, Lord : my soul is shattered
> With wave on wave of instant ills ;
> Vainly the everlasting hills
> With promised aid my eyes have flattered.

For lift thine eyes unto the mountains
  Whence cometh help, the Psalmist sung;
  He slumbers not nor sleeps who hung
His bow of hope o'er Sorrow's fountains.

The strength of Israel wields the thunder,
  He sitteth on His throne of might,
  Beneath His feet is bowed the night,
He gives the Word, and far asunder

Part the swift clouds, the earth rejoices.
  O Lord, our fathers hoped in Thee,
  Hoped and were holpen, but for me
Comes no sweet comfort of kind voices.

My heart is sad, my sight is weary,
  The leaden skies above me scowl,
  Wild winds upon the mountains howl,
And all the world is dull and dreary.

Poor stanzas made to test the double rhyme in " In Memoriam " metre.

I rather hoped to go with Ch. to Hereford, and to hear—two days—" Samson " and " Last Judgment " on one, " Requiem," Haydn's " Spring," and " Lobgesang " on the next. But she may not go, and I will not go alone. What I shall do when I get back to Clifton plagues me. Auntie and Ch. will be away the greater part of the time visiting. I shall be alone all these long days.

Friday, August 23.—Very unwell. Stephens and I left early for Penmaenmawr. Dined there, and rambled about the mountain. We got into a fine craggy gorge, where we amused ourselves with hurling down rocks and climbing about. Stephens nearly fell some 100 feet by the giving way of one of the slaty brackets on which he stood above the precipice.

The walk was pleasant, but did my head no good.

Saturday, August 24.—Just the same dull pain. Began "St. Ronan's Well." Went to Aber at 4.15. Saw the fall, which is decidedly good, and of course in good water after all this wet, and climbed a hill full of bogs, from which we descended on the Bangor road, and had a six miles' walk home. On the whole we did about ten miles, walking very fast, so that my head ceased not aching. My depression is extreme—powerless, yet short of time, and all abroad about my histories. Aristotle is on the shelf.

Sunday, August 25.—Up at 6.30. Off by 7.15 to Chester. Fine morning. Got there and had breakfast in time to reach the cathedral at 10.30. Service begins 11. We sat between the two sides of the choir, which was decidedly good. It seems to be Bangor's model. They have much the same division of the "Venite," and the same jumble of Tallis unaccompanied, and the ordinary responses. There the resemblance ceases, for Bangor's imitation is a burlesque. The Chester choir sang firmly, solidly, and well together. Without great brilliancy or command of piano, which marks the very best choirs, it gave a good sustained chaunt and a well-sung anthem. Pergolesi's "Gloria," sung to the words "I was glad when they said unto me," was the anthem. The words did not suit the music. Perhaps their responses are their worst part, weak and slurred. Dr. MacNeil preached—a sermon wholly unworthy his reputation—on " Behold, I show you a mystery "—fanciful, illogical, violently abusive of divorce courts, yet withal in parts forcible.

Thursday, August 29.—After an early dinner we set off for Port Dinorwic, between this and Carnarvon, intending to make our way toward Llanberis. The morning had been dull, but the clouds drew up as we went on. The road was stupid, but our splendid view of Llanberis Lake and Snowdon, purple with evening clouds above it, fully repaid us. When we reached home, and were sitting down to tea, Palmer came in. He wants us to walk with him over the Glyder range to Capel Curig.

Friday, August 30.—I felt uncertain this morning whether I should go with Stephens and Palmer, as the walk embraces two first-class and several inferior mountains. The weather, too, seemed uncertain. However, Palmer at eleven persuaded me to go, and we set off in a car for Bethesda. The morning was fresh and windy. From Bethesda we crossed the Ogwen, and went straight up the first great hill on the right of the valley. It is called Carnedd Filiast, and a stiff pull it was that brought us to the top. The view over the plain of Carnarvon, Bangor, Conway, and Anglesea was broad and sunny. From this point we walked along the backbone of a great wedge of mountain that separates the Ogwen and

Llanberis valleys. On the one side descended walls of breathless precipices to the Capel Curig road, on the other lay the Llanberis lakes and the three great peaks of Snowdon, ever changing as we moved. The lights were perfect, clear and blue, with mazy moving clouds. Palmer had described the walk as being one "along the ridge," by which it seemed he meant going up and down over the various peaks of a considerable range. I got very tired at the last and largest, Glyder Vawr, whose sides are steep and full of rolling stones. The wind, however, aided and freshened us. It carried Stephens' hat over an abyss, but that did not incommode him. The tops of the Glyders Vawr and Vach are quite barren, and strewed with gigantic piles of rock fallen from aiguilles that still remain. Their titanic slabs reminded me of Druid circles as much as the cliffs of the Saxon Switzerland of Egyptian temples. Snowdon was very grand from here, as was Hebog, and the distant sea and Cader Idris—a fine sweep of hills. Thence, having gazed down beetling cliffs and clambered dizzy pinnacles, we tramped down through bog and moss on Capel Curig, which we reached about six. I was famished, not having eaten since eight, and drank only a little sherry on Glyder Vawr. Besides, the walk was the longest I ever took. We got slippers and I bought a pair of stockings, and became comfortable for a good dinner. Then we drove home in the yellowing gloom. Llynogwen, and some lonely fishermen fishing in the cold clear starlight, struck me much. Home about ten.

[The Bangor party came to an end on September 1st, and Symonds returned to Clifton with his friend Mr. Stephens, to whom all his favourite places and things—the cathedral, sea-walls, Cook's Folly, Nightingale Valley, the old oak in Leigh Woods—were shown, one by one, and the effect recorded with obvious contentment in such phrases as, " Stephens everywhere pleased." From Clifton Symonds went on a visit to Wiltshire, where "we went out cub-hunting. Charlotte had a little white pony. I was mounted on a splendid black called ' Euxine.' I rejoiced to feel the strong, spirited animal beneath me." Symonds' intellectual life continued active as ever, and its growth fostered the habit of self-analysis.]

September 29.[1]—Goethe's " Life "[2] is a well-sustained biography. The genius of the man has an electrical effect upon me, galvanising these dull nerves into something like life and enthusiasm. Lewes' aim is to give a succession of vivid pictures, and this he achieves. So good is the portrait painting that every line thrills me. The reading is a continual process of self-comparison, how impotent and humiliating to myself. This discontent with my own personality is weak. If I had a really great character I could stand alone, and be content to remain what I am without sighing for genius.

[1] Diary.   [2] By Lewes.

If I had faith I should see myself as part of the divine scheme, and anticipate a time in the hereafter when mere human ability would be all useless and men stand on the same level. That, now, I cannot hold ; and the belief that what we are we shall be, that the vital force within us may be carried into fresh forms, but will never be increased or diminished— prevents me from seriously entertaining thoughts of suicide. To rush from a state of discontent I know, to one I do not know, and to be the worse perad-venture for the change, that is unreasonable. Read-ing this life teaches me how much of a poet's soul a man may have without being a poet, what high yearnings may plague him without his ever satisfy-ing them, what a vast appreciation and desire may exist where there is no expression or formative will. And in all these cases the force is wanting, power is absent, spontaneity is torpid. Suscepti-bility to beauty, capabilities of acute pain and pleasure, strong æsthetical emotions, these do not constitute a poet, though a poet must have them. Again, deficient ability for mathematics, for history, for politics, an impressionability that opens the mind to every subject without allowing it to master them, melancholy dejection and thoughts of suicide, the effervescence of sentimentalism, the vacillation of religious doubt, these do not spoil a poet, though they make a lesser man contemptible. Power, all-pervading power, pushing the soul into activity be-yond receptive susceptibility, covering all deficiency

by concentrating itself on the passion of the moment
—this makes the difference between the man of
genius and the dilettante driveller. Not so with
men of talent; they differ from men of genius in
kind; and talent, however small, is always definitely
appreciable. A man may have the susceptibilities
of genius without any of its creative power; but if
he has any atom of talent he cannot be without
practical energy. I may rave, but I shall never
rend the heavens: I may sit and sing, but I shall
never make earth listen. And I am not strong
enough to be good—what is left? I do not feel
strong enough to be bad. Then again of Love.
Oh! woe is me! for it seems that if I had but Love
I might get strength.

" Ihr Anblick giebt den Engeln Stärke."

I wish I could concentrate all my vitality into
three years, and at the end perish, having lived a
life of worth and energy through that short time.

Saturday, October 5.—I am twenty-one to-day, the
end and goal I have so often thought of. Up to this
point I have been struggling, saying, "When I am a
man I shall do this, understand this, be great; now I
am a boy, and from a boy little is expected." The
sum of intellectual progress I hoped for has been
obtained, but how much below my hopes. My
character has developed, but in what puny proportions, below my meanest anticipations. I do
not feel a man. This book is an evidence of the

yearnings without power, and the brooding self-analysis without creation that afflict me. I am not a man. Papa gave me all De Quincey's works; Auntie, £5; Ch., Goethe's Autobiography and Faust, 3 vols.; E. and M., a ring; Ch. and E., a thermometer; Aunt M., a bookstand; Aunt Ch., a pair of candlesticks. Besides these, Edmond sent me some flowers, and Mrs. Buchanan a pretty pencil-case and key for my watch chain. Ch., James, Lucy, and I walked down to morning cathedral and heard the "Benedictus" from the Requiem.

Just before dinner Jowett arrived. I was sitting in my study and heard him ask Newsome, "Where is the drawing-room?" So like him to forget. And when N. said, "Downstairs," he answered, "Oh, yes, to be sure." Mr. Hill, Alfred, and Florence, and Mr. Leech dined. Jowett, of course, did not talk at dinner. Papa had to leave us about 8.30 on his way to Tortworth to see Lady Ducie. He will sleep, and return by train to-morrow. In the evening Jowett, Mr. Hill, and Mr. Leech sat together. Alfred entertained me. He told me about the process of sculpture, which I should like to remember. The artist first models in clay. A thin preparation of plaster and inky water is laid upon this for several layers, and when they have hardened, great masses of plaster are dabbed on. When the whole thing is quite hard the clay is withdrawn from inside, and fresh plaster poured in after a preparatory oiling. Then the workmen knock off the outer plaster with a chisel, working carefully as soon as they arrive at the inked plaster. The cast thus obtained is called the artist's cast. This he gives to the pointer if the bust is to be executed in marble. The pointer is an inferior workman, who rough-hews the marble in this manner. There is a great frame containing two squares, in the centre of one of which is placed the cast and of the other the marble block. Fitted to the frame are two moveable pointers like pencils. Whatever point the one pointer touches in the one frame the other touches in the other frame. So the man works on and on, moving the pointers till the one touch the cast at some point, then he stops and renews the process in another direction till the whole block has been rough-hewn. At this point the face is roughly traced out and its expression just discernible. This is handed over to a superior workman, who copies from the cast and touches it up. If the artist can handle a chisel he sometimes puts on finishing touches. Munro does. Flaxman never did. To take a cast from this there is a process called "piece moulding." Threads of silk are disposed over the bust, and then plaster laid on. Before the plaster is quite dry they cut it by lifting the thread and take it off in pieces. These pieces they build up in a box and pour in plaster for the casts. One matrix will serve for six, and the thread ridges are very much prized by artists. They fear chalky knots in marble more than blue veins.

After the guests were gone I talked a little to Jowett. He deplored the class-lists, but thought that there is no practicably better way of electing examiners.

Sunday, October 6.—We breakfast at nine. I was glad of this, for it is hard to entertain Jowett. His forte is an *aurea taciturnitas*, and he has a habit of shutting up a subject by a single sentence. The conversation is one conducted by question and answer. I start a subject and ask a question. He makes an answer and stifles the subject. Auntie and Ch. do not aid.

At 10.30 we walked through the garden to the cathedral. Jowett admired the view of our house very much. He talked of the lamentable want in education. Men of ability and power often do not come out on account of adverse circumstances. Few "Nameless Great" and unknown Shakespeares.

I was amused with the sensation Jowett made. His beauty would not fail to attract attention; but besides this, people recognised him from Richmond's portrait. We sat under the organ. He admired the restoration and the choir. We just looked at the Chapter House on the way home. Jowett and I walked up and down the garden. I told him of my birthday. He said the most important era in a man's life is when he leaves college. Then to Mr. Rhind. Jowett was shy and silent. He told us a little of his visit to Berlin, many years ago, when he saw Schelling, Neander, and others. Jowett is peculiarly sensitive about not being coddled. He will not be sent out in a carriage if he can help it, and toiling up Constitution Hill from the cathedral, he said, "Our young legs don't mind this, do they?" puffing all the time. He told me Tennyson had written little lately; has been four months in the Pyrenees; his boys very beautiful; not precocious. Tennyson never writes letters. Jowett has only had two short notes from him. He reads a great deal. He looks on "Maud" as on a young and misunderstood child—would be pleased with papa's verdict, that it is his most subtle poem. Jowett had mentioned some one as "over-educated." I asked what he meant. He said that the intellect might be developed beyond the character and will. It happens in the case of Germans mostly.

October 7.—Jowett and I went to Seed's, where he had his portrait taken. It was very good of him to let it be done, for he hated it. He stood so funnily—like a doll, straight and stiff. The man tried to drill him into a position; he was meek, but awkward. I told him to stand naturally. The man wanted him to set his necktie straight—trying to destroy all personality; but I would not let him. It took a long time, and Jowett looked cross and uncomfortable. When we came in, Jowett read out to Ch. and me the song of the Jews and Karshish the Arab, from Browning. He reads

quietly and undramatically, but well. This nearly
made us late for dinner. He is very absent. In
going to his room he tried the backstair door first,
and then wanted to come up to my landing.   One
reason why he makes me shy, beyond his own silent
shyness, is that he is so uncommunicative of himself. I feel that he is self-wrapped, and that he will
not lift the curtain. He lives within a veil, and is
all in all to his own thoughts. Egotistical people
are easier to get on with, partly because you despise
their egotism. He has written the notes to the
whole of the Republic, and is now re-writing them.
He is trying to raise as many modern points of
interest as he can, and the allusion to the dependence
of intellectual and moral qualities on each other is
one. A long discussion about the merits of Bacon
and Galileo, and about Pascal, occupied the greater
part of the evening : Jowett refused to carry speculation beyond the grave—the realm, he said, of faith.

October 9.—Jowett sat up late again with papa.
He talked about himself. He feels that he must
go on in his work of liberating the minds of men.
He complains of headache, powerlessness of brain,
want of sustained thought, imperfect memory, as
I do. Jowett sees a danger of young men being
sentimentalised or criticised from production. His
point of view in all these things is evidently what
young men can be made into. At six we drove
off; Jowett looking very funny in a barrel-bodied
greatcoat. I put him into a carriage full of people

returning from an archery meeting. Jowett waved his hand and smiled rather slightingly, and then, he was gone. I returned to myself.

"Jowett[1] went off yesterday, looking very cherubic in a barrel-bodied greatcoat, and a hat put back from his immense forehead. The last sight I had of him was sitting in the railway carriage, irradiated by the soft splendour of its lamp, and hugging a chaotic mass of coats and umbrellas, from the midst of which he waved a finny hand in token of good-bye. I turned like Sir Bedivere 'revolving many memories,' and heard the first act of the Colleen Bawn. But my inner life was too perturbed, and the acting was too bad to admit of any longer patience, so I left the theatre just as the plot thick-ened, fully convinced that had I acted any one of the parts, not excepting the Colleen's, I could have done better. Then I came home and had it demonstrated to me by papa that my income[2] was enough for any man to live on. I daresay it is, and I could live on much less. After which I had a very bad night, and woke this morning 'a wiser and a worser man'—often the result of vivid phan-tasmagoria and strong emotions suffered during sleep. If for two or three successive nights I saw

---

[1] To his sister Charlotte. Clifton, October 10, 1861.

[2] His income at this time amounted in all to three hundred and fifty pounds a year. It was composed partly of allowances from his father and his aunt, Miss Sykes, partly of income from some property of his own.

such a murder enacted as I saw last night, or felt such a central passion, I must become a bad man. It would be the beast within me gradually gathering strength for madness.   There now is my life inner and outer for you since I saw you.   I have asked James to ride with me this afternoon to Sutton Court.   This is a capital Jowettian pen."

October 10.[1]—One of the most provoking things about ourselves is that we form pernicious habits, and do not know they are so till they have become necessary.   The cathedral soothed me at first like a delicious opiate; now it tyrannises over me and irritates me like opium after long indulgence.   The common defect of all æsthetics is that they raise a yearning which cannot be satisfed by themselves except in creation.   For a while the yearning is melancholically seductive.   But after a time the yearning remains when the pleasure of contemplation has grown insipid, and we seek a "human element."

[In October Symonds returned to Oxford.   His Diaries, as fully kept as ever, record the same round of breakfasts, luncheons, dinners, intellectual talks, walks, rides, hard work for Jowett—"he asked about my work, said an Essay a day was too much; I must be careful not to break my camel's back".—quantities of poetry, ballads and poems in the "In Memoriam" stanza; daily visits to Mag-

----

[1] Diary.

dalen or New College Chapel; an interview with an electro-biologist, and another with a phrenologist.

Much of the poetry remains unpublished, in the Diary; these verses, for example, written on October 22, 1861 :—

> "O love, sweet love, I sit and sing to thee,
>   And from sere reeds sought in the winter brake—
>   Hoarse reeds through which the winds wail mournfully,
>   And the waves wash—a funeral pipe I make ;
>   For thou art dead, sweet love, and never more
>   Melodious movements of the breathing spring
>   Shall thaw thy blood, or spread thy pinions frore,
>   Or stir thy cold stiff throat to carolling.
>   These reeds shall bloom and rustle to the breath
>   Of minstrel winds in summer ; birds shall sweep,
>   And painted flies shall flicker ; but thy death
>   Is unrelenting as the marble sleep
>   Which holds Endymion, whose eternal swoon
>   Breaks to no kisses of the passionate moon."

There are jottings, too, of conversations with his numerous friends, as, for instance, these on Diaries : "Diary good for thoughts, not for things. Ordinary log-book a poor affair. Useless to eliminate what others ought not to see. Danger of over-doing emotion. Mrs. Clive might have made a most powerful novel out of Haydon's Diaries." As a groundwork to all this life and activity, as a never-failing note of pain, run the records of ill-health : "Still weak and unwell, I cannot read, a cloud is over my brain ;" "return of old cramped head feeling ;" "a long internal agony of doubts, analysis, questionings." "Curious talk about my want of sympathy, ambition, mad suicidal fancies. God preserve me."

" I [1] have not much to tell you. Last night I saw Jowett, and asked him how he liked his portrait. He said ' it was well enough, he supposed,' and that was all I could extort from his modesty. He is ascetically unconscious of his appearance, and does not possess more than a slip of looking-glass too narrow for his chin, much to Green's annoyance in shaving when he occupied the rooms. Some people supposed that this is affected to subdue youthful pride, for there is an old story of his being detected, the night he got the Balliol, expatiating in a scholar's gown and arranging his soft brown curls before a mirror in the Master's lodge.

" This morning I wrote to Mrs. B—— in answer to a note from her, and said I should come on Saturday. Whether I shall be able I still doubt, for after a ride this afternoon, the swelling on my face has so increased, that I look ridiculous. If it does not abate sensibly to-morrow I cannot show my head among strangers."

" I [2] went to have my head examined by the phrenologist the other day, and, though he gave me enough encouragement, I think he is a great quack.

" Some shrewd things he said. On first feeling my head he pronounced that I came of a long-lived

[1] To his sister Charlotte. Oxford, October 31, 1861.
[2] To the same. Oxford, November 17, 1861.

J.A SYMONDS - OXFORD.

race, and booked me for ninety. The first part
of this judgment is true. Then he proceeded to
explain that my vitality was intense and worked
vehemently. He told me my historical memory
was defective, and that though I had tune I had
no time. Both these observations are true; my
memory for facts is lamentable, and I cannot dance
properly, though I am sensitive to music. Here,
I think, he stopped. The next was vague. And
I have noticed that phrenologists always guess
pretty accurately about memory, time, and tune.
All the moral faculties were well developed except
faith. The æsthetical parts of the intellect, form,
size, colour, order, number, were large; so was language, causality, and comparison. My want of
caution and acquisitiveness seemed the most dangerous part of my character, though a good secretive-
ness and firmness made up for them in some measure.
I asked the man many questions after he had examined me, about Shelley's small head, &c., and here
his impotent quackery came out. He defined genius
as scrofula. After that I knew how much the man
was worth."

[To any one who reads this extraordinary record
of a young man's life, the courage, the persistence,
the force of will which enabled Symonds to achieve
what he did, must be a matter for marvel and for
admiration. He was right when he wrote, much
later in life, in Dec. 1889, " People will eventually

say, this man did much work, good work, under extraordinary difficulties."

In this term the shadow of the "final schools" begins to make itself distinctly felt.   The references to class lists, examiners and their qualities, become frequent.   Symonds, a confirmed Platonist, is afraid of one of them whom he calls a "little Aristotelian pedlar;" and remarks, "The teaching of Jowett educates young men, but unfits them for the schools. Plato is learned by them, and they are examined in Aristotle.   All we want is fair play for both.   Conington thinks Jowett as perverse in his own way, and unfair to Aristotle."   His walks with his two intimate friends, Mr. Stephens and Mr. Courthope, are largely occupied with the subject of the "Schools."   The Christmas vacation brought Symonds back to Clifton, and he writes thus to his sister] :—

"You[1] shall have a letter from me at the expense of Conington (who ought to be written to) and of my essay on the Helvetian Republic.

"To-day I had a wondrous *Sehnsucht* to hear our choir once more.   So I arose and went, not knowing what my lot would be.   I was fortunate, for I heard 'The King shall rejoice;' given I suppose in honour of Canon Girdlestone, for it must be his last Sunday. Afterwards there came Mendelssohn's Christmas Hymn; holy song, ever associated with my better

[1] To his sister Charlotte.   Clifton, December 9, 1861.

feelings, and a sense of dreamy winter nights.
Other choirs may sing as loud, but none can sing so
sweetly and so softly as Mr. Corfe's.   They brought
the tears into my eyes, as I called to mind 'The
days when I remember to have been joyful and free
from blame.'   It cannot be so again ; for doubts
have come up to blur my trust in much that Christmas tells us of; and I have long long lost the
strange early feeling that hung about our cathedral
music.   Still to-night I seemed to go back to purer
days, and the fresh children's voices smoothly whis-
pering the degradation, or loudly heralding the God-
head, of Christ, brought back again odd memories.
I shut my eyes, and the old scene of the cathedral,
years ago, came back upon my sight.   It seemed
that I was standing in the sombre shadows of the
dimly lighted nave, and heard the organ sighing and
sobbing plaintively to some Beethoven melody.
Then came sweeping by the white-robed procession
—canon, priest, and chorister—led by the sacristan
with his silver rod and the holy dove upon it.   The
black mass of people divided to let the gleaming
thread of waving surplices pass on.   At the cloister
door they paused; the choir parted, and standing cap
in hand they bowed while the canon walked between.
Then the airy band dissolved, and their flowing
skirts went flitting here and there amid the crowd.
The cluster of globed lamps that swung across the
pillared gloom seemed hazy with its own imperfect
light.   Vast caverns of the deepest black marked the

branching of the spandrils, where stray gleams of light rested on carved angels' wings. Far off in the long north aisle, the kneeling statue of that mourning lady glimmered on the silent windows. Over all the dying organ made one deep harmony, and tuned my soul to the solemn beauty of the scene. Then it ceased, a shuffling of feet, and a moving of the people to the northern door, and outside the winter night was grey on the gaunt and leafless green; behind us the prophet-painted panes shone dimly in the waning lights within the choir.

"All this I seemed to see, and I felt as young and awestruck as I used to feel when papa took me on a winter afternoon from Berkeley Square. But with this childish feeling was mixed a deeper and a holier sense of sublimity, such as I felt two years ago.

"Nothing more remains to tell, except that I feel 'dree,' and that the *Seelensehnsucht* has rather coiled itself afresh.

"Do not try to answer this; you cannot write sentimental letters such as Miss Girard and I delight in. A matter of fact answer to a sentimental letter only irritates the receiver, who wonders he could have written such trash as to call forth such a contemptible reply. You may write a letter, but attempt not an answer, unless Weston has revived holy memories and made your soul melodious with melancholy pleasure. Good-night."

[Symonds at this period came under the influence of two very remarkable people, Mrs. B—— to whom he paid a short visit at Cheltenham, and Mme. Jenny Lind Goldschmidt, who visited his father at Clifton, and for whom he conceived the highest enthusiasm and veneration. At Cheltenham the emotional side of Symonds' religious temperament was profoundly stirred by burning conversation—discussions upon faith, long analysis of mental sorrows and pains—which he carried on in company of his distinguished hostess: "She talked vehemently of how she suffered in her mind. As she lay there exquisitely slender and mobile, full length on the sofa, she did look torn by demons. She told me of the torture of her thought, how religious, social, political doubt weighed on her. She never lost her feeling of God, but could not help thinking of Him as a tyrant. Sympathised with me, when I said such thoughts goaded one on to suicide as a means of finding out .the truth." The impression created by this visit to Cheltenham was very great, and the result of it may be traced through many subsequent days of the Diary. In a later conversation with his hostess, after drawing a picture of unsatisfied ambition, he adds, "The consciousness of genius is the only thing desirable in life, and impotence is the strongest procuress of suicide. I went away filled with the idea of the noblest womanhood I had ever met. The most gorgeous golden sunset, and a perfect double rainbow made a fine background to my thoughts of that great lady. Hope rose behind despondency."

The following elaborate account of Mme. Gold-schmidt's concerts, and the notes of her conversation, show how deep a hold the great singer took upon the æsthetic and emotional side of young Symonds' nature.]

Saturday, January 25, 1862.—When I came down to breakfast papa threw me a letter across the table, which I soon saw to be from Mme. Goldschmidt, offering to come from Saturday till Monday. Our rapture was great. We instantly began devising what we would do with her, and how careful we would be not to let a whisper about her singing escape us. Now for the concert. The instrumental music lacked brilliancy of tone; Mme. Goldschmidt came on second in "On mighty pens." She was quite in black, and looked to me an old worn lady with a large head and small person. She wore no crinoline, and her dress with its loose waist reminded me of grandmama's. At the first tones of her voice, I quivered all over. It is not her wonderful execution, her pathos, varying expression, subtle flexibility, that surprised me, but the pure timbre which so vibrated and thrilled my very soul that tears came into my eyes. The volume of sound she threw out, and then diminished to a whisper which permeated the room, the crescendoes and diminuendoes, nightingale metallic shakes, brilliant ascents, and floods of swift successive notes, I expected. But I had not realised such quality of voice. In parts, above and below, it is going. Besides this she sang a Rondo of Mozart's to the violin of Blagrove, which was long, pathetic, delicious. Such wonderful expression. To hear the voice and instrument shake together, now loud, now low, now dying, now increasing, was marvellous. A duet from Rossini's "Il Turco in Italia," with Belletti, was also good. In the second part, her scena, "Care Compagne," from the Sonnambula, fully realised what I had imagined. She concluded the concert with the bird and echo songs. The former was far the best, it resembled nothing I have ever thought of. It was a bird, but no bird had throat so flexible, no nightingale so prolonged her low preamble, so piped and fluted to the night. You saw her throat throb like the bird's. Sims Reeves sang three songs tenderly and with exquisite finish. He also sang a grand march duet from Donizetti's Belisario with Belletti, which the people got encored. Mme. G. was most enthusiastically welcomed. I could not see her face well, but she moved rapidly, bowed low, and seemed vivacious.

By the 6.10 from Bath came M. and Mme. Goldschmidt. Auntie, Ch., and I were ready to meet her. Papa brought them up from the station. She came running into the room, saluted us in an *empressée* way, ran out again to speak to a servant, and bustled about with her tippets all about her and the loose small skirts. I could not but look at her as an old lady—the face so worn, with such lines and bones and sinews, such eager, deep-set eyes, thin, mobile mouth. They dressed rapidly, and then came down. She wore black velvet, with a white tippet. The only portrait I have seen of her does not resemble her at all. It makes her fat and round faced, instead of thin and somewhat angular. She instantly began talking to me about the concert, and wish I had called on them that I might have been better placed.

I took Edith to dinner. There were two places next Mme. G., with their backs to the fire, where I wanted to sit ; but Edith made me put her by papa, on the other side, so I was next Mr. G. This crossed me. She did not talk very memorably. Papa was asking her about pictures. She admired, at Dresden, the great Madonna, Titian's Tribute Money, and Carlo Dolci's Christ Breaking Bread, more than any. " The Madonna," she said, " is not painted—it is thought—it is there—you see it—you cannot call it painted." But of ordinary art-criticism she had none. Simple feeling was all that gave her a preference for one picture over the other.

When we went into the drawing-room it was about nine. Papa and I talked to her a little about the difference between German and English temperaments—their fine musical organisation—our better appreciation and taste cultivated in the oratorio. He then sent me to get the lamp and reflector. When I came back, I was surprised to be asked to open the piano, as Mme. G. would sing. I suspected something wrong. So I made papa entreat her not to sing. She said she was not tired, and made Mr. G. sit down. Then she gave us an air from Mozart's " Nozze di Figaro "— slow and sad, full of pathetic crescendoes. After that she accompanied herself to a Norwegian song, representing the echoes of horns on distant hills. This sounded to me sad too, but I have a faculty for recognising the tender in all music. Some low, thrilling notes, which she sustained to an almost painful length, were the most remarkable part of the song. They sounded more like a spirit in the air, so subtly diffused. I noticed what a thrill her voice had. It made the piano-strings tingle audibly, and my ears were moved in the same way. As she sat there singing, she became beautiful, and her profile seemed really classical. After the second song, papa showed her photographs in the camera. The only one she really cared for was the Ajax. Before going to bed she seemed cold and tired. She poked the fire. When she said " Good-night," she took papa by both hands, and her eyes danced again. I noticed that she wears four large gold rings on the middle, and one on the third finger— no others.

Sunday, January 26.—We breakfasted at nine. Mme. G. stayed in bed.

We dined at six, I sitting next Mme. G. She

talked pleasantly, told stories, laughed heartily, and showed herself a good, domestic, merry-hearted lady. Neither her face nor her conversation tell you what a genius she has. She is still foreign, talks bad English, holds her knife *à l'Allemande*, cuts up her meat, and eats it with a fork, rests her knife on a piece of bread. There is something childish about her. It was pleasant to see her tuck Ch.'s arm under hers as she tramped out of the dining-room. About eight she came down, looking good and lovely, but old, in a black bonnet. I presented her with "The Escorial," and she renewed her invitations to me to go to Bath to-morrow night with papa. Then we bundled her up in countless wrappers, and off they went. It seemed blank and strange when they were gone, and we continued talking about her.

I have said a good deal about her appearance, but I ought to add what struck me most. First, the face is terribly thin and worn. The eyes are small, and very glaucous grey. They soon screw up when she looks attentive. The nose is immense and broad at the base. The mouth broad, and lips thin, with the skin about it pink and irritable. Her hair is profuse, and yellow. Her throat is immense, with a huge larynx. The whole face is mobile and expressive. She says that for three years she was nearly mad with neuralgia—did nothing, remembered nothing, could not bear to see any one. The grape cure cured her.

Monday, January 27.—Papa settled at breakfast that he could not go to-night to Mme. Goldschmidt's concert, because he is so busy, and because he does not wish to be seen by the Bath people. I shall go alone, Mme. G. having rather discouraged Charlotte's coming among the artistes.

I had some coffee at 5.30, and then set out for Bath. It now remains that I should describe one of the most eventful evenings that I have ever been so fortunate as to pass. I arrived in good time, and drove at once to 6 Pulteney Street, where the Goldschmidts were staying. I gave my name, and was shown into a drawing-room, with an open piano, several screens, music inscribed "Mme. Lind," and a Swedish book upon the table. Here I waited till Mr. G. could see me. He gave me some tea, and talked about music, &c., as he ran over some of the accompaniments he is to play to-night. I complained of the poverty of the songs to which music is set ; he said the difficulty of putting grand poetry to music is great — people like merely to have a sentiment suggested by the words. We especially laughed at "My own, my guiding star," with its phrase "bless my sight." They are going to have "Di sangue tinto" again by express demand. I remarked that a decided rhythm always takes. About 7.40 we set out, he and I going in one fly, and his man John taking another for Piatti and Belletti, who are like great babies, and require to be got to the concert-rooms in time.

We called for them at the hotel, and then went in ourselves.   Mr. G. took me at once to say good evening to Madame.   We found her in a kind of tent in the desert—a great space round a fireplace, screened off from one of the ball-rooms.   Here she had just finished dressing, look-ing-glasses and all her apparatus were scattered about.   She came forward and took me warmly by the hand—inquired after Ch. first, then after papa and auntie.   The concert time was drawing on, so I went into the room.   Madame began by singing an air from Handel's Susannah.   The words were good, "without the swain's assiduous care," and into them she threw a marvellous variety of sentiment. "Deprived of sun" was barren and triste, with a mournful pleading in the voice, and "cheering air" produced a smile as though to draw a picture of what the poor plant might have enjoyed.   Then on the word "wither" her whole frame languished, and the sounds came dying out.   "Shall human mind demand less pain?" she gave with fire and indig-nation.   She really grew most beautiful—her face rounded, her eyes flashed, she stood transfigured before me.   She was tastefully dressed in a low white dress covered with black gauze.   I hung on every note, and seemed to see the lovely girl dying among her friends, panting out her life with deep woe and pangs of love.   Whether this was the right picture, never having heard the opera, I can-not tell.   Piatti then played a graceful piece, and

Belletti sang. Last in the first part Mme. and Sims Reeves sang the great duet "Sulla Tomba," from Lucia di Lammermoor. He seemed to catch her fire and inspiration, and it went most gloriously. In part second Sims Reeves sang "My own, my guiding star"—a silly song, in which he was horribly affected. Mme. then came on for the last time. She gave "John Anderson" with an indescribable pathos and variety of expression. Her face and person acted it—the tottering downhill and sleeping at the foot was sad; the energy of sentiment she threw into "blessings on your frosty pow," and the beautiful way in which she modulated "John Anderson" gradually diminuendo into "my," and then closed with a loud yearning crescendo, heightened by her delicious foreign accent, almost made me cry.

Going out I saw Mr. Wm. Cave and the Winthrops. I stood talking to them till Mme. was ready. She appeared in her old black bombazine with innumerable tippets. We went to the door, but the carriage was not up. Mme. waited in a cold passage, to my dismay. The stupid official whose duty it was to see to getting it ready made profuse apologies. She repelled him with a cold and haughty bow. I never saw any one become so suddenly stately. Then she turned to me with a frank pleasant smile. A good crowd was collected round the door to see her get out. They did not behave well, and laughed at her enormous wrappers

and thin petticoats. Going back she looked up at
the stars. She talked hurriedly, and seemed excited. She said what a friendship she felt for
papa, and spoke most strongly about his kindness.
There was the same crowd collected at their
door. She hurried in and gave at once directions
for tea to be made. I like to hear her quick,
energetic tones, her pleading voice as she asks to
confer some little favour on you. She never says,
"Will you have some more tea?" but "May I
have de pleasure to give you some more tea?"
After all that applause and splendour, after the
genius of her singing, and the profound emotions
she must have felt as well as excited, she did not
forget the duties of an ordinary hostess. She made
every one comfortable, and cut the beef and the
bread as if she knew what pleasure it would give
me to be helped by her. I said, "You treat me as
if I were your son." She answered, "Yes, and I
do look on you almost as if you were; but it is no
virtue of your own. You owe it to your papa,"
with an arch smile that seemed to indicate behind
the truth of what she said a suspicion that she did
not dislike me for myself.

[The following notes of Mme. Goldschmidt's conversation must have been made soon after a visit
which she paid, some time later, to Dr. Symonds
at Clifton Hill House] :—

" If I had nothing but music in the world it would be enough.

"I become a different thing when I sing—different body, different soul.

"I cannot understand how people do not see how the senses are connected.

"What I have suffered from my sense of smell! My youth was misery from my acuteness of sensibility. Very sensitive people may go wrong, may make mistakes; they cannot be very wicked. I only learned what crimes were possible by being accused of them.

"Some poetry will not do for music—not Shakespeare, nor Shelley, nor Tennyson. I repeated ' Blow, blow,' and she said, 'That might be set to a Volkston.' I repeated, 'I sang of the dancing stars,' and she said, 'There is too much thought there: it has all the passions of the heart—dancing stars, too, how incongruous!' Every line of Milton could be sung. For music we must have one feeling, one harmony, not a series of broken lights. Dryden can be sung, he is simple and definite. Even Handel could not compose for Tennyson. His thoughts are nice, but his words will not flow in music, and he has too much condensation of ideas.

"'Tennyson takes all the solid sharp words and puts them together. Music cannot come between. He does not flow. He cannot like music.' 'Heine's songs run into music at once; they are music.'

'Italian is all music—every word.' Noticed how she dwelt on the connection of words and music."

April 27.—Papa read out "Guinevere" to-night. She seized every strong point, and acted it in her features, following the poetry with expression. She cried bitterly, and at the end said, "I feel like Arthur or Guinevere. I must be one or the other." It had affected her like tragedy. Then papa asked her to sing, and at first she could not— "The vibrations will clash," she said. You cannot modulate from poetry to music, in other words. How deeply this remark lies at the root of art, of the independence of the arts.

Soon, however, she got up and sang airs from the "Penseroso," and an air of Mendelssohn's to Heine's song, "Auf Flügeln des Gesanges." She accompanied herself, and modulated most exquisitely with various shades of melody.

Her hates are vivid as her likes. She takes both at first sight, judging faces, she says, unerringly. Miss E. called to-day; she bowed, and instantly left the room. X—— came to stay, and she saw his coarseness at once. He is incult but clever; like ——, a self-reliant, vigorous man, full of impudence, a man who told Tennyson to his face that his "Sea Dreams" had no artistic coherence.

She is very humble and careless of self. "My poor, humble self," oddly pronounced, is often on her lips; but she never cringes or loses dignity. Simple and unassuming, she does and says what she likes, walks with countesses, tells Colenso what she thinks of him, and queens it.

She comments on the charm of having a definite line in life, an art to live for; yet she would not have any of her children brought up to music as a profession.

She cannot bear Goethe. His and Hegel's influences have made the Germans, she thinks, irreligious. Biography she does not like, because it destroys great men, revealing the faults their valets see. "What good can we get from seeing how Bacon fell? Ah, that did give me pain. I would sooner have known evil of some near friend." So terrible to her is any blot on the ideal.

[Symonds pursued this acquaintance, which was so delightful to him, and to which he was wont to refer with the greatest pleasure. He paid a visit to M. and Mme. Goldschmidt at Oak Lea, their home at Wimbledon. Of this visit he made the following record] :—

May 19, 1864.—At ten M. Goldschmidt called for me in his carriage, and took me first to York Hotel, in Albemarle Street, where we found Mme. G., and then with her to Mrs. Grote's, in Savile Row. They introduced me to Mr. and Mrs. Grote. Mr. Grote talked to me. Mrs. Grote looked tall, stiff, and fierce. A large party of literary and noble people came. It soon began to thunder. The storm overlasted many of Mme. G.'s songs, and of Mr.

Blagrove's pieces. They sent me home at about
eight in their carriage. Mrs. Grote almost turned
me out of the house by saying good-bye to me.
Both M. and Mme. were very kind, introducing
me to their friends, Mrs. Grote's brother, Mrs.
Ernest and Miss De Bunsen, and talking to me
themselves. I contrasted this grand London party
with the little soirées at our own house, and Mme.
amused me by doing the same, and expressing her
surprise at the simplicity of life, dresses, and hours
which she had found at Clifton.

May 20, 1864.—I called at ten on Mme., and
found them just rising from breakfast. She alluded
to Mrs. Grote's desire to get me away last night,
that she might be alone with what she calls "the
tribe"—her own relations.

At 2.30, M. and Mme. called in their carriage,
and drove me down to Wimbledon. Oak Lea is
a pretty, new, red brick house, built by themselves.
It stands at the edge of the park, looking toward
Sydenham. Mr. G. told me that Mme. had wanted
to call it Larkfield; but he had feared the allusion
to herself, and Miss Winkworth had suggested Oak
Lea. Over the door they have a shield, with a
lark rising, and their motto, Excelsior. This, too,
they have on the carriage. The house is most
beautifully appointed, and elegantly furnished. No
expense has been spared to make it comfortable
and graceful, without being luxurious.

The drawing-room is not large, but lofty; it

opens into a conservatory, and above the fireplace
there is an oval window pierced into the same. It
is papered with bright blue, and has a red carpet
and brilliant crimson silk curtains. Mr. G.'s study
opens into it.

My bedroom looks out to Sydenham, and has a
little window whence one sees the pride of their
garden, an oak. In this room is a large silver-
mounted mirror, inscribed, "Wahr und klar," given
Mme. G. at Vienna. Everything is elegant.

Soon after we reached Oak Lea, Dr. and Lady
Augusta Stanley called; her first visit. It was curious
that I should meet her here for the first time.
Stanley does not seem to have noticed the card
I left at the Deanery. He introduced me to
Lady Augusta as a great friend of Hugh Pearson's.
She, as M—— rightly says, is "so aristocrat that
she has come out at the other end, so to speak."
She is almost brusque and jolly and hoydenish,
from her excess of desire to contemn the con-
ventions which she can without danger overleap.
We walked in the garden, and she admired everything, seeing it for the first time. I talked to
Stanley about Italy. He is looking fagged, but
his rosette suits him. Lady Augusta has very
black hair and eyes; she is not handsome. As
he said good-bye to Mme. G. he asked her, "How
do you like her?" She tells me that he says of
his wife, "She is gilding my house for me."

The dinner was beautifully cooked and served,

of the very best and most récherché kind. Their
style of living is certainly expensive. I admired a
magnificent silver copy of the celebrated vase with
ivy leaves from Pompeii on the table, and Mme. G.
told me a story of the silver service which we used.
She found it on her table the night before she left
Stockholm, and now it reminds her of the happiest
days she ever spent, enjoying her art among the kind
Swedish people, with the world still fresh before her
fame, when appreciation and not flattery was given
to her. She has carried this service with her everywhere. She said she could only thank the givers
with her tears.

Sunday, May 22, 1864.—To-day we had breakfast at nine. Mr. G. read prayers from the Church
Service. I am struck with the great ease and
simplicity that foreigners show in revealing what
they really think and feel about such matters as
these family prayers. At breakfast we talked by
some chance about street-music, and also about
Meyerbeer. Mme. G., who knew him, says he
only cared to catch the public; he was vain, and
very much afraid of death. In his will he ordered
that he should be kept four days in his own room
after death and bled, and have mirrors applied to
his nose and mouth, to prove whether or no he
had really died. We talked a little about musical
critics and their extreme want of the feeling of
responsibility.

We went to see the lodge where the gardener's

wife lives. A blackbird hung in a cage outside the door. Mme. G. went up and talked to it : " Come, pretty bird, pretty, pretty little bird, do give us a little song ; we want to hear you sing so much, you pretty, pretty little bird," in such a coaxing way that the bird, who had been shy at first, got down and came close to her, and put its head on one side to listen. Then Mme. G. sang to it, roulades and long shakes and high sharp notes, which made the bird most inquisitive. But he continued silent till she turned to go, and then he gave a loud, shrill chirrup as if to call her back. A little white dog, called "Dandy," then came out, and was greeted with the same kind of language. Inside the cottage I noticed a portrait of a lady in a curious evening dress. I could not see it well. Mme. G. said, "That's a portrait of myself." I afterwards found out it was painted by the celebrated Count d'Orsay, who had also made a bust of her. She could not endure him, and would not sit to him, so he did them from seeing her at the opera. How little did the vain creature fancy that his portrait of one of the greatest *cantatrici* that ever lived would be put by her after a few years in the cottage of a gardener.

Mr. G. and I walked with Mr. D—— towards Fulham. After leaving him, Mr. G. told me about his history. He rose quite from the ranks, and first became celebrated by a bust of Mme. G. made for Her Majesty's, and now belonging to Lord Dudley. Then the Queen sat to him for the City,

and in course of executing her portrait he quarrelled
with Prince Albert, who wanted to alter his design
and make the Queen's hair *à l'Imperatrice*, to which
D—— would not consent.   The bust of the Queen
in the conservatory at Oak Lea is a copy of this
portrait.   We talked about music.   Mozart and
Handel alone wrote thoroughly for the voice.
They lived among singers.   Beethoven and Mendelssohn never did.   They lived among instruments.
Beethoven never learned his art thoroughly as a
youth.   He could not write a good fugue, not
understanding double-counterpoint.   The masters
of the good old days had been regularly apprenticed.
Handel's fertility he accounted for by—1st, his
having this command over the technique; 2nd, his
bachelor's life; 3rd, the simplicity of his scores.
To write one of Handel's works in the score of the
present day would take twice as long as it took him.
His scores are often only three lines, with much left
to the organ conductor.

After she went up to bed, Mr. G. showed me
Beethoven's will and two MSS. of Mozart.   The
will was written long before his death.   It proves
that he was deaf at twenty-eight, and that he suffered constantly from it.   This is a key to much of
the music which he wrote subsequently.   I always
thought that yearning, passionate pleading, vehe-
ment reproach, and haughty self-reliance, with
frequent melting into the most tender expressions
of intense love, never to be gratified, were the most

frequent feelings expressed in Beethoven's music. This will reveals some of these "Motives."

May 23, 1864.—I did not sleep well, though my bed, with its lace fringes and downy foreign pillows, was most comfortable. I woke unrefreshed.

We breakfasted at half-past eight; we talked a great deal about shyness, from which Mme. G. says that she has suffered all her life, in such a way as to cause her torment. She only got over it a little by remembering that no one would care what her "poor humble self" did and thought. At ten we set off to drive Mme. and myself to Bushey Park and Hampton Court. Going there we talked a great deal of a subject which she is fond of discussing—the sympathy of sensitive natures, and the magnetic influence by which they attract one another. She seems peculiarly alive to this, and to care more for a certain delicacy of mind and taste than for high intellectual gifts. She spoke with special kindliness of one lady introduced to her at Mrs. Grote's, who said, that after hearing her sing "Fear not," in the angel's recitative in the Messiah, she had learned what it was not to fear. This led by natural transition to marriage, which, when complete, she called "a glimpse of Eden:" but she seems alive to the extreme rarity of true and harmonious marriages, and to think the false ones worse than any isolation. We drove up the great chestnut avenues of Bushey Park, which she described as "Milton." They are Miltonic.

Then we got out and walked, and she spoke of
another favourite subject—the possibility of making
dumb animals our friends.   This led to many an
unanswerable problem, and she told me that between
the ages of twenty and thirty, she had plagued
herself with religious difficulties.   What was the
meaning of sin? how did God come to make men
weak enough to err? if she got to heaven how
would she keep from falling when the angels fell?
and so on.   But years brought her faith and love.
I notice that she breaks into German, French, and
Italian as the feeling varies.   I could never have
fancied that metaphysical subjects really troubled her.
It was the mystery of her own personality, and of
the suffering of the world, which weighed upon her
mind.

We came to a house where the Duchess of Kent
used to live, and she told me of a party she once
went to there.   It was in 1849.   She met the Queen,
and the King and Queen of the French.   She
noticed how the Queen was always seeking for
Prince Albert.   Once in the evening they stood
back to back (she made me act it with her), and
the Queen did not know it, though Prince Albert
knew.   For a long time she looked for him with
her eyes, and at last she turned round and saw him
there, and her features broke into a smile, but he
remained quiet, and ready to do what she willed.
Mme. G. said that look came back to her when she
first heard of the Prince's death.

Then we went into Hampton Court. Here it was rather tiring; she looked at everything and ran about. I got dreadfully exhausted. She talked regretfully about her art, and what she had sacrificed. The artist must live in a world of ideas; he is made useless for the common life, he is a child in things of this earth, he dreams, and is good for nothing. "Yet," she said, "I ought not to have come down into the world: I ought not to have fallen down: I ought to have stayed. When I have a quarter of an hour to myself I go alone into a room, and then I dream—all things of beauty come before me—and it ends in a good cry; for the one thought I have is of the sorrow of sin which destroys beauty. We who have an ideal see that, and cannot bear the discord." This reminded me of Consuelo, and I have taken it down as closely as I could, barring my own interjections, questions, &c.

We drove back to Oak Lea to luncheon. Then Mme. G. drove me to the Putney omnibus, and, with most warm leave-taking, I parted from her.

[On March 22nd, 1862, Symonds came out second to Caird in the Jenkyns. And on April 7th he left for Great Malvern on a reading party with Mr. Stephens. Late in May he went in for his "greats," and, though ill and nervous, supported by sleeping-draught and pick-me-up, he secured a first, with papers which, as he had resolved at Coniston, were described by an examiner as "all that could be

desired." "Among the many letters of congratulation I got, Jowett's to papa was the most pleasant.
He says an examiner told him I was the best man
in." He took his degree on June 26th, and on June
the 29th, on the verge of starting for a foreign journey
with his father and sister, he makes the following
characteristic entry : "Certainly Oxford honours are
a poor thing. The glory of them soon departs, the
pleasure fleets away, and we have another struggle
rising up at once. Yet I can never be too thankful
for having been able to give papa so great satisfaction. All the trouble I had was well compensated
by his pleasure, and the thought of that is my most
solid gain."

Here, at the close of Symonds' undergraduate
career, I may introduce his own summing up of
the advantages and disadvantages of the University system, as they presented themselves to him
through his experience, and some characteristic
notices of the two minds, Conington's and Jowett's,
which most affected him in his undergraduate
days.]

The[1] fault of my education as a preparation for
literature was that it was exclusively literary.
Neither at Clifton, nor at Harrow, nor yet at Oxford, did I learn any one thing thoroughly. I failed
to grasp the merest elements of mathematics, absorbed nothing of physical science, did not acquire

[1] Autobiography.

modern languages with accuracy, and even in Greek
and Latin scholarship (upon which I spent so many
years), attained to only superficial knowledge. The
system of teaching at Harrow was itself wretchedly
inadequate. At Oxford I did much harder work;
but there even philosophy was studied mainly from
the rhetorical point of view. We were taught to
write upon a vast variety of debatable topics, and
to acquire some smatterings of what the several
schools had uttered on them, but there was no
robust mental training, no process by which the
man was compelled to think. Worse than that,
aspirants after honours were habituated to deal
cleverly with words and phrases, and to criticise
without substantial knowledge. They never grew
familiar with the solid facts of the world and human
nature, except by natural instinct and proclivity.
This absence of intellectual gymnastic prepared me
for an amateurishness in literature which has ever
clung about me.

As I have said, there was an almost total defect
of discipline in tough studies, both at Harrow
and at Oxford. In a sort of blundering way the
docile among us were made to recognise the force
of duty; and that was pretty nearly all we gained.
In other words, we learned to work for less tangible
rewards than wages. But we learned very little
else of solid value. Yet I am bound to admit that
this great educational defect had, as the French say,
its educational quality. This quality was freedom

of choice, modified by sympathy and circumstance
in self-formation. We were comparatively unspoiled
by drill of any kind. Our minds were made less
by the curriculum than by our friends, the subjects
we were instinctively adapted for, and our spontane-
ously selected lines of reading. Plodding along at
the curriculum, and taking great interest in the
whole of it at points where it coincided with my
literary bent, I obtained thus, not indeed the method
of study, but the zeal for study, and contracted habits
which made study and production of one sort or
another the duty and necessity of my subsequent
existence.

The weakness of the training displayed itself,
nevertheless, even in this liberty of choice. Some
of my contemporaries were by nature provided
with strong political interests. Outside the curriculum they grew and flourished, and evolved their
personalities by reading the newspapers and taking
part in Union debates. Others, like G. A. Simcox
and A. C. Swinburne, pursued an ideal of more or
less effective genius. But many of the rest of us,
who had proclivities but no commanding bias,
wandered too helplessly about between duty to the
curriculum and indulgence of individual undisci-
plined instincts. I could mention men who might
have been musicians or painters, but who wasted
their time at Oxford in aimless strumming on the
piano, and silly sketching, because there was no
career of industry provided for them. They served

the curriculum badly. Their natural talents found no strengthening exercise.

With this latter sort I can class myself. I went philandering around music, heraldry, the fine arts, and literary studies ruled by sentiment. I wrote weak poetry. I dreamed in ante-chapels. I mooned in canoes along the banks of the Cherwell, or among yellow water-lilies at Godstow. I rode across the country, larking on half-broken hacks. I indulged day-dreams, and acted trivial tragedies of love, and hate, and reconcilement with my miscellaneous set of friends. But in all these things I got no grasp on any serious business.

It may be questioned here whether I was framed by temperament to profit by a methodical system of education. That, I admit, is a grave problem. But I do think that there were forces in me which might have been more wholesomely developed, and debilities which ought to have been more austerely repressed.

[These opinions upon the university system coincide to a certain extent with those which Symonds records as being held by Mr. Congreve, the Positivist Philosopher.]

Against [1] the Oxford system generally Congreve spoke strongly. "Oxford," he said, "is a pleasant social place, but an enervating intellectual atmosphere. Jowett's habit of finding 'a kind of truth,'

[1] Autobiography.

the study of dreamers like Plato, the making of
verses, the pride of hot undigested philosophy ;
all tend to mere Saturday reviewing, want of aim,
and the sleet of words which oppresses the world
in the shape of magazines and ephemeral literature.
History is the proper training ; the examination
should be changed, men should be able to take up
distinct lines, and, as much as possible, should be
examined by their teachers.   Coaching in Oxford is
mere cramming by young men without experience, of
young men they do not comprehend, and who themselves desire nothing beyond what will pay in the
schools.   A Bachelor fresh from the pressure of the
Science Schools is a painful anomaly.   But he settles
down after a time, for he finds that he must unload
his brain of its heated contents.   The Balliol
system of writing is bad ; a man may use his pen in
taking notes for his own purposes, but he should
never frame his thoughts in words for others till he is
mature, and has facts to tell the world.   Magazining
is only a temporary disease.   The great books of the
world might easily be read through, if people would
consent to miss the drifting mass of light literature."

Meanwhile, the society of friends and counsel-
lors whom I was free to choose, kept exercising
a salutary influence.   Though I could not share
Green's powerful political and philosophical interests,
I felt the force of his character.   Conington directed
me upon the path of literature by principles of
common sense and manly prosaic taste.   He snubbed

and at the same time stimulated my vague sensibilities to beauty. He made me reflect and distinguish in matters of art by bringing clearly into prominence his scholar's sense of what is great or delicate in prose and poetry, against the background of his insusceptibility to nature, music, painting, sculpture. I began through him to see that literature is something by itself, not part of an iridescent nebula, including all our cult for loveliness. This lesson was salutary, and I owe much to the years of close intimacy I passed with him. Yet I am glad that I was created with a temperament less exclusively literary than his. I am thankful that I preserved a sense of the remote connections between all our sensibilities, for this has prevented me from isolating literature, although I recognise its independence. Jowett, when I came under his notice, proved a far more potent master of my mind than Conington. I immediately recognised something quite unique in his mental and moral personality. He wore the halo then of martyrdom around him, and dazzled young-eyed enthusiasts. " Essays and Reviews " had made a scandalous success, and the Oxford Conservatives were refusing to endow the Greek chair which Benjamin Jowett held.

I feel inclined to break this paragraph, and to indulge in some detailed reminiscences of Jowett. When I went up to Balliol, in the autumn of 1858, my father told me to call on Professor Jowett. He was not my tutor, but my father had recently sat

next him at a Magdalen Gaudy. I think I took
a letter from my father to the great mysteriously
reverenced man. I found him dozing in an arm-
chair over a dying fire. His rooms were then in
Fisher Buildings, looking out upon the Broad. It
was a panelled room, with old-fashioned wooden
mantelpiece. He roused himself, looked at the
letter, looked at me, and said half dreamily, " I do
not think I know your father." Then, after an
awkward pause, he rose, and added, " Good-bye,
Mr. Symonds." I had gone with all a boy's trepidation to call on him. I took with me, moreover,
something over-added of the shyness which my
dependence on my father engendered. This dis-
missal, therefore, hurt me exceedingly.

I saw nothing more of Jowett for at least a year.
But just before I went in for moderations, he sent
for me, and asked me to bring him Greek and Latin
prose and verses. So far as I remember, I was
allowed to select pieces. The few evenings in which
he coached me made me feel, for the first time, what
it was to be taught. He said very little, gave me
no " tips." But somehow he made me comprehend
what I had to aim at, and how I had to go about it.
In some now to me unapprehended way, he showed
me how to use my reading in Greek for the purpose
of writing. I am sure that the iambics I produced
for those few lessons were better than the thousands
I had laboured at before. Such influence, if continued, might have educed the scholar in me, but I

went into the Schools, obtained a first-class in moderations, and Greek iambics were shelved.

Jowett's influence over my mind, however, continued and strengthened. When I began to read
for "Greats," I took him an essay on some philosophical or historical subject every week. The work
for this essay absorbed the greater portion of all my
energies. I neglected everything, except my sentiments and fancies, for its sole production. And, in
a certain way, I grew mightily under the discipline.
I used to wait with intense eagerness, after reading
my composition aloud, for his remarks. They were
not much. " That is very good, Mr. Symonds ;"
" That is not so good as what you read last week ;"
" You have been too prolix ;" " There are faults of
taste in the peroration ;" " You do not see the point
about Utilitarianism ;" " That is an admirable statement of Plato's relation to the Eleatic philosophers."
I can hear him saying these sentences now, bent
before his fireplace in the tower-room of the new
buildings. I treasured each small word up, and
somehow felt the full force of them, expanded their
leaves until it filled my mind and penetrated the
substance of my own thought about the essay. He
taught me, indeed, to write ; not to think scientifi-
cally, but to write as clearly as I could, and with as
firm a grasp as I possessed upon my subject.

When the essay was over, Jowett made tea, or
drank a glass of wine with me—far more often we
had tea of the uncomfortable college sort, lukewarm,

out of a large metal pot, in big clumsy cups. Conversation did not flow. Occasionally the subject of the essay led to some remarks from Jowett, but rarely. More often there was spasmodic talking about things in general—Jowett never suggesting a topic—I blunderingly starting one hare after another—meeting silence or a quenching utterance—feeling myself indescribably stupid, and utterly beneath my own high level, but quitting the beloved presence with no diminution of an almost fanatical respect. Obscurely, but vividly, I felt my soul grow by his contact, as it had never grown before. That was enough, and more than enough. I did not then, and do not now, know what the process may have been. I almost think the paucity of speech, the sort of intellectual paralysis produced by what I knew to be not unkindly and not stupid in the man I revered, was more effective and more stimulative than lucid exposition or fluent conversation would have been.

One evening he said to me, "I cannot hear your essay this evening, Mr. Symonds. I have just heard that Clough is dead." This was the first time, I believe, that the name of Clough reached my ears. Jowett proceeded: "He was the only man of genius, whom I knew to be a man of genius, that I have seen among the younger men at Balliol."

On another evening he sat staring at the fire, and would not speak, and yet did not seem to want me

to go. At last he said, " When I don't say any-
thing, people fancy I am thinking about something.
Generally I am thinking about nothing at all.
Good night."

At another time he said, *à propos* of nothing that
I can remember, " Mr. Swinburne is a most curious
young man. He used to bring me long and elo-
quent essays. He had a very remarkable power of
language; but it was all language. I could never
find that he was following any line of thought."

Jowett's breakfast parties were more paralysing
than his coaching hours. Nothing is anywhere
drearier than a lot of people meeting at a breakfast. Here they met, stiff, awkward, shy, from their
very reverence for Jowett. He sat, sipped tea, ate
little, stared vacantly. Few spoke. The toast was
heard crunching under desperate jaws of youths ex-
asperated by their helplessness and silence. Nevertheless, it was a great event to go—although nobody
shone, neither host nor guest.

Walking out with Jowett was, for me at least, no
pleasure; yet I coveted the honour. It seemed
always impossible to start a subject which would
survive the exchange of four remarks. Jowett had
the way of killing the innocent foundlings of his
own and his companion's brain by some crushing
and yet inconclusive observation.

Still, though Jowett had this influence over my
mind, though Conington had another of the same
generic sort, and though my father exercised one

which was more penetrative than any, I feel bound to record that the most controlling influences of my life, the most enduring, those which are at present potent over me, belonged to none of those three men.

CHAPTER V

MANHOOD. FROM DEGREE TO FELLOWSHIP

Journey to Venice.—Mals.—The Ortler.—Meran.—First impressions
of Venice.—Padua.—Verona.—A rising in Milan.—The books
he read on the journey.—Illness at Visp.—Home again.—First
intimations of a literary career.—Autobiographic poetry.—Analysis of Haydn's " Creation."—His psychological altitude.—Stands
for a fellowship at Queen's.—A visit from Jowett at Clifton.—
Stands for a fellowship at Magdalene.—And elected.—Offer of
a travelling tutorship.—Attack upon him.—Breakdown in health.
—Goes to Malvern.—Wins the Chancellor's prize with an essay
on " The Renaissance."

[IMMEDIATELY after taking his degree, Symonds
went abroad with his father and sister; this time
through Munich, Innspruck, and over the Finster-
münz to Venice.   The Diary is again copious.]

Wednesday, July 9, 1862.[1]—*Gasthof zum Goldenen
Adler, Mals.*   Last night's inn at Landeck was fair.
To-night's we have not tried, but it is the only inn in
Mals by the Adige.   Our bedrooms have the ques-
tionable advantage of looking over the cowhouses,
hearing the deep lowing of the kine, and receiving
the incense of their odours.   To-day we left Landeck
early.   The morning was glorious, and not a cloud
rested on the mountains.   The ascent was gradual,

[1] Diary.

along the right bank of the Inn, until we came to a narrow defile, where 10,000 Bavarians of Napoleon's army were buried under rocks and trunks by the Tyrolese. Here we crossed the river and went along its left shore, under cliffs that momently grew in height and sublimity. Snowpeaks and glaciers began to be more frequent. The road winds always upward, but very gently; so that when about halfpast twelve we reached Hoch-Finstermünz, we did not seem to be much more than 1000 feet above the stream.

After lunching we left the Inn and took a little valley to the left. The view grew tamer. It was extremely hot, and I wished to sleep. However, as soon as I began to nod, my umbrella fell, and I started up awake. Through a comparatively prosaic valley we jogged on, till about three in the afternoon our attention was arrested by the glimpse of a fine snowpeak far beyond in front. Soon another to the right unclosed itself, and yet another still more high. As we drove on, these great snow spires and pyramids and walls of ice kept extending their lines until we reached the little Reschen See. There we paused to contemplate this unrivalled scene. Before us lay the lake clear and blue, reflecting an unclouded sky. Beyond stretched a wide valley deep in the broad line of new-mown grass, from which on either side rose the pine-clad hills, on one hand deep in shadow, on the other bright with light. Their ranks were so long and gradual, that the air tints at the end were of a delicate bright blue, above which blazed the snowfields we had seen one by one unrolled. The great central pyramid is called Ortler, the highest peak in Austria. I do not remember any view more beautiful than this one—the shapes of the mountains, the colours of the plain, and the sky were so harmonious. We kept the mountains in sight till we came here. After a very bad dinner we saw the rose-hue of the Alps on the Ortler-spitz.

Thursday, July 10.—*Hotel Kaiserkrone, Botzen.* We got up at four this morning and started at five. Directly I got out of bed I felt the oppression of my headache on me, and it has lasted all day long, making me taciturn, depressed, insensible. Behind us we left snowpeaks and glaciers, and drove down a picturesque but comparatively tame valley. To our right, at first starting, were some noble mountain flanks. On our way we passed a little village that was entirely burned down about seven months ago. It was in painful process of restoration.

Hot, dusty, and tormented with flies, we jogged on, ever descending. My headache became furious. At about 12.30 we reached Meran, picturesquely situated among lofty light-blue mountains. I was too far gone to think of views, and the heat could have contented nothing but a lizard or a lazzarone. We dined and dozed till it was time to go. About half-past two we set off for Botzen, threading a valley rich with most luxuriant vines, with maize and fig-trees. The trellised grapes, hanging in full thick bunches, and sending out their petulant craving arms to clasp each little twig, clinging to brambles, dusty by the roadside, rather than to nothing, were a study. A great storm swelled behind us, making the amphitheatre of mountains purple, and twice their natural size.

As I am writing now the thunderstorm is going on. It is not very severe, but all the bells in Botzen are ringing on its account. It is pleasant to get a decent hotel and dinner again, after the stably bedroom and miserable food of yesterday.

Friday, July 11.—About four this morning I woke with lightning in my eyes. A furious thunderstorm was raging, and all the bells of the town sounded their tocsins, in concert or at intervals. Very near the hotel was the cathedral tower, from the bells of which proceeded a most lugubrious tolling. The large bell was rung continuously, the vibrations of one stroke interfering with those of the one before, which had risen to a higher key. Thus between each clang there sounded a horrid jar. These bells, the fury of the thunder, the wind and rain and hail, kept up a terrific concert. At five we rose, and started at half-past six for Venice. The thunder attended us as far as Verona. The hills were purple and rainy. They looked the finer for their confusion. The thunder seemed to relieve my head, and I wrote the following :—

As when the moon some sultry summer night
Broods in the bosom of a labouring cloud,
And scarcely shoots a swart uncertain light
Through the dull volumes of her vapoury shroud;
But on a sudden breathing winds arise
And part the gloom, and she looks forth again
To scan the silent earth with silver eyes,
Disclosing valley, tower, and bosky plain:
So for three days my soul in darkness dwelt,
Shadowed by unintelligible gloom,
Till, stirred by secret impulses, she felt
Her light revive, she burst the dismal tomb,
And burning clear beheld that all is fair
And good and perfect in the tranquil air.

At Verona we had only time to take luncheon. The storms had now ceased, and until we reached Venice it continued quite fine.

Hotel de l'Europe, Venice.—I can hardly describe what I have seen of Venice, though I seem to have seen much, and have before my eyes a gorgeous confusion of glaring lucid skies, sombre palaces, broad flights of stairs, surrounded with black gondolas, dark narrow passages joined by low broad bridges, wide streets of dancing waters, great glorious moons, the vast pavement, cupolas, campanile, and standards of St. Mark, little lighted streets, romantic fruit shops and fishers of the Adriatic, gondoliers singing by moonlight on the great canal, ragged boys, like Anzoleto, washing their feet on marble stairs, pale faces peering through the curtains of their boats, and the deep glories of *il firmamento lucido.* From the railway we stepped into a gondola and came to this hotel, which is close to the Piazza of St. Mark, and looks upon the Grand Canal. We have three bedrooms looking on a side street, and a sitting-room on the Canal *au premier*. The hotel seems clean, and the table-d'hôte is good. After dinner we went out, and were rowed down the great canal to the sea that separates Venice from the mainland, where we saw the yellow sunset, and behind us the full copper-coloured rising moon. Then we rowed back, and turned up by the Rialto, through some small canals, dark and full of picturesque chiaroscuro, till we came to the Bridge of Sighs and the Piazza. There we got out, and walked in the mellow evening light, and returned to our hotel on foot. The moon shines now gloriously on the water, and occasionally I hear a gondolier singing.

Saturday, July 12.—It will be difficult to give a detailed account of all we have seen and done to-day. We rose to breakfast at half-past eight. Then we instantly sallied forth on foot to the Piazza. The morning was superb, the sun blazing and the sky clear, yet it was not too hot. We went into St. Mark's at once. The building is low in comparison with many around it, but its great dome-bubbles, its arches filled with gorgeous mosaics, and its bronze horses, are unlike anything I have ever seen. The interior is sombre, and its general effect not overpowering. Seen, however, in detail it may be regarded as a repository of Oriental spoils and splendours. The whole of this great church is covered on the roof with mosaic of all ages, on the floor with marble tessellated pavements brought from the East. It is crowded with chased columns of Oriental, Greek, and Italian marbles, some of them most elaborately sculptured, and the greater number crowned with gilded capitals, luxuriantly carved in leaves and birds and flowers. The church dates from the ninth century, and is the ducal chapel—not a cathedral. The gigantic Byzantine mosaics are of the greatest interest, but too numerous to be remembered in detail. I paid most attention to some huge angels, standing with spread wings and sceptres, some veiled cherubim in the pendenti, the four Evangelists represented with the heads of their respective beasts, and lastly, a great figure of Christ. Their chief interest is historical. Giotto and Cimabue and Bellini are related to these Byzantine remains, as Xenophanes and Thales to the mythologists, and as they stand to Plato, so may we trace the connection between Lionardo or Titian and the first successors of the Byzantines. Some of these mosaics are in *vitro*, or a composition like glass, such as we saw at Milan ; some are in stone. The church was full of Pagan altars and sarcophagi, as well as Christian remains. Constantinople and the East have been ransacked for its adornment. There were many people about, and some devoutly praying, but all these were in Madonna's chapel, which alone was lighted up.

Next we visited the Doge's Palace, entering by
the Scala dei Giganti, so called from the colossal
statues of Mars and Neptune, executed by the
Florentine, Sansovino.   That of Mars is really
very grand, and the best return to antique art I
have ever seen, in spite of Thorwaldsen and
Canova.   We first went into the great Council
Hall.   There is the "Paradise" of Tintoretto,
chiefly remarkable for its being the largest picture
painted in oils.   Its colour is very much injured,
black and livid, and its composition is greatly confused.   He has no notion of grouping, nor is there
the cosmos in chaos of Rubens.   All round the
room are great historical pictures by Tintoretto,
Veronese, and others, but those on the roof are
most remarkable.   It is hard to conceive that the
lustrous beauty of Venice in the clouds, surrounded
by angels, with the ducal state, attended by ambas-
sadors and senators beneath, proceeds from the
same hand as that which painted the "Paradise."
These pictures are, in fact, types of two different
manners of Tintoretto—the one is clear, gorgeous,
and careful, full of the most brilliant hues and transparent colouring : this you do not see out of Venice,
and perhaps the most remarkable specimen of the
manner is the "Bacchus and Ariadne" in the
Doge's Palace.   The flesh tints here are above
Titian—the yearning beauty of the Bacchus' face
is truly poetical, as also are the green vines round
his middle, and dark waves of hair.   The other

manner is dark, confused, and metallic. Such
so-called Tintorettos as we see in England and
Germany belong to this style. In fact, one feels
in Venice that one has seen the real Tintoretto for
the first time : his foreign specimens are either
executed in careless moments or spoiled by time.
Veronese's great picture on the ceiling, of "Venice
crowned Queen of the Sea," is superb. The flesh
painting, particularly that of the back of a woman
sitting in the middle of the picture, surpasses
Rubens. The hues of the angels' wings, and all
the light upon the dresses in the picture, are more
gorgeous still. Papa and I lay on our backs to
see it.

I am writing on Sunday morning alone, papa and
Charlotte being in the English Church. I feel
rather like the lady in the Palace of Art.

Indeed the excellences of the Venetian School,
like those of the best music, seem at first sight
rather to harmonise the soul and impregnate it
with beauty than to root themselves in the memory.
The Venetians have little beauty of form ; there is no
high ideal at which they aim ; and this distinguishes
them from the schools of Lionardo and Raphael.
In the same way their composition is not designedly
symmetrical. They present no artificial grouping.
Like Rubens, life is their chief study. To represent life and action is their aim. And like Rubens,
they feel the beauty of colour far more than that
of form. Tintoretto, for his rapidity of execution

and vast sweep of brush, is the Venetian Rubens;
but he is surpassed in colouring by Veronese, whose
gorgeous hues, lucid medium, and splendid disposi-
tion of light and shadow, place him on a par with
the great Antwerpian.   Yet in both Tintoretto and
Veronese there is a majesty and warmth of hue
which Rubens never reaches.   Their rich amber
hair and glowing flesh of ivory *morbidezza* are more
lustrous than the pure gold tresses and rosy whiteness of the Flemish beauties.   And though the
Venetians always represent life and Nature more
than the ideal, they do not fall into the disgusting
excesses of Rubens; their passion is more refined,
nor is their canvas ever defiled with such brutality
as the " Murder of the Innocents " at Munich.   It
is the luxury of life in the burning South that they
have caught, the pomp and gardens and blue hills
and mighty palaces of Italy ; all these seem concentrated in the sentiment and colour of their pictures.
If we ask ourselves why some of the greatest Venetian masters are so little known, the answer is
simple—the essence of their works cannot be represented by engraving.   Raphael is better often in
a line engraving than on canvas, because his chief
power lies in form and expression and not colouring.
Michel Angelo's gigantic figures and elaborate
grouping can in like manner be easily transferred
to copper.   But the Venetians, wanting in ideal
beauty and wanting in composition, excelling as
they do all artists in the breadth and colour and

perfume of luxurious reality—in the pomp and pride of life—become mere skeletons when separated from the hues they have thrown around them like an atmosphere. This I felt in the Academia, which we visited after dinner. The names of Vivarini, Carpaccio, and Bonifazio I had barely heard of, but I found them great artists. Vivarini is the Venetian Perugino; his figures have a great dignity and sweetness; in the Church of St. John and St. Paul is a fine St. Christopher and St. Sebastian, and above it a Pietà exactly like the grand Mantegna at Berlin. Vittore Carpaccio has painted a long series of pictures representing the history of St. Ursula. There is no power of perspective in them, but great beauty of colour, dignity of attitude, and grace of feature. His meeting of Ann and Joachim is a splendid piece of bright colouring, and so is his apotheosis of St. Ursula. The details of his pictures are full of those everyday incidents that we remark in Benozzo Gozzoli and Pinturicchio.

The passage of the Venetian school from the Byzantine influence is extremely interesting. One great enthroned Madonna, by Giovanni d'Alemagna, illustrates the modification of her grim visage and almond eyes in its earliest stage. Scenes from the life of Christ, painted in the missal style, with gold markings for the drapery folds, carry on the growth. Gian Bellini is still under its influence. Among the many beautiful pictures of his in Venice, there is

none in which the Virgin is not stiff and conventional, with a stern forbidding aspect, and long
narrow eyes.   By far his finest work is in the
Church of St. Paul and St. John.   There the saints
and fathers of the Church about the throne are
emancipated from Byzantine ugliness.   Madonna,
as the most sacred personage, retains most of the
conventional aspect.   Of Gentile Bellini, there are
one or two historical pictures interesting, because
they show how unchanged Venice is.   Even the
pigeons flutter in those paintings about St. Mark's
as they do now.   From Bellini to Titian is a vast
leap.   The Assunta wholly satisfied me.   Such pas-
turage of colour, such superb action, such dignity of
adoration I have never seen.   I would sooner have
this picture than the San Sisto.   Titian's Virgin,
of course, is not so unearthly, or even so beautiful.
But she has a full warm splendour, and a humanity
which the other lacks.   The harmonies of colour
and power of movement were intoxicating.   This
is to me a far greater picture than Pietro Martire.
No engraving does it justice.   The details are all
perfect, and the execution most careful.   I think
that the variety and beauty of the cherubs surpass
Correggio, and certainly no one but Titian painted
such a figure as St. John.   The action of the
wounded monk in Peter Martyr equals, but does
not surpass it.

Sunday, July 13.—After rather a disturbed night,
we had breakfast at half-past eight, and papa and I

went up the great Campanile, which commands a
splendid view of Venice.   There is a white and grey
look about the town, which rather disappoints one.
Then we rowed to the Church of St. John and St.
Paul, rightly called the Westminster of Venice.   It
is a grand Gothic church, of the transition period,
from Romanesque to pointed arches, full of the tombs
of old doges and generals.   The old sleeping doges,
with their fine Dantesque profiles and close-fitting
caps, are ideals of repose.

I wish I could give some notion of the luxury
we enjoyed in gliding through the narrow canals.
There, though the sun was blazing in an unclouded
sky, those tall houses almost meeting overhead gave
a delicious shade.   From light to shadow we passed
as the gondola swung round the corners to the
warning cry of the oarsmen.   To feel the air so
soft and warm upon one's cheek, to feel the un-
dulation of the green smooth water, to see those
ancient palaces and profound glooms of deep-cast
shadows over marble traceries of vines and eagled
lions and angels was truly Venice.   Sometimes our
black gondola, like a great crocodile, dispersed a troop
of little swimmers.   The boys here are amphibious,
and run about quite naked, but for a wrapper round
the middle.   They leapt and ran on land, broadening their chests with play.   In the water, they dived
and swam and flung themselves about like ducks.
Without shame or restraint, fair to look upon, but
oh, how animal.   One woman's face attracted me

greatly. She was leaning from an upper window; against the dark background shone her light hair, tightly braided over a melancholy white face, not thin and sallow like so many of the Italians, but full and fresh-coloured, with blue eyes. From scenes like these, which I cannot describe, we passed into the Scuola di San Rocco. This is filled with pictures of Tintoretto, to the number of seventy-five. They are all in oils, but so executed as to take the place of frescoes, nor can much more time have been spent upon them than upon the ordinary fresco. Their impasto is very thin, and the stroke of the brush most rapid. No detail is finished, but general effect is every-where regarded. They seem to have been injured by time and neglect, and their hurried painting has no doubt rendered them more susceptible of light, for all are faded with the exception of one roof piece. They display the usual fault of Tintoretto— no unity of design or grouping—and his constant power of rapid action. Some are very naturalistic, especially the carpenter's house, with its broken wall and beds, which form the scene of the Annunciation, and the stable of the Nativity. The action of flight, and the whole strength of angelic personages, are most remarkable throughout. Satan in the Temptation is a proud beautiful youth, with gaudy wings and bracelets. How different from the Old Man in Milton and Rembrandt. The grand Crucifixion seems to me devoid of unity, and excessively confused. In detail it is very fine, and the power of action displayed is enormous. One man engaged in nailing down the bad thief is a study from Michel Angelo. Another raising the good thief in the foreground presents a beautiful and bold line from arm to arm.

After dinner, as it was fine and calm, we rowed out to the Lido, and crossed the island and gathered shells upon the shore of the Adriatic. The sky behind was gold, pink, and purple. We read Shelley's Julian and Maddalo, and saw the madhouse.

Alighting on the Molo, we had ices at Florian's in the Piazza, among a great crowd. The band played round a circle of gaslights in the centre. *Beati Venetiani!* if warm skies and summer fêtes were all. Yet one could not help looking back with sorrow to the picture of Gentile Bellini, and thinking that doges and senators had swept over that pavement where now the little Venetian girls were dancing to the sound of their despots' military music. The boys who sold *fiori di mare* and match-boxes laughed and sang, and parodied the music; they kissed their hands to us, and pretended to kiss Ch.'s dress, and begged for the biscuits we had left.

Tuesday, July 15.—We left about ten, highly satisfied. Venice has fully answered my expectations, and has not been hot or disagreeable, from the Canal water.

This day was scorching. I never felt so much misery and relaxation from heat. We stopped at

Padua during all the midday. First we saw Giotto's Chapel. The building is a plain oblong, with a Gothic apse thrown out. Its roof is oval. I notice that these Italian Gothic churches are often pierced upon the south side only. The design, as well as the frescoes, are by Giotto. His colouring—pale and serene—is very different from the stern drawing and gorgeous hues of Vivarini. The expression in some of the faces is wonderfully naïve and well delineated. I noticed here, also, that the most sacred personages are always least free from conventionalism.

After seeing this chapel, we went into the Church of the Eremittani in the Arena close by. It is a fine, dark Gothic building, chiefly remarkable for containing some grand frescoes of Mantegna. These interested me greatly, for I was able to see what a sudden emancipation from Byzantine forms and conventional modelling Andrea had attained by pure study of the antique. His figures are sharply defined, technically excellent, somewhat hard in colouring, and always remind one of statuary, of bas-relief. After having luncheon papa and I went out, in furious heat, to the old University, the halls and staircases of which are decorated with the names and arms of centuries of students and doctors. We saw some English there. The anatomical specimens made of wax were what attracted papa. At the door of St. Anthony's—*Il Santo* they call him here—we bought pretty rosaries. This church is one of N. Pisano's, fine and solemn. It is an

attempt to unite the Gothic crucial design with
Byzantine cupolas, after the fashion of St. Mark.
Nor is the attempt unsuccessful—especially from
the exterior. Inside the church is white and bare,
and severe, too much like a Belgian building.
Indeed, the arrangement of the false chevet is
wholly Belgian. The paucity of windows in these
Italian Gothic buildings is remarkable. This pecu-
liarity probably caused the development of fresco,
for those large blank spaces needed decoration.
The shrine of St. Anthony is most gorgeous, with
marble bas-reliefs and silver cressets. Opposite,
on the south side, is a chapel of St. Felice, wholly
clothed with fine Paduan frescoes of the fourteenth
century. Afterwards we dined, and then got to
Verona, where we found it stifling. Our hotel—
Delle Due Torre—was very comfortable and picturesque.

MILAN, *Wednesday, July* 16.—The night [at
Verona] was more burningly hot than I ever remembered. After an early breakfast we went out
and saw St. Anastasia and St. Zeno.

Then to the theatre, which is most interesting.
The seats of the circle, the corridors, and the
vomitories are all perfect. It certainly helps one
to realise the scene of Roman *circi*, though the size
disappointed me. Verona is a picturesque old town,
full of palaces, and surrounded by beautiful blue
hills. I ought to have mentioned that we saw
the tombs of the Scala family : Gothic canopies

charged with figures, and surrounded by wrought-iron chain-rails.

The people of Milan are very unquiet to-night. They have been excited by a speech of Garibaldi, in which he denounced Napoleon, called him "traditore," "mosso da libidine," "capo di briganti, di assassini." The Milanese hate the French, and are beginning to weary of the Sardinian government, and because they have to pay heavier taxes they regret the Austrians. This promulgation of Garibaldi has roused them against France and Sardinia, and made them furious for a Republic. To-night they propose a demonstration; all the soldiers—cavalry, infantry, and National Guard— are in readiness to suppress it. While I was writing, a confused murmur reached our ears. We got up and ran to our window, which looks both up and down the street. Instantly, we perceived that a large band of men, with lighted torches, were rapidly advancing up the street. A crowd formed in front of them. We saw men behind and at the sides. The bright red torches swayed about, burning and smoking with a glare upon the houses crowded with faces. Something seemed to interrupt their progress. A great noise arose, and the crowd increased. It was picturesque to see them toss their flambeaux up and down to make them shine, and in the distance each man looked like a shape of flame. Eschmann came up and told us that this was one of four divisions of the demonstration; 400 of another had been taken prisoners, and these were surrounded with soldiers. The soldiers forced them to break up, the crowd dropped away, and so ended the *émeute*. I often wondered what a demonstration meant. This is a pretty and picturesque specimen.

BAVENO, *July* 17.—At 12.40 we left Milan and arrived at Arona, after a hot journey, about half-past four. I felt well all to-day. A thunderstorm was brewing on Maggiore, which looked lovely notwithstanding. Its waters seemed quite an old friend, and so did the face of the Hotel Belle Vue at Baveno, where I am now writing. After dinner we rowed in the grey light on the lake.

It may be interesting to record the books I took with me, bought and read during this tour. To begin, I had, of course, my Bible and Prayer-book in one, and my little "Daily Food." Then, there were the Revelations and Job, each separate, the Greek Bucolic poets and Hermann und Dorothea in one volume, Plato's Republic in Greek, the Epistolæ Obscurorum Virorum, Kugler's Hand-book to Italian Painters, Shelley's minor Poems, La Comtesse de Rudolstadt (Deuxième Série), Green's Essay on Novels, one volume of Shake-speare containing Cymbeline, Lear, and Othello. I bought Valvédre, by George Sand, at Paris, at Munich a German and Italian lesson-book, at Venice an Italian Dictionary and a book called "L'Art Moderne," by Gautier. Then also papa gave me a pretty Virgil. I have read more or less of all these books except Green's Essay and Job, and, besides, I have read parts of the Cornhill, Macmillan, Murray, one part of Orley Farm, some of the Golden Treasury, Tennyson, La Jolie Cordière, by Saintine, some Paradise Lost, and Tom Jones.

Friday, July 18.—*Hotel de la Poste, Isella on the Simplon.* Papa and I sat up rather late last night discussing Rubens and the Venetians, after I had read a portion of my diary to him. I had a bad night in consequence, for I revolved in my head an essay on Art.

We engaged a very nice *vetturino*, with a comfortable carriage and two horses, to take us over the Simplon. He is an Italian, and seems brisk and polite. He drove us to-day much faster and better than our Tyrolese. His dog, who guards the luggage and runs beside the carriage, amused us much. We set off about half-past seven, and reached Domo d'Ossola at twelve. I remembered the purple hills on our right from last year very well. The colour seems to be caused by the multitude of minute ferns and mosses which cling to the rose-coloured marbles and granites of the rocks beneath. These hills form part of the same geological series as those which contain the quarries of Baveno. In these valleys one feels Virgil and the Sicilian poets more than anywhere. The wild fig-trees, the open areas where they thresh the corn, the quiet lawn and rivers, the Mincio that drains Lake Garda, the vines trained on elm and mulberry trees, seemed all familiar from the Eclogues and Georgics. Nor did the harsh chirp of the cicala fail to awake bucolic memories.

I wrote a letter to Stephens, which, though it recapitulates much that I have written in my diary, I shall partly transcribe, as summing up my views and giving heads for an essay.

"Art and man I always like better than Nature cold and simple. I feel at home in a town, because men are everywhere the same, and *homo sum*, &c. Scenery, when invested with association, becomes an object of passionate attachment to us, but I feel an alien among woods and lakes and mountains until that glow of sentiment has been thrown over them. This is peculiarly the case in driving rapidly through fine views, which one strives to remember without having time to understand or love. I can fancy a slow progression on foot, with a study of wayside flowers and changes of the sky, would cause Nature to grow more into my soul and become my friend.

"Rubens I have learned to admire more than ever. He is the Handel of painting. It is true he nowhere breathes the dignity and solemnity of Handel, but he has all the musician's power and rapidity of movement. His rhythms, so to speak, are, like Handel's, clear at first sight—vigorous, broad, and often passing into vulgarity. Like

Handel, he rarely sets himself to be beautiful, or
sacrifices to the Graces; but a careless sweep of
his brush throws off a perfect piece of elegance,
just as Handel seems by pure power to evoke a
touching melody.   Again, Rubens is as devoid of
Raphael's subtlety as Handel of the refinements of
Beethoven.   The musician, it must be confessed,
has a sublimity which the painter lacks; but I doubt
whether passion and the pomp and glory of this
world had sunk so deeply into Handel's soul as
into Rubens's.

"The great Venetians — particularly Tintoretto
and Veronese—have the same aim in Art as Rubens,
but they attain it by different means.   Composition
and form they sacrifice to colour; and instead of
copying an intellectual Ideal, they revel in the
pomp and pride of life.   Passion and splendour are
their theatre, but it is the passion of the South and
the splendour of Italian skies.   Their women have
less clear white loveliness than the Flemish; but more
fire pervades their deep ivory beauty.   There is
dignity in the Venetians where we often find brutality and coarseness in Rubens, and suppressed flame
where he creates pure light.   The Venetians reach
the soul by higher channels, but they have not the
variety and cymbal clash of Rubens: they could
not lead Roman triumphs, or Bacchus mad with
drums, upon their canvas; and their technical skill,
especially in perspective, is inferior to the great
Flemish master.

"To turn to Lionardo implies a long journey. We leave the mere portraiture of life and passion for the cherished reproduction of an ideal. Nature here is second to the intellectual conception, though she is still all important. Nature is φρόνησις to the σοφία of the ideal. Lionardo's spirit rests upon his scholars, whom he seems to have saturated with his genius. One type pervades them all. And this type is the ideal as it appeared to Lionardo. Nature bows to it, and mathematical proportions are studied to enhance its perfection by dignity of grouping and due balance in the subject. Colour is comparatively neglected—a strange variance from Venetian art, where the figures are arranged as nature groups them, without premeditation or calculation, and where colour is everything — an atmosphere of loveliness."

Saturday, July 19.—*Hotel de la Poste, Visp.* We left Isella at seven. I slept well, with the exception of one nightmare, which woke me up with the dim consciousness of a presence in the room. It was pitch dark, the matches were under two keys in my portmanteau, the noise of the stream prevented my hearing anything else. As often happens in nightmares, the dream continued its influence into my waking moments, and I could not but think some one was in the room, the more so that I knew no reason why I woke up suddenly with this impression, and remembered that my window opening on the outer staircase was unclosed. To get up, close and bolt it in the dark, required *sang froid.*

Tuesday, July 22.—Hotel Gibbon, Lausanne. I was so unwell on Sunday that papa gave up the notion of Zermatt and the Gemmi. We stayed at Visp all Sunday. I was in bed most of the day.

Yesterday we left at ten and drove to Sion. I thought my headache had come from the jolting of the carriage, or from sitting with my back to the horses. So papa kindly gave me a back seat, and I did not increase my headache. We arrived here at nine. I was extremely wretched, as indeed I am this morning, though now I can eat, which I could not before.

Hotel Byron, Villeneuve.—I am now feeling better, though I have had a miserable day. Every inch of my body aches; the two mustard plasters, one on my back and one on my stomach, which were put on at Visp, make every posture uncomfortable; my scalp is sore and my bones tingle; queer shudders run down my back; my head is full of neuralgic pains; my eyes feel boiled, and are regular centres of agony, to move which is to set two instruments of torture in motion. On the whole, I have felt like a parboiled lobster, saved even as a brand from the burning.

[It was necessary to record this last passage, because, as we shall find later on, Symonds attached great importance to his illness at Visp. Indeed, the whole journey was of moment in his career, for the theme of his letter to Mr. Stephens continued to develop in his mind, and led presently to a formal opening of his "artistic" studies.

By August 1st Symonds was home again, and on August 2nd he is "enjoying the calm air, the green leaves, and sunshine of the place. Yet it feels cold. I began a book, lettered 'Art and Literature,' to-day, with a long article on the characteristic of the Venetian School." On August 3rd we find this: "Stayed in all morning, partly because of my cold, partly to write Theodore, a self-analytical expansion of my verse of July 7th. I wrote 200 at a sitting, so they are doggerel." August the 4th: "Wrote at Theodore." August the 5th: "Left for Malvern. On my way I completed Theodore."

I think that these entries, referring to Art and Literature on the one hand, to the writing of poetry on the other, are of great importance in the history of Symonds' career as a man of letters. It seems that now, after his success at Oxford, after the stimulus of a highly intellectual journey with his father, he was beginning, unconsciously perhaps, to feel his way along the path of literature, and to test his natural bias within that sphere of activity towards which he was being insensibly drawn. And the unconscious questioning continued for some time. At Malvern he debates with his reading friends, Mr. Robinson and Mr. Courthope, the subject of "Art and Originality." It began with the

question of how far a painter might borrow from a
poet or historian without being a copyist. "I con-
tended that all great poets were as much a part of
the world's development as original. I showed how
they took colour from their school, and affected it
by their own individuality. I wished due attention
paid to the historical point of view. I do not feel
certain about all this. The history of the Van
Eycks goes against it." This is followed on August
20th by this significant remark: "I am discontented, because I do not feel myself a poet, and do
not see why I should not be one. It is vain and
foolish—in part a jealousy of Conington's appreciation of C——." After this there is a return to
criticism, to artistic analysis, of music, as usual,
enriched by the knowledge of painting, which he had
acquired abroad; and from Sutton Court, his brother-
in-law's house, he writes to Conington the following
remarks, suggested by a fine performance of the
"Creation" at Gloucester. "As I sat and thought
of the first chapter of Genesis and heard Haydn's
music, it seemed to me that I listened to a wise commentary. I called to mind Plato's definition of chaos,
Milton's description of the angelic symphonies of
light, and the chariot of God's Christ. I tried to
remember what Raphael and Michel Angelo had
modelled in form and colour to represent the power
of God in the Creation; but there was nothing which
spoke to me of utter desolation at the beginning, of
mysterious breathing as the Spirit went forth upon

the waters, of a low, still, permeating voice that gave
the fiat, and of a definite blast of God's will, ending
in the restless outgoing of intolerable light—like
those strange inexplicable chords and combinations
of symphonious instruments. Analysis of the reason
of this virtue resident in sound, seems to me impossible. I can only mark out the province of sound
from that of the other arts, and say that it is most
powerful wherever the idea of motion is prevalent.
Thus it would occupy a place like that of Plato's
astronomy, and its science would be the science of
motion, oral and visible, ruled by laws of abstract
harmony. Music is at the same time the abstract
science of all harmonious motion, and also its concrete expression to us. In its latter character it
communicates those impressions of delight which
are peculiar to it, and which still remain unanalysed.
As such it represents the motion of the heavens,
the life of the earth, and the energy of man; as
such it controls the tempest of the heart; the discord of anger and of fear, the harmony of love and
adoration, the windless calm of obedience and contemplation. Further it cannot go. Form and
colour it leaves to painting, sculpture, and architecture, which are the geometry of art. Poetry is
the metaphysic of art, dealing with the abstractions
of music and the plastic arts, and adding to them
her own province of pure intellectual thought."

[This is a highly characteristic passage; it shows

us the man deeply affected through his senses, which produce in him an emotion sublimated to its least definite and most pervasive form in music, and then instantly turning round to analyse this emotion. It illustrates the governing qualities of Symonds' personality, acute sensibility, and intense intellectual activity; he felt profoundly through his æsthetic sensibility, but his intellectual vigour would not let him rest there; he desired to know as well as to feel. This was his spiritual attitude at this most important period of his life. Had it not been for the grievous misfortunes which were so soon to overtake him, he would have pressed forward toward some union and fusion of these two qualities in him, his capacity for feeling, and his desire to know—with what result we can only now surmise.

As it was, the internal clash and conflict of two such powerful appetites inside a delicate frame, were wearing and grinding the man to powder. The next night is disturbed by violent dreams, and the day following his pain is poured forth in a torrent of splendid Augustinian Latin. Then the storm of passion dies away upon the close of this prayer: "Make me calm without stagnation, wise without the delirium of little learning."

It is not improbable that the resolution of his internal difficulties would have been achieved through the victory of the æsthetic and the absorption of the intellectual qualities, that he would have reached his knowledge through feeling. The following passage

seems to indicate the advent of some such amal-
gamation :—"I felt in a good mood for musing"
(he is in the cathedral); "things came in upon
me as they sometimes do rushingly. I could not
analyse or dwell upon impressions, but I felt past,
present, and future bound in one, and all around
me full of hurrying suggestions. It is a delightful
but an exhausting condition, and one of much ner-
vousness; for the soul trembles, unable to grasp all,
yet desiring to hive sunshine for leaden days. The
grandeur of the Athanasian Creed, as Tallis's music
rolled it forth in sonorous ebb and flow and constant
reconstruction of decaying chords, seemed to me
more soul-crushing and full of intellectual pomp
than I ever remembered it. The Greek spirit,
terrible in its decadence, swept on upon its metaphysical chariot, bearing the image of a sublime
creed, yet crushing remorselessly the bodies of all
upon its path." There it is the Athanasian Creed
intellectually grasped through the emotion of music.
On the other hand, the following analysis of Mendelssohn's Motett on the 22nd Psalm seems to
illustrate the opposite process or tendency; here
the æsthetic import of the music seems to be
reached through an intellectual appreciation of the
words.

"I have just come from hearing Mendelssohn's
divine Motett on the 22nd Psalm. It is the most
dramatic, sublime effort of music that I ever heard.
Mendelssohn seems to have been inspired in writing

it with the whole spirit of the Greek tragedians—
that spirit which he caught during his labours on
the Antigone, that spirit which breathes throughout
the conversation between the chorus and the Princess
as she is journeying to the tomb. It always seemed
to me that that passage is the most pathetic in all
the range of the Greek drama—the solitary sadness
of Antigone taken up and echoed by the chorus
which repeats her lamentations in other words ; the
wail of misery, succeeded by the passion of momentary struggling, and at last relieved by a sense of
self-devotion, of nobility in death, of heroic and
mythological apotheosis—strikes the deepest key
which pagan music can command. Self-sacrifice to
the gods, and obligations of kindred, and an equality
of fate with men renowned in story, are the theme
of the Antigone. And if they can move us so, what
are our emotions when we gaze upon the desolation
and hear the agonising cries of Christ, when the
interest involves the universe, when the victory
gained is for all time? This passion, the deification
of suffering and conquest wrenched from agony, great
painters have attempted to describe in pictures as
majestic as the Crucifixion of Tintoretto, or as
desolate as the lonely Cross of Rubens or Vandyke,
sole against the lurid clouds with Him that hangs
thereon. It is not, however, the province of painting
to evolve the various steps in a great dramatic conception, to call up collateral points of interest, to
suggest the commencement of the passion, follow

it to its climax, and finally pronounce the moral of
the conclusion. Painting arrests the passion at one
point, and leaves the imagination to do the rest—
it can never be consummately dramatic. Nor can
poetry alone. It needs the accompaniments of
scenery or dress, or the aid of music. But in such
a situation as we are alluding to music is supreme.
The monotonous minor of the opening cry, 'My
God, my God, look upon Me,' introduces us to the
solitary suffering of Christ. The voice is low and
wailing, and we shudder till the attendant chorus
takes up the theme, 'And art so far from the voice
of My complaint?' For the next two verses the
same order is continued, the commos or conversation between the solo and chorus, in which the
chorus acts as echo and interpreter of the lonely
outpouring of the tenor voice, being sustained.
Then for two verses the Protagonistes is silent,
the theme of God's mercies in the olden time being
suited to the reflection of the chorus. He bursts
forth again with the words, 'But as for Me, I am
a worm,' commenting with true Greek feeling
upon the sentiments of the chorus, applying them
to himself, and showing the futility of their poor
consolations. In the succeeding voice the agony
of lamentation is wrought to a terrific pitch; we
reel and tremble beneath it, and feel that the sun
is darkened, and the stars give no light. Then
is apparent that power of synthetical dramatic representation, which music possesses above all the

other arts; for to heighten the passion, which must
in poetry and painting have been confined to the
expression of agony in the Sufferer, or sympathy in
His friends, we have the chorus of yelling Israelites
represented to us, 'He trusted in God that He
would deliver Him.' Up swell the derisive minors,
clash the trebles in exulting derision, a storm and
fury of discord and triumph swells from organ and
contending voices. It lulls, and the solitary tenor
proceeds once more, supported by the sympathising
chorus. In the words, 'and then thou shalt bring
me to the very dust of death,' we reach the lowest
point of abasement. But now it is time that the
tragic horror should be tempered, and again notice
the resources of music. Without altering the artistic
unity of the piece, without bringing down a *Deus ex
machina*, without revolting the judgment with any
sudden transition to premature victory, retaining the
old minor, out swells a solitary treble, the first treble
which has spoken alone during the whole anthem,
and calls in an air loaded with pathetic pleading and
excess of beauty to God, 'Be not Thou far from
Me, O God.' This is taken up by the tenors and
basses; gradually the pleading air acquires a solemn
and almost triumphant beauty. Hope has passed
in like a ray of light, but it is tempered and subdued.
We feel that victory though it is, it has been bought
with intense woe, and that the sorrow is not past.
The hope is one of calmness and resignation, more
than of expectation or confidence. And this feeling

is kept up till the end of the piece, which concludes
with a chorus—'The earth is the Lord's,' solemn
and sublime, yet still minor. The human will has
been subdued, and homage is paid to God, who
out of pain works deliverance. We are still before
the cross, and He who hangs thereon is still bleeding, panting, suffering. But He has bowed His
head, and knows the end, and feels that all is good
and merciful, and that He is one with God."

No doubt it was the fineness of his brain-structure
which made Symonds at once so capable of æsthetic
emotions, and so analytic of those emotions. But
in this very fineness lay a danger. Throughout the
Diary we begin to meet such ominous entries as, "a
strained feeling in my head;" and notes of this nature
become more and more frequent. In fact, a breakdown of brain-power was menacing his career. And
the struggle was the more wearing for Symonds,
in that the spiritual conflict between emotion and
knowledge was being carried over into the world of
conduct and of action. A passage from a letter to
a friend indicates the position clearly enough : "It
is one of the most terrible results of introspection
that I find the weakness, vicious tendencies, morbid
sensibilities, and discontent deepened and intensified
by all that I have learned in study, and by all that
I have lost in faith. Old realities have become
shadows, but these shadows still torment me. There
is a restlessness of passion, an unending want of
what can never be, that seem the peculiar Nemesis

of a scholar's life. I envy you to be living in the world of things and not of thoughts—that is, to use the former as your battle-field of life, and to turn the latter round at times for your recreation. I, on the other hand, hear the great world of fact and action roaring for ever around me unintelligibly; my own sphere is one of phantoms, and my own battle a mere schiomachy. Thoughts and words are the men and things I deal with; but they are direful realities, full of suasions to passion, and maddening with impossible visions of beauty. This constant contact with the intangible results, in a word, is the state of Faust. We must go from thought to action, from the darkness of the study to the full light of the world—if we are strong enough. And here is another Nemesis of study—bodily weakness. Oh, woe to such as make their own dreams avenging Furies, and are unable to escape, to be at peace! Like Faust, life for such men is only found through vice, and they become human only after Medean baths of witchcraft and sense-searing indulgence."

The situation seems clear enough; in one region emotion and intellect are at war, in the other thought and action. Emotions generate a passion, an appetite; intellect analyses the emotions into thoughts; thought is unsatisfying to the appetite which emotion has created, and that appetite demands the translation of the thought into action, but health bars the way. This is a state of mind known to men like Leopardi; but it was terrible that one so young as Symonds should already have attained such lucid vision of the case. This letter seems to me to prefigure his future life. He did take to action ;— to creative action, in the vast amount of literary work which flowed from him during the next thirty years; to civic action in the duties which he performed so well, first at Clifton, and then at Davos ; to enjoyment of life in the unconventional freedom which Switzerland and Italy afforded to his active temperament. But there was a long and dolorous journey to be taken before he attained to the liberty of action which was in fact the full effectuation of his own personality.

Three fellowships were open for competition during the Autumn term of 1862. Jowett recommended Symonds to stand for them in turn. Queens' came first. He entered for it on October 3, and failed to get it. "*October* 8.—Waited all day for the election. At six, I heard that Elton and Maidlow were elected. Facts are more significant than feelings. Reached home about 1 A.M."

While under examination, he wrote this to his sister] :—

"Thank[1] you for your letter. It was very nice to get so many birthday congratulations in my solitude.

"Twenty-two years is a good age—an age

[1] To his sister Charlotte. Oxford, October 5, 1862.

certainly at which I ought to be better, stronger, more fixed in character, and more developed in organisation than I am. If birthdays are of any use, they serve at least to remind us of such truths as this ; and so little by little we become accustomed to take our lowly places in life, and not to fret onwards for what is not to be. I do not see any reason why we should expect unhappiness in the future. Every year lessens our discontent, hardens us to the chances of the world, dries up some spring of yearning or vain fancy, and so makes us more equable, and more ready for the future. It is not in what we have to bear, but in the way that we can bear it, that our happiness or misery consists. Nor do I believe that any pangs can be at the same time so acute, and so disgraceful, as those which in seasons of calm weather we create for ourselves in our own hearts. The prayers that in youth we make for genius, wealth and beauty, as we grow older, become prayers for peace, so that each year brings us nearer to the aspiration of St. Augustine : 'O Lord, grant us Thy peace. O Lord, grant us the peace of Thy Sabbath. O Lord, grant us the peace of Thy Sabbath which has no evening.'

"There is something strange and touching in these prayers for rest, and in the passionate longing, which, amid the noise of business, or of pleasure, comes over all of us, for a windless calm of dependence upon God. In the examination on

Friday afternoon, I could hardly translate one sentence of an old Greek poem, it touched me so. A mother had been cast adrift with her baby on the waters, and the child was sleeping, but the mother strove with terror for a time, and then bent over the little face, and cried, ' Sleep, baby, and let the seas be still, and let our woes unmeasured cease.' It seemed to me that this was a type of the useless unreasoning prayers which every one is making on the waves of life. They know that the seas must rage and the troubles must fall, but yet there is that within them which bids them think of peace, and somehow assures them that it is not far off. Nor is it far off, for death is always near, and we doubt not but that he comes as a friend to all men, ringing vesper bells, and sounding no alarm in the darkness of the night.

" If these lines are too exalted and visionary, a birthday and a solitary Sunday must excuse them. I have answered one thought in your letter. For the other, if I am much to you, you know that you are much to me—how much we neither of us can calculate. Wait and see whether I be elected at Queens' before you give me anything. A photograph for my rooms in case of my getting them would be a most acceptable present. If not, M. Müller is the book I should like.

" *P.S.*—This letter need not be all read out ; for though no secret, it is too dithyrambic for the breakfast-table."

[The next fellowship was at Magdalen; and in the meantime Jowett came to stay at Clifton Hill House.]

October 15.[1]—Had a pleasant tête-à-tête with Jowett. He talked about fellowships, and about staying up at Oxford. That he does not wholly approve of. He calls it living in a hothouse, and says men get braced in London. About health, he thinks young men of my age are apt to pule. To read conscientiously for years on one subject requires peculiar gifts. Great perseverance and freshness are needed; for after a time the acquisition of knowledge becomes tedious, and its reconstruction ceases to be anything but restitution. He spoke about the habit some men acquire of using words without thoughts. They write beautifully and cleverly, but neither they nor their readers can tell what they mean.

[The examination at Magdalen began on 21st October, and the following entries occur] :—

October 25.—" I have been doing a Latin Essay, 'Ut pictura poesis,' a nice enough subject had it been English. I noticed, when I was doing verses, that a little greenfinch had got into the hall and could not find its way out. The bird's feet were entangled with cobwebs from the ceiling, and it clung wildly to the wires of the oriel by the daïs.

[1] Diary.

I found the poor thing tame and exhausted; I took
it in my hands, and removed the cobwebs, and then
I let it fly forth from the open window into the clear
autumnal sky, fresh with sunlight after rain. The
creature sat dazed upon a battlement, and then
hopped to another, and pecked a little moss. At
last it felt its freedom, chirruped, and was away
toward the woods. So would that some one might
release me."

[Symonds very much wished to be elected at
Magdalen; the stately buildings, the magnificent
chapel services, the aroma of the place suited his
taste. "Quam dilecta sunt templa Magdalenæ.
Nunquam aliquid adeo desideravi," he had written
during the examination; and while waiting for the
announcement of the issue, he was highly nervous.
Characteristically he interjects, " By the way, how
ridiculous Pantheism seems at a moment when I
am so keenly individualised!"

The suspense was soon at an end; Symonds was
elected unanimously. " That night I dined in hall
as a stranger. All the Fellows took wine with me.
It was the festival of the restitution of the Fellows,
and after hall the whole College, on and off the
foundation, drank of a great cup, standing and saying, ' Jus suum cuique.' In common room Knight
made me a short speech, which I answered with a
few words. The bells rang a merry peal for my
election." On the 27th he was admitted Proba-

tionary Fellow, and on November 1st he went into
his rooms in College, cloisters 8, one pair left. He
took leave of his lodgings at Nalder's, 56 St. Giles,
in this letter to his friend, Mr. Stephens: "It is a
sad and solemn thing to leave a house where one
has thought, worked, and felt intensely, with pain
and with pleasure, with success and disappointment,
under depression and hope; and where, for the
most part, solitude has been the condition of one's
communings. The recollection of your friendship
will always make Nalder's a pleasant place in my
memory. Yet here I have been absolutely at times
alone, not in respect of company, but in spirit.
And this, I think, is what now appals me. . . . As
I grow my sensibilities become more tender, and
this year has been a marvellous one for me. For
its successes I have all reason to be most humbly
thankful, and for its soul-searching sorrows I have
also reason to thank God."

Immediately after moving into Magdalen, Symonds received the offer of acting as tutor to young
Lord Pembroke, then at Eton. He was uncertain
what course to take, and went home to consult his
father. The conversation that evening naturally
raised the whole question of a career. Symonds
stated his "ambition rather for literature than for
anything else, and carelessness for politics and Par-
liament." The upshot was that he determined to
remain in Oxford, try to find tutorial work, and to
eat dinners in London.]

" I [1] will begin a letter to-day, and shall probably not send till to-morrow. We had a solemn dinner last night in the Bursary, on the occasion of what is mysteriously called ' Pippin Audit ;' of the origin of this, and many other phrases connected with the College, no one, not even Dr. Bloxam, who has devoted a lifetime to Magdalen Antiquities, can give any account. Certain it is, that on the last day but two of January, there is a formal audit of the College accounts, and in the evening a great festival is held, marked by a bowl of roasted golden pippins. If the College business is treated with no more lucidity than the steward evinced in his speech last night, I am afraid that many incomprehensible questions about our finances might easily be answered. Such a meeting is pleasant in its way, it makes one feel the magnitude, and I wish it made everybody feel the responsibility of such a body. Thirty thousand pounds have been received by them for good or ill as their annual revenue in the day time, and in the evening they celebrated their society by a sumptuous festivity. I was glad enough to escape a little before tea, and to walk with Bramley round the walks in the moonlight. Indeed, if the great gates were not always locked, or if I possessed a key, I should often walk there at night. The broad meadow and the cloister trees chequering the path with moonlight, the sparkle of the water, the dim rows of elms in the park, and shadowing deer beneath them, the

[1] To his sister Charlotte. Magdalen College, January 30, 1863.

antiquity before him, did not really know as much of ancient history as we do. Perhaps he sunk under the weight of materials, and certainly, if all the classics had been preserved, it is difficult to understand how modern literature would have sprung up. I think we have quite as much of them as could really be of use.

" I took a walk with John before he left. I thought him very able, and much improved in ability since he went into the schools. I do not think his ill-health has been any disadvantage to him mentally, but rather the reverse, although this seems strange.—Ever yours sincerely,   B. JOWETT.
" Many thanks for the photographs."

But after three weeks the crisis arrived; Symonds' health gave way suddenly, and, as he says, " I have never been a strong man since."]

" My [1] illness declared itself one night in the form of a horrible dream, the motive of which was that I saw a weak old man being gradually bruised to death with clubs. Next morning I rose with the certainty that something serious had happened to my brain. Nor was I mistaken. During the next three years I hardly used my head or eyes at all for intellectual work, and it was fully ten years before they recovered anything like their natural vigour ; while in the interval I began to be consumptive. I do not doubt that the larger part of

[1] Autobiography.

this physical distress was the result of what I suffered at Magdalen, coming after the labour of reading for my degree, and the obscure fever I had at Visp."

[Immediately after this collapse he went to Malvern, in company with his sister.]

" I [1] am very glad to hear that you so much like to go with me to Malvern. I am sure I should enjoy it immensely; and though I ought to hope it will not be necessary, I cannot help feeling that I should be disappointed were I to decide upon staying here. It is hard for me to judge what I ought to do, for, though I was very uncomfortable yesterday, I feel stronger to-day, and so it goes on. Much of my time I spend in our chapel. The calm of music, which once I used to enjoy, but which I thought had vanished for ever, seems to have returned to me, and I take advantage of our daily services to employ my time without exercising my mind. In the interval between morning and evening prayers I ride—sometimes twice a day, once to exercise my mare, Doefoot, gently, and again to stir my own blood. There is a humility and resignation, and even a kind of tranquillity in weakness, which seems to answer in an unexpected fashion that prayer of ' Dona nobis pacem Domine!' which we are ever scattering in stronger moments. I shall

[1] To his sister Charlotte. Magdalen College, Oxford, Feb. 25, 1863.

decide for myself on Friday about Malvern, unless papa thinks it wiser at once to settle on our going, in which case I should be glad of an authoritative letter, recommending a fortnight's change. What will become of Doefoot I hardly know."

[At Malvern Symonds and his sister lodged in Cleveland House; and there, though suffering acutely from his brain, and with "eyes weak and inflamed, so that he has to wear shades and spectacles," he completed the study of the Renaissance which won the Chancellor's Essay. With the recitation of this composition he closed his residential career at Oxford. The reference in his Diary is characteristic: "*June* 24, 1863.—Since I wrote last in this book I have got the English Essay Prize. Papa and Charlotte heard me recite it before the Prince and Princess of Wales. I have made a new and pleasant acquaintance—L. G. M——."]

CHAPTER VI

MANHOOD. FELLOWSHIP TO MARRIAGE

My[1] health continuing miserable, I left Clifton, at my father's bidding, and much against my own will, for Switzerland, upon the 25th of June 1863. At that time, though I had enjoyed the valley of Chamonix and the glaciers of Mont Blanc, I did not care for Alpine scenery. The prospect of dragging my pain and weariness and aching eyes among a crowd of tourists through Swiss inns disgusted me.

In Cecil Bosanquet, brother of my Harrow friend Gustavus, I had a kind and amusing travelling companion. He knew I was ill, and must have seen

[1] Autobiography.

that I had something weighing on my mind. But I did not confide to him my troubles. I had done so to no one, who was not brought into the affair by necessity.

This summer in Switzerland turned out so decisive for my future, that I shall dwell at length upon its incidents, drawing from the diary I still kept pretty regularly.

Friday, 26.—We came from Dover to-day to Beauvais. The cathedral is only a choir and transept carried to the most audacious height, ornamented externally on every square inch, but plain inside. The impression of strength which it conveys is purely intellectual. The brute materials of stone and iron are compelled by human energy into assuming functions alien to their nature. The lightest and most graceful structure, which seems to be spun from cobwebs or made of lace, is built up, stone by stone, and cramp by cramp, in obedience to the daydream of some unknown architect. This illusion disappears when you walk outside, and see the heavy buttresses, leaning one upon the other far into the road, and all required to give the slight effeminate semicircle of the apse stability.

Next day we came to Rheims. Sunday following, we decided to stay. "At ten we went to hear High Mass. They have a rage here for austere Gregorian music, which I believe to be now prevalent in France. At first the service seemed to break the harmony of art, which flowed from

branching arches and embowered capitals, from
lofty organs carved with angels windy-winged and
spreading hair afloat upon the breeze of sound,
from distant altars and candles flickering in daylight through the incense-clouds. The music was
severe and cold. But as the consecration of the
elements drew nigh, I could perceive that the whole
effect of the service was reserved for that chief mystery. Then the great organ awoke from slumber,
softly and silverly preluding with simple modula-
tions from key to key and stop to stop, without aim
it seemed, but most mellifluous, in long luxurious
cadences. And now one solitary treble voice began
an air of sad, pathetic pleading, as though it were
beseeching Christ to descend and manifest Himself
to His beloved. The organ reserved its sweetest
stops for an accompaniment, using the tremolo, and
altering them from tone to tone of deeper pathos
as the voice swelled up or died away in its entreaty.
At first the instrument subserved the song, but soon
it rose in rivalry, and toward the end it gained complete ascendency, thrilling in solitude through the
whole silent church, as though its mighty heart felt
the down-coming of the Deity. The multitudes of
men and women bowed in adoration. A bell rang.
The music ceased. A priest lifted wafer and cup.
And through the incense, above the altar, to the
eyes of ardent worshippers, there swam the vision
of Christ crucified. ' Fac me plagis vulnerari, cruce
hac inebriari, ob amorem filii.' But mute devotion

is not enough.   We must welcome God incarnate
and triumphant with songs and trumpets, and the
cry of exultation.   So the choir strikes up a resonant
fugue, 'Benedictus qui venit in nomine Domini.'
Such was the æsthetic import of the Mass for me."

The 30th of June we spent at Strasburg, and I
was determined to ascend the spire, after spending some hours reading Plato's Symposium in the
cathedral.   It was necessary to obtain a special
permission from the Mayor.   C. B. only got a
short way above the platform; I persevered by an
act of will, remembering Goethe.   The guide preceding me, we rose through a spiral cage, very
narrow, with open sides, down which we looked
into the streets of the town.   A false step might
have sent one flying thither.   This staircase narrowed at each of eight stages; and just at the top,
in order to enter the crowning canopy, one had to
stand in empty air upon the foliated apex of a
pinnacle, and thence to take a spring, clutching
at a bar above, and swinging up to a little stone
platform.   This gymnastic was trying to the head,
especially on the return, when the whole descent,
forested with spires, was seen naked beneath us.
In the state of my health at that time, with the
brain so troubled, this ascent of the Strasburg spire
taxed nerve and energy too much.   But I was glad
to have made it at the expense of some headache.

Basel, Lucerne, Pilatus, nine days in the pine-
woods of Seelisberg, six days at Engelberg, Rosen-

laui, Interlaken, such was our route. These lines,
written at Engelberg, describe my inner mood—

> Ill and alone on alien shores,
> At noontide when the hot sun fires
> With blinding light the silver spires
> Of ice-tops, when the sick stream pours
> His everlasting torrent down
> The tumbled wreck of splintered stone,
> And black impending pines alone
> Assuage the mountain's horrid frown,
> 'Tis sad to sit and dream of thee,
> Dear England, deep in greenery.

[And this letter to his sister describes his outer
mood.]

"My[1] plan, if the weather permits, is to reach
Meyringen by the Joch to-morrow. Should the
weather prove bad, I shall go on at once to
Interlaken from Meyringen. This doubt about the
weather began yesterday, when we had a furious
storm of rain and wind. I find that the chief
pleasure which I take in scenery is derived from
what artists call 'effects,' and these are usually
some peculiar aerial conditions of sunlight, mist,
or cloud, under which the landscape is viewed.
When the sun has reached a certain position with
respect to our valley it pours a full flood of light
into the gigantic chasm, and then every atom of
craggy outline, every Alpine slope of grass, and
all the interminable depths of pine forests which

---

[1] To his sister Charlotte. Engelberg, July 19, 1863.

descend upon the pathway of a roaring stream are brought into intense relief. The whole valley looks like a golden cup, wonderfully embossed and chased within its concave, into which has been poured liquid light.

"Generally I avoid writing about mountains. Clear uniform sunlight fatigues me. It has a topographical utility, for it enables one to discriminate all the members of a range or network of valleys. But it makes nature dead. And for this reason I believe that a common English landscape contains all the elements of the sublime and beautiful. No Alpine views have touched my soul or elevated my feelings more than certain aerial effects of coming and departing storms, which I have watched at sunset on Shotover. None have so thrilled me as the beauty of morning and of evening in the skies and vapoury distances of Clifton.

" I wish so much that there were some chance of your coming abroad with papa. When several of us are away together the unhomeliness of travelling is not so felt as it must be when one is alone, and has so many absent ones to think of. I believe that nothing will induce me to leave England again for Italy, when I once have got home. Please thank papa for his letter, which was like 'sun in winter.' I should have written to him to-day, but that I find my paper full."

I [1] did much walking every day, however, and

[1] Autobiography.

found real pleasure both in the Alpine scenery and
glorious Alpine flowers.   The thought of Hesperus
and Hymenæus, combining with Goethe's " Ueber
allen Gipfeln ist Ruh," haunted me at Engelberg, at
Meyringen, at Interlaken.   The evening star was
strong and beautiful in that warm summer-time ;
and I wrote "prose sonatas" on the theme of
Hesper for each of those places.   I will transcribe
the last of them.

July 22.—The day has been dull and sultry.
Clouds have draped the mountains, and the sun
has never shone, and in the air is coming thunder.
An hour after sunset we strolled forth between
two lakes, and leaving one behind us followed
the stream which joins them.   Shortly before it
finds the lake of Thun, there is a bridge on
which we rested.   Before us stretched the leaden
plain of water, bounded by shadowy hills.   The
torrent rushed beneath, and all its tawny flood was
livid with the yellow glare reflected from a chasm
in the clouds.   Between this sullen splendour and
the calm grey hills there ran a narrow tongue of
land on which no gleam was thrown.   Dismal and
black it lay in the midst of two waters, the turbid
torrent and the distant lake.   We stayed there
long, watching the light upon the changeful stream,
and growing almost in love with death.   Surely
this was the place to tempt a suicide.   Cool plash-
ing water, dark and impenetrable, surface-gilt with
glare of sunset dismal as decaying life, kept ever

murmuring in the sultry air : saying, "The land is desolate, the skies are dull and hot as a consuming furnace, but I am ever fresh and dewy and forgetful ; I am Lethe ; come to me, bring nothing of the world, and you shall find your rest." So I pondered and made the torrent speak ; for in my heart were thoughts too deep for tears and woes too keen for utterance. Then far above our heads, above the cove of buried sunlight, broke the clouds, and Hesper swam forth, clear and hopeful, in his liquid spaces of aerial gold. Pure were the heavens around him, and their crystal chasms seemed cooler, happier than the leaden waves. As I gazed into their brightness it was as though I saw the choir of heaven's cathedral, wherein sat angels innumerable, harping on their harps and singing songs above the reach of words. Though I could not understand the burden of those songs, the spiritual melody went to my heart, and there translated its sweet message into mortal consolation. "Seek not the tomb," my heart responded, "live your life as God shall give it. Trust in Him, and try to be of better cheer. After the dull day comes glory and peace." The dissolving saffron of the sunset glowed and faded to the tone of Mendelssohn's music, "If with all your hearts ye truly seek Me."

Next day we walked up to Mürren from Lauterbrunnen, where I was destined to abide, with one brief interval, until the 31st of August, a memorable period for me. At Mürren I learned to love

the Alps with a strong passion, which, though it
has sobered in the course of years, still vibrates and
endures. I also came to appreciate the Swiss people,
and to admire the simple dignity and wholesome
habits of the peasantry. My health revived daily.
In spite of frequent drawbacks and persistent trouble
in the brain, I grew stronger and lighter-hearted.
The promise of Hesper at Interlaken seemed in
part likely to be realised.

In those days there was only one little wooden
inn at Mürren, the Silberborn, kept by Herr Sterchi
and his family. Life was very primitive, few people
staying in the house beside ourselves ; troops of
tourists coming up from Interlaken to lunch, and
going noisily away again. The George de Bunsens
were our companions for some time, and while
they were still there an English family arrived. I
can remember looking out of Cecil's window and
spying their advent one bright afternoon in early
August. It annoyed us to think that the hotel
would now be fuller. "They were Mr. Frederick
North, M.P. for Hastings, and his two daughters"
(so runs the Diary). "Both the young ladies were
devoted to sketching. The eldest was blonde, tall,
stout, good-humoured, and a little satirical. The
second was dark and thin and slight, nervous and
full of fun and intellectual acumen. The one seemed
manager and mother, the other dreamer and thinker.
Neither was remarkable for beauty, but the earnest
vivacity of the younger grew upon me, and I could

soon have fallen in love with her. Her name was Catherine. Mr. North is kind and easy-going. They seemed to have travelled in most parts of Europe." Such is the entry in my precious priggish Diary about the woman whom I was destined to marry. I carried the thought of Catherine North, like a sleeping seed, in my mind through the next ten months, sought her out in London then, and did what will be afterwards related. The Norths stayed only a week, I think, at Mürren, but that was time enough to form a tolerably just conception of them. Alpine inns are favourable places for hatching acquaintance and gaining insight into character.

[Mr. Bosanquet having to return home, Symonds went down to Zurich to join his future brother-in-law, T. H. Green. He was fully resolved to bring Green back with him to Mürren, and the reason peeps out in the following letter to his sister] :—

" I [1] found Green here last night. He wants us to try a little inn near Zurich, called Uetliberg, which is only 1000 feet above the Lake. I may try this place, but I confess that already I regret Mürren. The heat to me seems intense, maddening; but it is nothing to what it has been, and people laugh at me when I say I feel it. This shows how imprudent it would have been to have gone to Munich now. Two or three days even of this heat would

[1] To his sister Charlotte. Zurich, August 12, 1863.

have quite undone all the good of Switzerland. I
should not wonder if we returned to Mürren. I
cannot make Green go as far as the Æggishorn,
which is strongly recommended ; and certainly
Mürren's monotony and beauty, and great internal
comfort, are better than semi-substitutes like Uetliberg. It is your birthday, and I must send you,
what you know I do most heartily, my very best
wishes. I wish I could also send you some
souvenir from Switzerland, but things cut in wood
I hate. Would you care to have one of the Bernese
costumes? I thought of getting that for you. It
is to me a most lovely dress.

"At Mürren there was a young girl of the better
class from Thun, who had come as a friend of the
landlord for change of air, and who helped his people
in the waiting on their guests. She always wore
this dress when she dressed for Sundays or for
dinner-time, and it suited her well; for she was a
blonde, very slight and graceful, and very girlish.
It amused me to find my ideal of Margaret realised
in her better than in Gounod's Faust or Retzsch's
etchings. In the evenings, after the servant girls
had done their work, when the sky was clear and
bright with stars, they used to sit upon the balcony
and sing their country songs. It was pretty to hear
them passing from high shrill shepherd ballads and
mountain *lieder*, to low soft chorales, then modulating
all together a 'Tra la la, tra la la,' in liquid notes
rising from their throats, or thrilling deep down in

the chest, like the voice of a bird singing to itself
at night. The landlord and his servants in these
country inns treat travellers more as guests than
anything else, and show them attentions, as if they
were bound to do so by the laws of hospitality. I
expect I had a very favourable instance of this at
Mürren, for the simplicity and good manners of the
people seemed perfect."

Green [1] and I next day walked up to Uetliberg,
and set ourselves down there in a little wooden
tavern for a week. He had just come from Heidel-
berg, and was full of German philosophy, politics,
and the higher poetry. I think he had it in his head
then to translate a book of Baur's upon the first
century of Christianity. We both worked during
the day, sitting at wooden beer-tables under the
thick beech trees, which, here and there, were
cut into vistas over the illimitable landscape. I
chose a gap from which the Bernese Oberland
was visible, while I penned an essay on Shakespeare's Sonnets (it has not been published,
but I possess the MS. still, and do not think
amiss of it). I used to send many thoughts on
airy wings to the Jungfrau, Eiger, Mönch, and
humbler Breithorn. I could see them all distinctly
when the vapour-veil allowed, and could mark
exactly the spot of Mürren. Even the Schilthorn
allowed itself to be observed upon the flank of
that vast snowy panorama. In the evenings we

[1] Autobiography.

used to take long walks among the glow-worms,
beneath the stars, watching the lamps of Zurich
burn like earthly stars low down beside by the
lake. It was a monotonous but pleasant life,
and I learned much from Green. Here it was,
I think, that he first shewed me Goethe's proe-
mium to "Gott und Welt," a poem which took
deep hold upon me, and began to build my
creed.

But a great longing came over me for Mürren.
I remembered its unrivalled purity of air—those
walks upon the Schilthorn, in the Sefinenthal, toward Trachsellauinen. I heard the aerial echoes of
the Alpenhorn ascending from Lauterbrunnen, or
floating from the Wengern Alp, and gaining melody
upon the way. I longed for the immediate presence
of the giant mountains with their glaciers. And the
simple folk kept calling to me. And R—— E——
was the soul and centre of these things.

Green wanted us to go to Gais in Appenzell, but I
over-persuaded him. I must return to Mürren, and
he must come with me. We agreed then on these
terms. He was to take the route by Rapperschwyl,
Einsiedeln, Schwyz. I hurried straight to Thun.
There I visited R——'s home, and made acquaintance with her mother, who seemed a little suspicious
of me. She had probably some right to do so, for
I doubt not that, in my simplicity, I let her infer
that I was going back to Mürren for her daughter's
sake.

I walked up to Mürren on the 10th of August in drenching rain.   And it rained and snowed incessantly for three days when I arrived.   R——, who knew that I had come again to see her, and who did not understand what all this meant, kept severely aloof, avoiding me on purpose.

August 22.—Green came yesterday; and at nine this morning the sun shone out.   We walked together in the deep snow, which lay thick upon those late summer flowers.   They, poor things, revived immediately beneath the genial warmth, and lifted their pretty heads from wells of melting snow-wreaths.   The whole world seemed to feel returning spring.   Birds floated in dense squadrons overhead, whirling and wheeling on the edges of the clouds, which kept rising and dispersing in the eager air above our valley.   Far away the mists rolled like sad thoughts that dissolve in tears.

Later in the day we went to sit upon those rocks, the crests of precipices fifteen hundred feet in height, whence the eye plunges so giddily to the Lutschinen torrent, and where it is so pleasant to rest among the tufted stone-pinks (Stein-Nelken) in the cool of afternoon.   "Descendunt montibus umbrae."   The shadow of the Schilthorn spread itself above the hamlet.   Jodelling goat - herds prepare to leave the upland meadows.   Peace spreads abroad while the row of dazzling giants, from the Eiger to the Blumlis Alp, still face the western sun, and shine until they too fade into amber, orange, rose.

So the Diary goes on its way, minutely detailing all the tiny incidents of this slight idyll. I picked bunches of flowers fresh every morning for R——, climbing daily higher up the mountains as the summer flowers retreated, until at last there were few left but lilac crocuses and deep blue harebells. Innumerable sonnets too were written.

The last day I spent at Mürren was a Sunday. Herr Feuz, who then sold alpenstocks and little models of Swiss cottages, asked me to stand godfather to a little girl of his, just born. R—— and her friend were to be godmothers. Of course I acceded willingly to his request.

[And this is the account of the ceremony sent to his sister] :—

" The [1] reason that I have not written to you lately is, that since Monday morning we have been travelling continuously by Winterthur, Schaffhausen, Constanz, Friedrichshafen, and Ulm to Munich. I tore myself away from Mürren on Monday, not without a spasm. Certainly I must in some sense be slow to take impressions, for last year I never could have believed it possible to grow so deeply attached to mountains, or to feel their spirit and their strength as I have done this summer. Everything

---

[1] To his sister Charlotte. Munich, Sept. 3, 1863.

seems cold and tame and lowering now : Munich
and its art is bare and vulgar : I cannot return into
my old self.

"On Sunday I stood godfather, as I told you I
had promised, to the girl of one of the Mürren
guides.   My 'gossips' were Mlle. R——— E———,
daughter of a jeweller in Thun, and Mlle. Katrine,
daughter of a retired innkeeper at Grindelwald.
They had come to spend the summer at Mürren
as the landlord's friends, and to help his wife.   One
of them is certainly the prettiest girl I have ever
seen abroad, and the other is what the German
Swiss would call 'ein recht schönes Deutsches
Mädchen.'   This being the case, and I being an
Englishman, you can fancy there was a little eagerness among the people of Lauterbrunnen to witness
the baptismal ceremony.

"We three had breakfast together, and then the
ladies got into a sledge, and I stood on the stand
behind, and we were dragged like lightning down
the steep descent to Lauterbrunnen, past the pine
trees and the precipices, past the Staubbach and its
hundred sister streams, chattering all the way in
broken French, and screaming when the whirling
of the sledge excited our alarm.   At Lauterbrunnen
we found the baby, and were entertained with wine
by its father, and then walked solemnly to church
adorned with bouquets.   All the village stood ready
to admire us, the Herr Pfarrer came out with his
great white ruff and black bedgown, performed the

ceremony after almost English fashion, and preached a sermon of which I understood but little. Then I took the young ladies to the hotel and gave them a luncheon, which chiefly consisted of veal cutlets and champagne. I was much pleased with the modesty and propriety of their behaviour. There was no affectation or self-consciousness about them. English girls of that condition would have giggled, blushed, and nudged one another, or have been half-frightened and speechless. But these maidens sat and ate their luncheon with perfect ease and grace, slightly deprecating the trouble I took about getting and serving them the meal, yet in nowise appearing out of their element. During the middle of the repast in walked Dr. B—— I noticed that his eyes were fixed on me with some curiosity. I suppose it was strange to see a young Englishman of one's acquaintance seated between two Swiss girls in their Bernese dress without a chaperone. Of course I talked to him, and told him of the christening, and he came out to see us off again to Mürren. When we reached the hotel we dined, Green and the father of the baby joining us. It pleased Green's democratic principles to be in such society; but I found it no less well-conducted and far more entertaining than that of my equals or superiors. More wit flowed, better things were said, and a finer politeness shown, than I have generally met with at the dinner-table. We sat together, as is the Swiss custom, till about nine,

talking, reading Goethe's ballads, playing at domi-
noes, and singing. Several of the other maids of the
hotel were imported to help the singing, and they
gave us many good mountain melodies which I wish
I could remember.

"I thought the account of this day would amuse
you more than a recital of everyday doings."

[Switzerland, Mürren, and the idyll of R——
E—— left a deep impression upon Symonds' tastes
and emotions; but they had not done much to restore
his health in any permanent fashion. He travelled
to Munich, whose "essential tawdriness" he began
to perceive, and thence to Nürnberg, Bamberg,
Dresden, and Leipzig.]

"This[1] piece of paper is enormous, and my pen is
very pinny. You may understand from this that
I am travelling with only a handbag, having sent
on my heavy luggage by express to London. If all
be well, I hope to be at Clifton on Wednesday.

"We have amused ourselves here greatly. The
Leipzig fair is going on, and the whole town
swarms with Jews and German merchants. All
the streets are laid out with booths, and the ground
floors of the houses seem occupied by dealers
from all parts of Europe. German, Italian, Polish,
Russian, and English names are mixed up with
texts in Hebrew; red-capped Hungarians and

---

[1] To his sister Charlotte, Sept. 27, 1863.

black-bonneted Jews walk about arm in arm. Our hotel is a great centre of commerce. Its ground floor is a cloth exchange. Jew dealers in cloth and linen occupy the first floor with shops. We live upon the third, where there is also an enormous hall, decorated for the occasion with arbours and grapes and river scenes, mountains, castles, moonlight, the German muse, and great tuns of wine, to represent Rhineland. Here at dinner and in the evening a band plays, and the commercial travellers lead a jolly life. Business and pleasure seem strangely mixed. I wonder where all the people live."

[From Leipzig Symonds went home, and was received full Fellow at Magdalen. But head and eyes still rendered any serious studies impossible. "At Clifton," he says in the Autobiography, "I saw much of Henry Graham Dakyns. He had come to be an assistant-master at the recently-established college. He was a Rugby-Cambridge man, the friend of Arthur Sidgwick, whom I knew, and of Henry Sidgwick, whom I was destined to know. Of Graham I need only say here that his perfervid temper of emotion, his unselfishness, his capacity for idealising things and people, the shrewdness of his intellectual sense, and the humour of his utterance (style almost of Jean Paul Richter), made their immediate impression on me."

Symonds left England once more for Italy,

journeying by the Riviera di Levante to Pisa, Florence, and eventually to Rome, which he reached in December. He had hoped that Mr. Arthur Sidgwick would be able to join him on his journey, and in a letter of invitation, dated October 9th, he writes: "I have to-day a desire to embrace at once all that is beautiful and deeply thought in Art, Philosophy, and Nature. . . . Thus I am caught in a whirl, and I do nothing but feel intensely a various and changing life."

From Turin, Florence, and Rome he wrote these three letters to Mr. Dakyns, in which he describes his mental and physical state]:—

"When [1] Milton spoke about false poets drawing their inspiration from 'Dame Memory and her seven daughters,' though he meant Mnemosyne and the Muses, his contempt arose from a lurking side glance at the *Sehnsucht* which clings to them. *Sehnsucht* is the passion which builds an ideal in the future, or the world of possibilities out of old and transfigured recollections. This is all I can now tell you about her, though at other times I could say much more.

"I have had a long and stupid journey. My eyes got worse when I was at Oxford, owing probably to our habit of sitting round a blazing fire after dinner; they were again weakened by a stormy passage, and when I got to Paris I could

[1] To H. G. Dakyns. Turin, November 3, 1863.

hardly see. Of course I can neither read nor look out of the window when I am in the train, nor can I read or write during the evenings at hotels, so you may fancy how much time I have for reflection. This, since I find abstract reasoning fatiguing and even impossible at most times, I consecrate to Dame Memory, not after the projectile fashion of *Sehnsucht*, but in a mildly retrospective mood. To these 'sessions of sweet silent thought' rise many forms, now divinised, and even past pain and loss and terror assume a tragic beauty, while the pleasures of the years gone by seem unimaginable. Life flies before me like a symphony, and I choose to alter the old adage thus: 'Præsens, imperfectum; plusquam perfectum, perfectum; futurum, infinitivum et optativum.' When tired of these I revolve verses which I know by heart. One great source of amusement I have lately discovered, and that consists in dwelling upon some historical scene and defining it to my own imagination. From Paris to Macon I thought incessantly of a passage in Suetonius descriptive of (I think) Caligula's wakefulness. It begins, 'Incitabatur insomnio maxime.' The result was that, having fully realised his position, I tried to write verses about it. I liked them at the time, but when I put them on paper they were all monotonous and feeble. I cannot get beyond the sensuous idea."

"I[1] am ashamed to leave Florence without writ-

[1] To H. G. Dakyns. Florence, December 9, 1863.

ing to you, though how I am to keep all my
epistolary engagements I do not know. Your letter
came to me some seventeen days ago, as I was
setting off one intensely cold morning for Vallom-
brosa. I read it there among the brooks strewn
with their yellow chestnut leaves, and it made the
place more vivid by contrast with the scenes which
it recalled to memory. Since then I have seen,
grown, and suffered much. I have seen pictures
enough to content my artistic yearnings. I have
grown in knowledge of my insufficiency and in
resolves—a barren growth. I have suffered from
terrible physical and mental weakness. An oppression, under which I hope you may never groan, a
darkness into which no angel can descend, has
weighed me to the earth. And neuralgia has gnawed
me until I am very feeble. 'Quousque tandem?' is
all I cry—in vain. Here I am burdened, and in
England I have no rest. I do not know what will
become of me. Would that you and others of my
friends had known me years ago, when I was fresh
and young and capable of being and doing good.
I have seen much of Congreve here. Rutson and
I take long walks with him and make him discourse. You know, of course, whom I mean—the
Positivist priest in London. This is an inadequate
description of the man, but it denotes him. He
is divided from Littré and Mill and Lewes, and
others whom the world call Comtists, by his priesthood. They take the scientific side of Comte,

regarding the religious as a senile dream. He
hinges his theory of the future upon the new faith,
that shall reorganise society. I never saw a man
more confident in his own opinions under worse
auspices. When I asked him how far distant he
thought the reign of Positive principles might be,
he answered, 'To the unbelieving, I should place it
at the expiration of three or four centuries; for
myself, I believe that our power will be established
in hardly more than the same number of generations.' Everything according to his notions points
to the silent adoption of Positive principles and the
irresistible march of its unerring truth. So far he
agrees with the enemies in his own camp. But
he goes beyond and says, 'Men need religion; the
health of Europe is decaying because there is no
religion; religion is necessary to bind society together. Why are our nerves weak, our bodies
feeble, our writings aimless, our whole constitu-
tions brittle? Because the moral organisation of
religious faith has been dissolved, no discipline
exists, each man thinks as he chooses, many think
nothing, others are broken by a thousand doubts,
literature expands into useless but exciting channels,
stimulus without an aim keeps up continual irrita-
tion, in short, there is no centre or circumference
to our society. In politics the State is becoming
disintegrated to the very individual. And all this
rottenness ensues from the want of a moral bond.
If I thought that Christianity could supply this

bond I would be a Christian, though I should not believe the creed. But it cannot; it never did; the religious bond of Europe has always been more polytheistic than Christian; and now we need something stronger.' I ask, does he think that Positivism can supply to the affective parts of man an interest sufficient to make each individual quiet in his sphere, confident of the future, and vigorous for labour? 'Certainly,' he answers; 'men will relinquish the immoral and degraded yearning after personal immortality; science will teach them not to seek for first causes like God.' Humanity then will reorganise as their great mother, as that without which they are nothing, to which owing everything they are bound to render every service, as the source of strength, the seat of aspirations, and the object of prayer. He allows that humanity can have no consciousness, and when I define prayer as implying the communion of two conscious beings he glides away and talks of contemplation. I have asked for bread, and he has given me a stone. Why not deny me bread and say, 'I have none, science has petrified my store'? I should be more content. But to offer me religion, prayer, a Church, a liturgy, a stool to kneel on, a pulpit to hear sermons from, and then to bid me fix my hopes upon a *summum genus* which I help to make—it is too absurd. If I ever become a Positivist, it will be of the Mill kind.

"In a week or two the cathedral at Bristol will

echo to the sound of Christmas anthems, and the
most sacred, mythical, and undogmatic mystery of
Christian faith will be celebrated.   I love that pagan
season of rejoicings with its multitudinous visions of
bright-armed and clear-throated cherubim in the
still air.   Yet it will come cheerless to me in the
strangers' land, for the spirit has departed, and the
charm that lingers is one of old association not to
be unlinked from place.   Besides, our paganism in
England is different from the rites of Rome imperial,
more suited in its dark, warm, mystic passion to
the children of knights who sought the Holy Grail,
than the thuribles and pontiffs of the Vatican.

"I wish I could be home again at Christmas, free
from Congreve, and the Sistine Chapel, with a child's
belief in angels.   How they hurried in the Gloria
in Excelsis, after the low symphony, until the
whole church rustled with their swift-descending
squadrons.

"Good-night.   Write to Rome, and tell me how
you passed Christmas."

"I [1] shall be leaving Rome without writing to you
unless I write soon.   You cannot tell how hard I
find it to say anything to any one from abroad ;
although I feel as if I ought to be able to suit your
tastes, with some subject of interest in Rome, I
cannot eliminate one from this tangled skein of rich
and rare experience that I have enjoyed.   If I have
ever wished for you, and you must believe that my

[1] To H. G. Dakyns.   107 Corso, Rome, Jan. 13, 1864.

pleasure would have at most times been increased
by the presence of one so sympathetic and so apt
to feel the beauty and the glory of the world, it has
been in the Sculpture-galleries of the Vatican and
the Capitol, and upon the sea of the Campagna.
The one is full of beauty, more definite and musical
and ever new than anything that I have dreamed;
the other breathes a pantheistic inspiration so lovely
and indistinct, and yet so omnipresent in its changeful tunes and half-heard melodies, that I learned to
gain a new insight into old mythologies and modern
dreams of nature's life.   This language is so rhap-
sodical that you can make nothing of it; but if you
were here I would defy you to put your feelings for
the Campagna into any words."

From[1] Rome Stephens [who had joined him after
Mr. Rutson went home] and I moved down to
Naples and Sorrento.   Feb. 11, back to Rome.
Feb. 14, by post to Narni, Todi, Perugia, and Assisi.
Feb. 15, by Citta di Pieve and Chiusi to Leghorn.
Home by Genoa, Marseilles, and Paris.

I have a diary of this Italian journey; but the
best part of my impressions was conveyed in a long
series of letters to my father and sister.   He wished
to arrange and publish them.   But the plan, wisely,
I think, fell through; and when I found them, after
his death, I burned the whole bundle.

Being unable to use my eyes for study, I read
very little and learned no Italian.   On the other

[1] Autobiography.

hand, I was able to walk as much as I liked, and could see everything which did not involve mental strain. Accordingly, with indefatigable curiosity, I drank in buildings, statues, pictures, nature—the whole of the wonderful Italian past presented in its monuments and landscape. I learned a great deal undoubtedly, which proved of use to me in after years. And the life I led was simple, reserved, free from emotional disturbances.

[The following passage from the Diary shows how Symonds felt at Castellamare] :—

February 1, 1864.—The[1] people are not unworthy of this land. They live a joyous life upon the slopes, between wind-sheltering mountains and the land-locked sea. They are different from the Neapolitans, more beautiful and lightly built, retaining as it were some old Greek loveliness of shape and dignity of carriage. Girls carrying pitchers on their heads have the neck and bust of a statue, and the young men look like athletes with deep ardent eyes. A peasant boy, like Juvenal's servant, waited on us while we dined in the old rustic fashion, and ate our dessert of dried figs, and plums, and grapes, preserved in their own leaves, the produce of the country. We found him playing bowls with oranges; and when our meal was finished he brought musicians, with violins and pipes of a true rural kind. They played us *Volkslieder*, love songs

---

[1] Diary.

and fishing choruses. This Neapolitan music has a peculiar richness of melody, depending on long lingering cadences, and notes sustained until their passion breaks into a shower of swift descending sound. The air is not elaborate or subtly modulated, but simple, oft-repeated, and full of yearning beauty. When one remembers that Handel borrowed his Pastoral Symphony and the melody of " He shall feed His flock," from the shepherds of the Southern Apennines, one understands how richly laden with pathetic loveliness these songs can be. One especially pleased me. Neapolitan girls sing it to their lovers, and its words begin, " Ti voglio bene assai." With youth, health, ignorance, and beauty this land would be perfection. Here I could bask in sunshine,

> " Till books, and schools, and courts, and honours seem
> The far-off echo of a sickly dream."

Truly, they now sound leagues away on alien shores. The world is wide, wide, wide, and what we struggle for, ten thousand happy souls in one fair bay have never dreamed of. I would give much to live, and love, and pass my life within the sound of these unvarying waves, and in the gorgeous interchange of light and gloom which dwells for ever on the furrowed hills. I know not why, but in Italy I feel a continual unsatisfied desire, and, therefore, ignorance must be an element of happiness. Shelley calls the great god Pan "a want," and all this beauty seems to me the sense of what can never fully be our own. It rolls without us, and we include it not: it lives its life, and we intrude upon it for a moment: it is serene and full of peace; we hurry over it, and question it and get no answer, and then we die, and still it is the same: it sounds to us like "the echo of an antenatal dream," and when we strive to arrest its fleeting loveliness, it disappears far off on wings that follow on the paths of sleep. This love of nature is modern; or, perchance, the ancients felt it deeper than ourselves, and hid beneath their moderate lines—

"Hic ver perpetuum atque alienis mensibus æstas,"

a fount of passion drawn from blood-red suns above sapphire seas, from gorgeous hues and heavy summer scents, from "swooning sounds" upon the pathless hills, and springtide chantings of innumerable choirs. Ruskin's paint-box of delirious words, my "orchestra of salt-box tongs and bones," speak nothing; even Shelley's rainbow woof of aerial images are unintelligible till we find ourselves within the sphere of inspiration. Silence and rest and voiceless enjoyment are the soul of Art upon these shores; here Nature lives her life, and each man must penetrate it for himself; she has no high priest, but is unto herself both oracle and Pythia, and even music can do no more than reproduce the passion which her pulses stir.

[But Symonds was not well, mentally or physically ; nor, indeed, was his travelling companion, Mr. Stephens.   He writes as follows about this journey] :—

How[1] I dragged my illness and my ennui through that wonderful world appears from some stanzas written at Sorrento on the 5th of February.   They are printed in " New and Old " under the title " Looking Back."   It is noticeable that this poem, undoubtedly the spontaneous utterance of a prevalent mood, dwells upon Clifton, wholly omitting any mention of the Alps or of Italy.   One of the most sublime and psychologically pregnant passages in the great Lucretian epic is the description of ennui :

> " Ut nunc plerumque videmus
> Quid sibi quisque velit nescire et quærere semper
> Commutare locum quasi onus deponere possit. . . .
> Hoc se quisque modo fugit (at quem scilicet, ut fit,
> Effugere haud potis est, ingratis hæret), et odit
> Propterea, morbi quia causam non tenet æger."

Lucretius prescribes the study of the laws of Nature as a cure for this disease of the soul.   " Live in the eternal thoughts and things," he tells us.   And in some way or other this is the right way, the only way, to escape.

I was deeply wounded in heart, brain and nerves ; and yet I was so young.   On the 5th of February 1864, I reckoned just twenty-three years and four

[1] Autobiography.

months. And like Alfred de Musset, in his " Nuit de Décembre," I could speak of my wanderings thus—

"Partout où, sous les vastes cieux
J'ai lassé mon cœur et mes yeux,
Saignant d'une éternelle plaie;
Partout où le boiteux Ennui,
Trainant ma fatigue après lui,
M' a promené sur une claie."

The physical illness—that obscure failure of nerve-force, which probably caused a sub-acute and chronic congestion of small blood-vessels in the brain, the eyes, the stomach perhaps, and other organs—was the first source of this ennui. But there was another and deeper source behind it, and of which, in fact, it was but the corporeal symptom. I had not recovered from the long anxiety caused by ——'s treacherous attack. Then excessive head-work, superfluous agitation concerning religion and metaphysics—the necessary labour of an ambitious lad at college, and the unwholesome malady of thought engendered by a period of *Sturm und Drang* in England—depressed vitality, and blent the problems of theology with ethical and personal difficulties.

Such, I think, were the constituent factors of my ennui. It grew daily more and more oppressive. As the clouds had rolled away in the congenial atmosphere of Mürren, so now in the great cities of Italy they gathered again. I returned to England weaker than I had left it.

[On his return from abroad Symonds settled in London. He rented rooms on the first floor at No. 7 Half Moon Street, his friend Mr. Rutson living in the same house. His health was still wretched, and he was unable either to do much work, or to enjoy much society, in what he calls "this great grinding world of London." Of his enforced leisure he writes to his sister]:—

"It[1] is a great pity that children are not always taught to play some instrument. I should find music a great resource now, when the periods of unemployed solitude are much more frequent and more trying— owing to the weakness of my eyes and head—than I had reckoned on. I have it seriously in my mind to take lessons on the piano, simply as a means of passing hours which must be devoted to reflection when the book has been laid down. The æsthetical element is sorely neglected in all education, but its loss is felt most by those whose temperament renders them sensitive to art, without enabling them to originate anything. I have felt very lonely, as you may believe, plunged into this absolute solitude of London, and capable of so little mental exertion during the day, and of no continuous occupation in the evening, after the varied and refreshing interests and pleasures of Clifton. I sometimes dread, when I am at home, that a time may come when I shall have to call in vain for kindness such as is there

---

[1] To his sister Charlotte. 7 Half Moon Street, March 31, 1864.

lavished on me, and find myself alone. Such desolation one knows in nightmares, but I fancy that it
surrounds many men whose hearts are tender, and
need love, but who have none to love them. Therefore I desire to take my present happier case as a
man should take any great gift of God, which comes
to him and makes him live. He must not refuse it,
or even question it; but if it ceases, he must not
repine, or curse his fate and waken to despair. It is
very hard to bear both blindness and weakness of
brain in solitude, for thought and reading are rendered
equally injurious to the chance of future strength.
Indeed, when a man has accustomed himself to
exclusively intellectual pursuits, and his head and
eyes fail him, he becomes very dependent on
the easy unexciting and unexhausting society of
home.

"But I am not going to croak, for I do not feel
altogether in a croaking humour. I have only been
reckoning up the difficulties of my position, which I
consider to be grave, and, therefore, all the more
honourable to their conqueror if he can conquer them.
Farther acquaintance with London life will teach me
how to employ my evenings better; though theatres
and lecture rooms, from their great heat as well as
glare, are bad for head and eyes to an extent that
will oblige me to use them very moderately.

"Mr. Fox is very attentive. He plays the part
of valet with the most punctilious, wearisomely punctilious, care. It is impossible to have a wrinkle in

one's clothes, or a book or brush out of place about one's rooms."

[Symonds, though suffering, writes to his friend Mr. Stephens: " But I am not daunted, and I look on this kind of life as salutary in many ways, especially as a corrective of sybaritic habits, and also as a prelude to what must almost inevitably be the isolation of many years in the life of all men." He employed such respite as his ill health allowed him in writing articles for the *Saturday Review*; in setting out his thoughts upon theology in the form of a Commentary to Goethe's " Gott und Welt," and reading the minor Elizabethan dramatists. But the letter just cited shows that a dread of solitude —of a solitude that would certainly increase with age —was leading him toward the thought of marriage. Music was still a solace to him, but as this summer wore on, London became intolerable.]

" What [1] have I been about all this long time when I have seemed to forget you ? Do not ask me, but do not think I have forgotten you. In this stifling city of bricks and dust and iron, I have often seen you knee-deep in the bluebells and anemones of Leigh Woods, under the tender screen of fresh green beech and hazel leaves, or in the solemn shadows of the rocks at night, looking across to those deep cloven dells. Longing, so intense that it supplies the sight it craves for, has filled me for the valleys of Switzer-

[1] To H. G. Dakyns. London, May 19, 1864.

land and the sweet strange languid spirit of Clifton.
If I were a painter I would draw that wild mysterious
Syren—with her veils of moonlight vapour, the
flowers and leaves and streams about her feet, the
towers on her dusky hair, the passionate heaving of
her hidden breast, the languor of her smile, the
sweet intoxication of her kisses, and those eyes which
I have never seen, but felt, prayed to, and questioned
restlessly from childhood.   Or if I were a poet, the
same should live in song.   Men should know how,
in the still green gardens of that lady, they might
meet with love, or melancholy more intense than
love, dreams subtle and distinct of joys impossible,
embroidered on the woof of common life.   I would
tell them, too, how universal Pan in days gone by
had wooed her for her beauty, leaving in her lap
the gift of charm invisible; of whispers half heard
in the summer trees, and shapes half seen at noontide in the shadows; how Ocean from his distant
caves had filled her ear with indescribable sea
sounds, and in the midst of her primeval woods
shed mystery.   Nor would I fail to interweave the
many songs which she has sung to me—the song
of Linus, whom the reapers loved, and whom they
sent at sundown to the well, but he returned not,
and they sought him all a summer night with cries
of, 'Ah, for Linus;' the song of Hymenæus whom,
a shepherd boy on Œta, the star Hesper loved, and
drew him up the heights and rapt him from the
eyes of mortals in immortal joy; the song of young

Endymion, of Hylas, and of Cyparissus; the woodland tales of Ida, where Œnone loved, and Aphrodite met the sire of mighty Rome. I, too, would tell of her deceitful moods, of the frowns and scourges which she has in store for those who worship her, and of her pitiful relentings when she goes abroad upon the sobbing winds and beats against the window panes, entreating to be pardoned and to be loved once more. Guileful spirit, beautiful and wicked, who has raised thy veil and seen thee as thou art? Who knows thee in the cold, dark night, when moon and stars are hidden, when no tempests are awake, when all is stern? Who has found thee in the open light of common day, or trodden unbeguiled among thy labyrinths? Then he may seek but he will find thee not, for thou dost dwell in the sunsetting and sunrising, in luxurious summer evenings and in latticed shadows of soft, silken leaves, spurning the real and palpable and hard and open places of the world.

"I do not know why I have run on like this. I often think or dream aloud on paper, and you must take this for a reverie. I do not know what to write to you, for I have nothing to tell. My life has been monotonous, and I have suffered as usual from weakness of eyes and head."

"Thank[1] you, my dearest Charlotte, for your kind and affectionate letter. The pain which I have been suffering during the last few days, the

[1] To his sister Charlotte. London, June 20, 1864.

solitude in which I have lived, and the multitudes of thoughts and feelings which have swept through my mind, have left me very weak and very sensitive to all kind influences. I am better now, and able to get about a little.

"It makes me very sad to think I am to see so little of papa again this summer, and that my health will not admit of my coming to Clifton—which I have dreamed of, as most dear and beautiful of all fair places, among the mountains of Switzerland and the ruins of Rome. You offer me kind consolation in saying that ill-health improves and refines the mind. But I do not feel it easy to look upon it as a blessing. It does not seem to me far other in the intellectual world than sin is in the moral— at least when it suspends activity so much as in my case. It is only a true and earnest Christian, one who lives for another world and believes in a life where nothing is that is not perfect, who can be truly resigned under the weakening of his physical and mental faculties."

"London [1] is like a brick oven seven times heated. The pavements and the walls seem to hold caloric funded, day by day increasing, radiating all the night, but not exhausted when the sun gets up to fire them afresh. Every one is going away. The streets are comparatively thin of grand carriages. Operas are being played at lower prices. The Ministerial fish-dinner comes on soon. And

[1] To his sister Charlotte. London, July 17, 1864.

of all things there is a beginning of the end. It is rather dull. But I have come to like London under almost every aspect. It is the only place where constant relief from the agitations of one's own self may be found by looking at other people ; because, in London, life never stops by day or night, and whenever you choose to go forth and roam about, you find people restless and energetically living in some fashion. A little while ago I had a very sleepless night, and it burdened me to hear all through the darkness, and through the still cold approaches of the dawn, and through the hot beginnings of the day, one ceaseless flood of sound, varying in intensity and kind, but never resting. It burdened me. But if I had been well and living strongly, it would have stimulated me with a sense of sympathy. How strangely different is this cast of circumstances from that which environs one in some place like Mürren. There nothing is heard but the sounds of innumerable waterfalls and never-ceasing winds. The air is not less full of murmurs, but not one recalls humanity. Here every sound attaches itself to some human being. In the one place God somehow seems close to one. In the other He is far removed, and seen but dimly through the mass of men obscuring Him. Yet the Self remains essentially the same.

" I am quite alone, more alone, with the past and present to myself, than perhaps I ever was. And writing to you is like writing to another world. I seem to hear my own voice falling thin and dry and hollow on your ear, as it were over the waste of a great water."

[The thought of Mürren recalled, "as by inspiration," the memory of that English family whose acquaintance he had made there on the ledge above Lauterbrunnen, among Alpine flowers, and face to face with the Jungfrau. With characteristic impetuosity Symonds called on Mr. North, pursued the acquaintance, asked and obtained leave to follow the family to Pontresina in August, proposed and was accepted on Sunday afternoon, August 14th; on the 16th exchanged betrothal rings with Catherine North on the top of Piz Languard, accompanied the Norths to Venice in September, and was married at St. Clement's Church, Hastings, on November 10th.]

CHAPTER VII

MANHOOD. DRAWN TOWARDS LITERATURE

13 Albion Street, London.—Studies law.—Question of a career.—Visit to Clifton.—Conversations with Woolner.—On Morality in Art.—Depression.—47 Norfolk Square, London.—First symptoms of pulmonary disease.—Birth of a daughter.—Determination towards literature.—Consults Jowett.—His advice.—A conversation with Jowett.—Visit to Clifton.—Dr. Symonds declares the lungs to be affected.—On Shakespeare's Sonnets.—His study of Clough. —The Handel Festival.—Sent abroad by his father.—Regrets for Clifton.—Letters from the Riviera.—Monte Carlo.—On Elizabethan freedom and licence.—Leaves the Riviera for Tuscany and Ravenna. — Returns by the Lakes to Macugnaga. — On landscape painting.—Over the St. Bernard to Switzerland.—Mürren revisited.—Symonds takes stock of himself.—Returns home.

[AFTER a few months the Symondses took lodgings in Albion Street, because it was quiet and near the park. Symonds ostensibly intended to follow the law, but in reality he was being steadily drawn towards literature. He writes to his sister]:—

"I[1] have not written to you once since I left Clifton, but you have written to me, and I feel guilty. Nor can I plead great stress of work, for in no way have I been occupied. Our time passes

---

[1] To his sister Charlotte. 13 Albion Street, March 21, 1865.

pleasantly when we are alone in the evenings.
If you were all here, I mean you and papa and
auntie, and if I could quell those questions which
continually rise in my mind about life, I think I
should be wholly happy.   Women do not, need not,
pose themselves with problems about their own
existence, but a man must do it, unless he has a
fixed impulse in one definite direction, or an external
force, compelling him to take an inevitable line.
I do not think, looking back upon the past, that I
half knew,—I know I never half thanked you for—
the help you gave me in music.   I ought to have
been taught it, for I believe I have more natural
taste for that than for any other of the arts, and I
should have taken the same line that you do, of
clear and intelligent and various interpretation."

[How his legal studies were faring may be
gathered from the following letter to Mr. Dakyns]:—

"You[1] may see by this that I am in lawyer's
chambers, but how much law I am doing I will not
reveal to you.   It is very little.   My wife is well.
I am well.   The quarter of a sheet concerning our
doings shall be given you.   We breakfast at nine, and
I begin to write as soon afterwards as possible.   If I
do not go down to these chambers, the writing continues till one.   It is about the Dramatists at present,
and will be for a long while.   After lunch we pay

[1] To H. G. Dakyns.   5 Paper Buildings, Temple, March 23, 1865.

visits and see pictures. In the evening, if there is
no party to go to, no play to see, no music to hear,
we read aloud. We have read many books, the best
being Lewes' ' Goethe,' ' Romola,' Villari's ' Savo-
narola,' and now we are reading Grimm's ' Life of
M. Angelo.' I want to keep my mind on that period
of European history. Gaps are filled up by Dante,
Heine's Songs, and the learning of some poems of
Goethe. With all this law does not agree. I do
not know whether it will ever suit me. At present
my coach cannot give me work. I am in a state of
suspense about law and literature. Am I to serve
God or Mammon? Am I to study and write or
to pursue this profession? Am I to be poor with
letters, or to run the chance of being rich with law?
Then, again, am I justified in assuming [myself]
to be one of the priesthood of art? Am I a
selected soul? If I give myself to literature, and
find myself inadequate, can I be content with a
fastidious silence? Is it my fate to be a bluebottle
fly buzzing in the courts, or a voiceless ephemera
upon the banks of an unfrequented river? I have
not faith, which is the oxygen of life, and lets one
breathe in spaces howsoever cramped. You see I
am settling the question of life; and if you can
give me any definite ideas on these vague problems,
thanks to you. It is a terrible and a consuming
problem. I feel so weak, so unable to do anything, or to take hold of any subject. In the room
with me at this moment are five men, all provided

with clear brains for business, all talking slang, and all wondering what strange incapable animal I am who have thus come among them. They can move stones with their little finger which my whole strength will not stir. But is it likely that they could touch the subjects which thrill my soul? Would there were some high court of equity to decide our vocations. It seems as if, till this moment, I had lived apart and now am launched among men. I have talked too long about a matter which, after all, is and must be my own, to be decided by myself. It is a hard world, my dear Dakyns, but a beautiful world if one could feel one's self at liberty to enjoy it."

[In the autumn of this year the Symondses were at Clifton Hill House, on a visit.]

August 7, 1865.[1]—To-day has been splendid. I worked at Lyly all the morning, and in the afternoon went with C. and Woolner to walk in Leigh Woods. They are just as beautiful as when I used to roam there years ago. The lights fall still as golden on those grey rocks streaked with red, on the ivy and the trees, the ferns and heather, and the bright enchanter's nightshade. Not a point is different except myself. This beauty sinks into my soul now as then; but it does not stir me so painfully and profoundly. I do not feel the hunger which I had; nor am I conscious of the same power,

[1] Diary.

the same unlimited hopes, the same expectations solemn from their vagueness.

C. has in a great measure effected this change. What is good in it I owe to her influence, and to the happiness which her love has brought me. She has raised my moral nature and calmed my intellectual irritability. But there is also a change for the worse. This is simply attributable to my long-continued physical weakness. No one who has not suffered in the same way can adequately feel how great is the sapping, corroding power of my debility. Eyes for more than two years useless. Brain for more than two years nearly paralysed— never acutely tortured, but failing under the least strain and vibrating to the least excitement. To feel as little as possible, to think and work as slightly as I could, to avoid strong enjoyments when they rarely offered themselves, has been my aim. I have done nothing in this period by a steady effort. Everything has come by fits and starts of energy, febrile at the moment, and prostrating me for days when they are over. Sometimes for weeks together I have not seen a ray of sunlight. At Florence, at Rome, in London, at Clifton, I have risen with the horror of these nights, have walked through the day beneath the burden of dull aching nerves, and have gone to bed in hopelessness, dry with despair and longing for death. Suddenly, in the midst of this despair, a ray of my old capacity for happiness has burst upon me. For a few hours my heart has beat,

my senses have received impressions, my brain has
coined from them vigorous ideas. But vengeance
follows after this rejoicing. Crack go nerves and
brain, and thought and sense and fancy die. The
leaden atmosphere of despair closes around me, and
I see no hope. Many are the men, no doubt, who
have suffered as I have suffered. Last summer I
spent six days in London, in Half-Moon Street.
I had just [been subjected to treatment] which gave
great pain, and made me very weak. If it suc-
ceeded it was to do wonders. In the midst of my
weakness I hoped. I sat upon one chair with my
legs upon another. I could not read. I could not
bear the light upon my eyes. I was too desolate
and broken to see friends. I scarcely slept, and
heard all night London roar, with the canopy of
flame in the hot sky, above those reeking thorough-
fares. At three or four, day broke. In the evening
I sat idle, and it was dark. All the while I hoped.
This cure shall do wonders.

But the old evil broke out again. One night I
woke. A clock struck two — it was the Victoria
clock at Westminster. I bit the bedclothes, and
bared myself upon the bed in anguish ; and at last
I sobbed. It was all over with me. I took up next
morning the old cross.

How long is it since I last kept a connected diary ?
Three years. When that blow came upon me in
the spring of 1863, I said, I will write no more in
this book. And I did write no more. My happi-

ness went first. Then my brain refused to work.
Then my eyes were blinded. I went to Switzerland.
How much of beauty I learned there. And at
Mürren I saw C. Then followed my summer
in London, and those days of mental, moral,
physical annihilation. At the end of them I arose
and found C. at Pontresina. On the 10th of last
November we were married ; and now we live
together in our house, both happy, and she will ere
long give me a child.

God give me strength. Thou knowest how I love
her, Thou only ; and Thou knowest how she has
made me happy. But this is not all. Give me
strength. Cast me not utterly away as a weed.
Have I not longed and yearned and striven in my
soul to see Thee, and to have power over what is
beautiful ?

Why do I say " Lord, Lord," and do not ? Here
is my essential weakness. I wish and cannot will.
I feel intensely, I perceive quickly, sympathise with
all I see, or hear, or read. To emulate things nobler
than myself is my desire. But I cannot get beyond
—create, originate, win heaven by prayers and faith,
have trust in God, and concentrate myself upon
an end of action. Scepticism is my spirit. In my
sorest needs I have had no actual faith, and have
said to destruction, " Thou art my sister." To the
skirts of human love I have clung, and I cling
blindly. But all else is chaos—a mountain chasm
filled with tumbling mists ; and whether there be

Alps, with flowers and streams below, and snows above, with stars or sunlight in the sky, I do not see. The mists sway hither and thither, showing me now a crag and now a pine—nothing else.

Others see, and rest, and do. But I am broken, bootless, out of tune.

Sinews, strong nerves, strong eyes are needful for action. I have none of these; and besides, I have a weakness ever present. It eats my life away. . . . Truly this is no fable.

I want faith. " Je suis venu trop tard dans un monde trop vieux." . . .

Yet I have ambition. Truly I wish and will not. Men like Woolner and my father make me blush. They will, they do, they enjoy. They have a work in life. They have brains clear and strong, nerves equable and calm, eyes keen and full of power. They have faith in God and in the world.

What is left for me to do? As long as C. lives and loves me, my home must be happy. There I am fully blest. But in this home I shall languish if I do not work. And for what work am I fitted? Jowett said, some time ago, for law or literature. I say, after some months' trial, not for law. And for literature, with these eyes and brain? What can I do? What learn? How teach? How acquire materials? How think? How write calmly, equably, judicially, vigorously, eloquently for years, until a mighty work stands up to say, This man has lived. Take notice, men, this man had nerves unstrung, blear eyes, a faltering gait, a stammering tongue, and yet he added day by day labour to labour, and achieved his end? Shall it, can it, be?

Is this possible? C. will help me. She is noble, loving, true. But will I help myself? Will this body bear me up?—this Will last out.

To study, acquire facts, gain style, lose the faults of youth, form a standard of taste, throw off dependence on authority, learn to be sincere, try to see clearly, refuse to speak before I feel, grow logical, must be my aim.

I have no faith, not even in myself; and the last three years have destroyed all sanguine expectations, all illusions, but they have not brought me deadness or content.

August 9.—Woolner is doing a bust of my father. He is a little man of great vigour—very clear in his perceptions and opinions, strong-willed, determined, moral, finely fibred. I like the outspoken sense of his remarks. He makes mistakes of criticism, and is very bumptious. I, for instance, hear him now through an open door: "Carlyle says the language of my poem is quite perfect . . . that's because it is so simple, and has nothing strained; idiomatic, just as one talks." This simplicity of self-satisfaction is amusing. He carries it so far that one forgets it. I particularly admire his fresh strong expressions of dislike and approbation. He knows a great many remarkable men. Tennyson is a great friend of his, and so is Browning. Browning tells him that he writes straight down, and never looks again at what he writes. Tennyson composes in his head, and never writes down until he is about to publish. Tennyson has composed as much as he has ever published and lost it again, owing to this habit. In particular, he once wrote a Lancelot, and now only a few lines or words come back upon his memory. Tennyson says form is immortal, instancing the short poems of Catullus. Browning hopes to live by force of thought, and is careless about form. Tennyson, Palgrave, and Woolner went to Tintagel. The poet there conceived four idylls about men, answering to his four idylls about women. Jowett put them out of his head by wondering whether the subjects could be properly treated. Tennyson makes mistakes about the poets he admires. He once wrote to Baily, and said he was a wren singing in a hedge, while the author of "Festus" was an eagle soaring above him. Woolner does not respect persons, but has a masculine respect for character, and likes people to keep to their trade and not to meddle. He has a profound contempt for Jowett's meddling criticism.

August 10.—Woolner told me last night that he is thirty-nine, Conington's age. At fourteen he began to dream of poetry as the best thing in life, and he still likes it better, and would rather cultivate it than any other art. His very correct eye led him to adopt sculpture as the easiest means of

getting a livelihood.   He cannot endure town life;
looks forward to spending his days among trees,
with a bit of water near him, in the country, design-
ing poems in form.   He read us out, in a coarse,
deep, energetic voice, parts of "My B. L."

We had a pleasant afternoon in Leigh Woods,
sitting on the point from which the bridge, the
observatory, and Clifton Downs are seen.   I read
C. pieces from the Golden Treasury, comparing
Wordsworth's, Shelley's, and Keats' love of nature.
We also discussed the morality of poetry—my ballad
on the ghost of the lady who seeks her lover,
Sebald and Ottima, Ford's Annabella, came uppermost.   It is most hard to fix the limit of right
and wrong in art.   My father condemns Faust.   I
hardly condemn Annabella.   Where the treatment
of passion in poetry has the object of showing vice
to be odious and to be a Sodom's apple in its
hollowness, I think great lengths are allowable.
Of course, Shakespeare's "Venus and Adonis" can
on no such theory be excused.   The Pygmalion
of Marston and the Salmacis of Beaumont are un-
pardonable panderism, no less odious than Latin
Priapics or the Centos of Ausonius.   So, too, are
the gross passages in "Pericles" and Fletcher's
plays—foisted in for the gratification of a prurient
author or a prurient public.   The coarse jests of
Aristophanes in many cases were of this kind.   In
others satire cloaked their offence.   The mere
beauty of such a scene as that between Ottima and

Sebald is not a ground against it. If it were not beautiful it would not be art; and if not art, it would be no better than a filthy newspaper. Its moral purpose could hardly here avail it : for a sermon would serve the end of ethics better than an ugly piece of realistic drama writing. Still, it may be doubted whether for the one who reads *de te fabula* in Sebald's loathing after sin, there are not hundreds who dwell only on the glow of passion in the picture, and think such joy but cheaply purchased by the loss of innocence and happy virtue.

> Had I as many souls as there be stars,
> I'd give them all for Mephistopheles.

I talked a good deal about the two classes of artists : those in whom feelings predominate, whose songs are wrenched out of them by suffering; and those who sit down to describe, work up and labour at their fixed conceptions. Pangs of intense emotion precede birth in the one case; deliberate intellectual labour in the other. Poetry with the one class is an ichor which they will not staunch, but which consumes them. They would rather die than cease to sing, and cannot sing without a struggle of passion. With the other class it is a true artistic genesis, contrived and carried out by strength of mind. Compare Alfred de Musset and Tennyson, Byron or Shelley, and Goethe, Beethoven and Handel, Raffaello and Michel Angelo. When the struggles of the one class cease they are silent : they only

"learn in suffering what they teach in song."
Heine called De Musset, "Un jeune homme d'un
bien beau passé." He gave up his passions,
struggles, yearnings, dreams at twenty-five, and
ceased to be a singing bird till fifty, because he had
ceased to feel acutely. Poets of the other class
work on, thinking of their materials, careless of
themselves, requiring only the stimulus of thought,
and needing no preparatory storms.

[Symonds' depression, due no doubt to ill health
thwarting a powerful and active nature, finds expression in the following letter to Mr. Dakyns]:—

"Your[1] letter was anything but meaningless. I
understood it, I think, quite well, and I can sympathise with your despondent reflection on the
'wasted idleness of existence.' In fact, that is
what I suffer from, and what I thought of when
I told you that I was not well. What happens
to me is that one tide of physical depression after
another sweeps over me, and not one leaves me
as I was before. Each weakens me; I feel my
strength of mind, and power of action and fancy and
sense of beauty, and capacity of loving and delight
in life, gradually sucked out of me. At the present
moment I do not know what to do. Life is long
for unnerved limbs and brains, which started with
fresh powers, now withered and regretful only of the
past, without a hope for the future. I do not write

[1] To H. G. Dakyns. Sutton Court, Pensford, Aug. 20, 1865.

this because I am not happy in my home. Far
from that. But happiness, domestic felicity, and
friends, good as they are, cannot make up for a *vie
manquée*. If a man has in his youth dreamed of
being able to do something, or has rashly promised
himself to strike a creed out of the world, or else to
be strong in scepticism—if setting forth thus, he has
failed upon the threshold . . . then he resembles
those for whom the poet wrote, ' Virtutem videant
intabescantque relicta.' But I am not in despair.
No one should give over hope. I am only disappointed at the failure of anticipations, and sorrow-
fully convinced that the weakness of which I have
been conscious is inherent and invincible."

[The whole of this summer of 1865 was unusually
rainy. From certain symptoms in the left side
Symonds was, subsequently, led to the conclusion
that the seeds of pulmonary disease were laid during
his visit to Clifton. The Symondses had given up
their lodgings in Albion Street, and on their return
to London from the West of England, they settled
into No. 47 Norfolk Square, which Symonds had
bought. The quiet of the situation was the chief
inducement ; but "the situation proved gloomy, and
not by any means favourable to health." On the
22nd of October their eldest daughter Janet was
born at Norfolk Square. Symonds, in the midst
of London life and occupations, was paying too
little heed to his health, "which had been very

delicate since the return to London. The nurse
warned me one day that my incessant cough was
what she bluntly called 'a churchyard cough.'" Yet
the diary all through this period is in reality highly
vigorous, full of active thought and acute criticism.
Symonds, in spite of difficulties which might well
have daunted a less resolute nature, was, in fact,
walking rapidly towards a decisive choice in life, as
is indicated in this important extract.]

Nov. 30.[1]—My own wishes about the future
become clearer. I have talked to Rutson, who, on
the whole, agrees with me. To take up literature
as a definite study—that is the kernel; to fit myself
for being a good "vulgariseur"—I am not an artist
or originator. To do this I want study of literature
and language, long study, while the Temple clock
is always saying to me, "Pereunt et imputantur."
Green thinks it would be base of me not to write,
having some money and so clear a vocation.
Jowett long ago told me I might be eminent in
letters. Conington thinks I might write a history,
but 'not unless he knows more than he's likely to
learn at present.' Green and Rutson both see I
am too much a mirror, lack individuality, need a
bracing subject, need to give up magazine writing.
I want to make my literature a business, to go down
to it daily, to Lincoln's Inn, *e.g.*, to read steadily,
putting on an Italian or German coach for one

[1] Diary.

portion of the day, analysing Justinian for another, and writing hardly anything. If I could do this, I have much time before me, and my home is daily brighter and better."

[In this doubt as to his vocation for literature Symonds consulted his old friend, Mr. Jowett.]

"Dear Mr. Jowett," he wrote, "I should very much value your advice about a matter which is occupying my thoughts at present. Since I left Oxford I have, as far as my health permitted me, been reading law. I must allow that I have not been able to read much, owing to weakness of eyes and other ailments; but these, I am thankful to say, seem to be leaving me, and I am more capable of regular mental labour. At the same time, I find that law is not a subject which attracts me, or for which my powers seem to be specially fitted. Indeed it is with difficulty that I can bring myself to study it at all. I have never, since I had any definite wish, ceased to desire a life of literary study, and this wish grows upon me. I know I am not fitted for anything artistic in letters, or for pure philosophy. The history of literature is what I feel drawn to, and to this I should willingly devote my life. It does, in fact, require whole self-devotion, and I cannot follow it together with any other occupation so exhausting as law. Where, then, I need advice is here. Is it prudent for me to give up a profession and to choose literature? I do not mean prudent in a pecuniary point of view, but in an intellectual. Am I flying too high if I consecrate myself to study? I do not think that any one could give me better advice upon this point than you. What weighs with me in favour of literature is—first, my health, which could be more humoured in a life of study than at the bar; secondly, my inclinations, which are most decided in favour of study; thirdly, my capacities, which seem to me ill-adapted for the bar. Still literature is a service not lightly to be undertaken. And the strong assurance, from one who knows me so well as you do, and who knows all the difficulties of a student's life, that I am unfitted for it, would weigh greatly with me.

" I have been writing, at spare times, a history of our Elizabethan drama as an exercise, which is now about one-third finished. But the point seems to have been reached at which I must definitely renounce writing, or make it the sole business of my life. Please do not trouble to answer this quickly. If I could speak to you ere long it would be better. My father told me he had some hope of a visit from you, and Miller said the same.—I am, ever yours most sincerely and gratefully, J. A. SYMONDS."

[The answer came.]

" MY DEAR SYMONDS,—I should like to have a talk with you on the subject of your letter. Could you run down and see me this day week? or if not,

I will try to come up and spend a day with you in London.

"I think that you are very likely right about the desertion of the Bar. Still I would urge you to be called, and to finish the elementary study of Law as a branch of literature or philosophy. In Hallam's 'History of Literature' it strikes me that you can see the advantage to be had from legal knowledge. But let me have a good talk over the matter next Monday week, if you can come. I dine at 5.30, or any other time that will suit you.—With kind regards to Mrs. Symonds, ever yours in haste,

"B. JOWETT."

[That Symonds was already some way advanced along the line of literature before he sought Jowett's advice, and that the issue was already virtually settled, seems clear from this passage in the Diary]—

September 9, 1865.—I[1] am going on with the "Dramatists." This study is something like picking pearls from a dunghill. I sift and sift heaps of refuse, and find some real jewel. The discovery gives me a thrill of pleasure when it comes. The poetry of that period stills my soul like the sound of music. But I doubt whether I can transfer my sensations to my writing, and make others interested in what delights myself. This doubt must attend purely literary work. The artist sees beauty, and arrests his visions, feeling them to be a joy for ever. The

[1] Diary.

historian of a period only tells what he has found, and cannot flatter himself that many people will welcome his discovery. What I should like to do would be to make my history of the English Drama a monograph on the development of the histrionic art. The literature of the English stage is the only complete one we possess. The earliest Athenian plays have perished. The Roman was an echo. The French received a violent twist, owing to the influence of Richelieu and the Academy. The Spanish in no sense equals ours. But the English Drama, from its germs in miracle plays, through its infancy in moralities, and its adolescence in Shakespeare and Ben Jonson and Fletcher, and its age in Massinger and others, is a complete organic whole. It is a flower of Art, national, perfect in its growth, as fit a subject for the physiology of æsthetics as Italian painting. To do this well, however, would require greater power and knowledge than I have at present. I can sketch out and survey the subject, but I cannot command it.

[The upshot of this visit to Jowett at Balliol was the] "advice,[1] that I should get called to the Bar, translate a book like Zeller, try to connect myself with some hospital work in London, and not lose sight of possible politics in the future. He thought me very fortunate to be able to pursue my life, but recognised the consequent responsibilities and

[1] Diary.

dangers of inaction. Literary life, he admitted, was, of all, the hardest, and needed much intercourse with men to keep it from pedantry and dulness: "You have a very good memory, remarkable facility, and considerable powers of thinking. It depends on yourself to bring these to perfection." He walked to the station with me, talking all the way. I had spoken of the difficulty of understanding what passed between the Resurrection and the preaching of Paul. "There may be many ways of explaining that—some mystical, some psychological—but we should leave certain subjects as necessarily inexplicable. All historic criticism is so doubtful; and if we got the whole truth, we might not be able to sympathise with that past age. What is really painful is to think of the structure of dogmas raised by men upon the one point of the Resurrection." "Yes; an inverted pyramid, the point remaining and the base always broadening, with men walking on the top, and fearing to tread too much on one side or another, lest they should bring it all down." "I've read a good deal lately of a French poet, Alfred de Musset." "Yes." "He saturated himself with German ideas, lost his old faith, and remained yearning after it and leading an impure life." "That's the lowest state of human weakness." "So it is, perhaps; but De Musset was a great poet, and many run the risks which lost him." "But men should keep their minds to duty." "That comes as an afterthought. At first when they throw off custom,

they go groping and grovelling among the ghosts
of dogmas. What you said at St. Andrew's about
clinging to the great and simple truths as anchors
has no meaning to them then.   They must run clear
before they can appreciate the value of those simple
truths." "I daresay you're right." "That's why
they cling to Comte and such systems in a modified
sense." "Do you really think any young men get
good from Comte?" "Yes, in a modified way; it
satisfies them to find a system, repudiating dogma
and basing morality on an independent footing.
Vivre pour autrui, and scientific exorcisms of old
orthodox ghosts, restore their tone. They don't go
farther." "The fact is, if you throw off custom, you
must sink below it or rise above it. The club men
you talked about, and common conventional Christians, do not really much differ." "But don't you
think that connected with old custom there are some
hopes and aspirations, and fear of hell, which raise
people above it?" "It does not do much for them.
They would rise far higher if they could abandon
custom, and look only to the great and simple
things—if they would do their duty and try to
benefit people around them." "But the means
are not always ready." "I don't believe that's
anything but indolence and want of invention on
the part of most men. Every one must have some-
body dependent on him or some sphere of use-
fulness." By this time we had reached the platform,
and I had to get my bags from the cloak-room.

The train came up. I thanked Jowett heartily for his kindness, shook him by the hand, saw his little form trot off among the porters, and was whisked away—full of thoughts, with hope and a purpose in me."

As [1] soon as my wife was able to move, a little before Christmas, we went down to Clifton. There my father examined me, and pronounced that there was mischief of a very serious kind at work at the apex of the left lung.

[That was on December 24th. Dr. Symonds applied severe remedies, and kept his son indoors for some time. The imprisonment and this fresh menace to his health were a sharp trial for Symonds. Alone, indoors, looking over Bristol on the evening of Christmas day, his thoughts all run back to his early Christmas memories, to his first strong affection; and the attraction of the cathedral where the others are—where he may not be—sweeps over him in his reverie. But however acute may have been the internal anguish, that high courage which sustained him through life, that root of determination and resistance which so pre-eminently characterised him, begins at once to make itself apparent; and when he announces the evil news to his friend, Mr. H. G. Dakyns, the message is cool, calm, brave.]

"I write to you most *ausführlich*, and express myself esoterically; so that when I should say to

---

[1] Autobiography.

Miss ——, 'I have had a cold which kept me a few days in the house,' to you I word the same thing thus: 'There is no danger, but it cannot be forgotten that my grandfather, and an aunt on the mother's side, died of consumption, and that my sister has to winter out of England.'"

[And yet, as Symonds had occasion to remark later on, the appearance of this lung trouble began almost immediately, though very slightly at first, to relieve the brain trouble from which he had suffered so acutely. He writes to Mr. Dakyns] :—

"If[1] you go to Farringford, I wish you would manage to talk to Tennyson about the Sonnets of Shakespeare, and tell me what he thinks about their emotional meaning. Palgrave has just published them with the omission of the twentieth, in some respects the most important of them all, and in a few words written by him at the end he appears to take the worst possible view of them. I have read and re-read those sonnets, and I have never been able to find any of the gross and shameful passion in them which Hallam and Palgrave find, and I may also add Coleridge. That they express humiliation and consciousness of some sort of guilt on Shakespeare's part and overmastering affection cannot be denied. It seems also clear that he knew his friend to be unworthy of him, and a man of loose life. Yet I find nothing shameful in the poems

[1] To H. G. Dakyns. Clifton, December 27, 1865.

themselves, nothing that indicates a disgraceful connection between Shakespeare and Mr. W. H——.
Even the twentieth stanza, which Palgrave omits,
and which in point of language is more gross than
any others, seems to me to prove the exact opposite
—the purity, I mean, of Shakespeare's passion. I
cannot but think that Palgrave may have consulted
Tennyson about his edition of the sonnets, and it
would interest me greatly to hear whether the author
of 'In Memoriam' has any views upon a subject so
disputed.

"You ask if the régime suits me. Six days
indoors, blisters, morphia, and partial starvation do
certainly not suit me, but, on the contrary, produce
a head heaviness and eye weakness which is not
enjoyable. The resurrection of power which I was
beginning to feel during the last two months, and
which had begun to express itself in the determination to make continuous efforts after higher art,
dwindles again. Yet I am infinitely happier than I
used to be, nor can I enough for this be thankful."

[No signs of intellectual languor are apparent
throughout the pages of the voluminous Diary; the
whole record is intensely alive with sympathy for his
friends; with minute discussions on the possibility
of substituting a true *Moralität* for mere *Sittlich-
keit*;—an echo of Jowett's remarks upon throwing off
custom; with thoughts on art such as this: "Beauty
stings a sensitive soul, and ichor flows from the

wound.   In those who have artistic power this ichor forms a pearl.   In others it drops silently away. Both suffer;" on friendship, such as this: "It is a bad thing to base any friendship on uncommon and merely emotional sympathies.   They may wear out. Friendship ought to be a matter of daylight, not of gas; red lights, or sky rockets."

His attention was much occupied by Clough, whose works he was subsequently to edit in conjunction with Mrs. Clough.]

"This morning, being very dull with snow and my bad night, I read through Clough's Remains. This book is more definite than Palgrave's Memoir in the Poems.   The letters belong principally to his ante-married life, but they are not *ausführlich.*   I am struck with this reticence, characteristic of his dry poetic style and social taciturnity.   His boyhood is the most interesting part of his life.   When he left Rugby he got into Ward's hands at Balliol, who upset his notions about things—'asking you your opinions' (so he speaks of him), on every possible subject, beginning with Covent Garden and Macready, and certainly not ending till you got to the question of the moral sense and deontology.'   Ward turned him inside out."

[That is a process which Symonds was meanwhile applying to himself; for all through the Diary, underlying his studies, underlying his affection for his friends, runs the perpetual strain of self-analysis,

comparison, criticism, reproach. I find this characteristic letter] :—

"*January* 31, 1866.—This is truly sad about
me ; my brain is teeming with thoughts that cannot
be expressed, because of my physical weakness.
Poems of some sort, could I but work at them,
would come from me. Yet, if I produce, my
thoughts tear me like vultures ; I have to leave the
lines unfinished, or to complete them with a spasm,
from which I sink back helpless. The poor palpitating fruits of this parturition look but lean or
rickety ; and yet I can never alter, nurse and
cherish them. If I died to-morrow, my name
would truly, as far as fame goes, be writ on water.
On the hearts of some I know it would be written,
but they too must die."

[Yet the approach of that illness, which was induced by the damp summer of 1865, and declared
itself in the winter, though it accounts for much of
the depression which pervades the Diary, did not
render Symonds incapable of such keen enjoyment
as this which illumines the following description of
the Handel Festival] :—

"I [1] promised to tell you something about the
two days of the Handel Festival which I went to.
Arthur Sidgwick was here, and this, you may be sure,
added to my pleasure, for he is a musician, and
loves Handel. Besides, I met multitudes of people.

[1] To his sister Charlotte. 47 Norfolk Square, Sunday, July 2, 1865.

The Pearsons, and the Stephenses, and all the Sonning folk, the Goldschmidts, Mrs. Gaskell, Mary
Ewart, and heaps of Oxford and Cambridge men.
But these were only accessory pleasures.   Sitting
in that vast garden under glass, within view of the
statues, and of fountains silent from their distance,
among a crowd of true musicians—the whole *Gesell-
schaft* of Handelmaniacs being congregated—was a
nearer approach to the real pleasure.   Then came
the tuning of multitudinous violins, and the roar of
the tremendous organ.   Then Costa took his place;
the orchestra began to prelude, disappointing me at
first by the faintness of the sound it made, but being
swallowed up ere long in a tide of overpowering
voices.   Then, for the first time, I heard the vocal
part of music transcend, predominate, and override
the instruments.   The concert opened with a chorus
from Saul, 'How excellent Thy name, O Lord'—
one of Handel's true movements, in which he mar-
shals chords like squadrons in an army, obliging
them to part and reunite, now marching in a solid
mass, now scattered into divers bands, and finally
assembling and advancing in unvanquishable num-
bers.   Several pieces from Saul followed, the greatest
of which, without doubt, was a chorus, 'Envy, eldest
born of hell.'   Even the words were fine:

> Envy, eldest born of hell,
> Cease in human hearts to dwell;
> Ever at all good repining,
> Still the happy undermining;

God and man by thee infested,
Thou by God and man detested,
Most thyself thou dost torment,
At once the crime and punishment ;
Hide thee in the blackest night,
Virtue sickens at thy sight.

It would be impossible to describe in words how
the mere music of this chorus represented envy as
a passion corroding the heart, and attacking the
very citadel of health and happiness. A tone of
grave reproof, measured hatred, sorrowful denun-
ciation, and just loathing pervaded every note ; and
the fury stood before one's mind, unmasked, made
manifest, and shown in all her foul deformity, by
the supreme radiance of music. Melody cannot be
ugly. A musician cannot paint an ugly thing. All
he can do is to give life to those emotions of disgust
and indignation which vice and ugliness inspire.
This Handel, in this chorus, has so powerfully done
that we feel sure that it is envy and no other fiend
who has inspired the awful rebuke of his reiterated
condemnations. From 'Saul' we passed to 'Samson.' Patti sang 'Let the bright Seraphim' fluently
and clearly. Some things from 'Acis and Galatea'
came next, and then we had the loveliest of all
Handel's choruses—a marriage hymn from 'Solo-
mon,' in which the songs of nightingales and the
breath of zephyrs are invoked to soothe the slumbers
of a king and queen. No one who has not heard it
could have believed Handel capable of producing

anything so light, and languid, and full of luxurious
repose. The Coronation Anthem, and parts of
' Judas Maccabæus,' closed the selection. On
Friday Catherine joined Arthur and myself. We
sat together and heard ' Israel in Egypt,' the
colossus of oratorios, the greatest choral work, which
sprang from Handel's brain in twenty-seven days.
You have heard it once, so I will not say much
about it. I enjoyed this day immeasurably more
than the other. I felt as if I had embarked upon
the great wide sea of music, and as if melody had
become an atmosphere. It was one, continuous,
complete. The effect of the ' hailstones ' and
' darkness ' was overpowering ; and I fairly cried
when the storm subsided and the change came—
' But as for His people He led them forth like
sheep.' Then came those mighty choruses which
describe the swelling and the raging of the sea,
the conflict of Pharaoh and his horsemen with the
waves, the breath of God that went abroad upon
the waters, the billows that rocked over the dead
chieftains, the murmur of the senseless ocean and
the cry of the lost armies, the shout of Israel's victory and the shrill voice of Miriam's exultation.
There is absolutely nothing in the whole realm of
art so dramatically magnificent as this second half
of ' Israel in Egypt.' Not even does the ' Persæ '
of Æschylus describe so vividly the fall of a godless
people and the triumph of a mighty nation. For
not only has Handel made us see the horse and his

rider, hear the Red Sea chafing on their chariots,
and listen to the cymbals of rejoicing Israelites, he
has also, by the power which music alone possesses,
sung hymns to God commemorative of His glory
and immediately representative of His power. My
words are vain. But you know what I mean.
Where poetry, as the vehicle of emotion, especially
of religious emotion, ends, there music begins.
What poetry hints at music expresses. What poetry
describes lives and moves before us in music, and
compels our spirits into sympathy. At the end of
all they sang 'God save the Queen,' and it was
over.

"I was more lost in meditation on the nature of
music than I have ever been before. Here was a
man Handel, a fat native of Halle, in the Duchy
of Magdeburg, articled at eight years old to an
organist, and from that moment given up to music
—a man who never loved a woman, who (to use
the words of his enthusiastic biographer) continued
irritable, greedy, fond of solitude, persevering, unaf-
fectionate, coarse and garrulous in conversation,
benevolent, independent, fond of beer, religious,
without passions, and without a single intellectual
taste. He had never received any education except
in counterpoint. He had had no experience. Yet
he could interpret the deepest psychological secrets;
he could sing dithyrambs to God, or preach moral
sermons; he could express the feelings of mighty
nations, and speak with the voice of angels more

effectually than even Milton; he could give life to passion, and in a few changes of his melody lead love through all its variations from despair to triumph—there was nothing that he did not know. The whole world had become for him music, and his chords were co-extensive with the universe. Raphael's capability to paint the school of Athens, after coming from the workshop of Perugino, was perhaps less marvellous than Handel's to delineate the length and breadth and height and depth of human nature in his choruses. We shall never comprehend, *nous autres*, the mysteries of genius. It is a God-sent clairvoyance, inexplicable, and different in kind from intellect."

[Dr. Symonds wished his son to pass the cold spring months at Mentone. Symonds left home with some of that reluctance which always seized him when he had to part from Clifton, and all that it implied for him.]

February 11, 1866.[1]—Of all things let me not fall into the error of Sir Egerton Brydges, and incessantly distress myself about my poetic gifts, complaining that they are not recognised, wondering whether they are real, abusing those who deny them, uneasily questioning myself and others as to their validity. Let me enjoy and be content with that. Poetic feeling is not artistic power. The emotions which I experience while hearing music, in beautiful

[1] Diary.

scenery, before fine pictures, in cathedrals, at the
thought of noble men—these enable me to understand and to enjoy, intensify the glow of life, and
raise me to a higher sphere. But from them to
actual plastic art there is a mighty step to make.

Friday, February 16.—I am sick at heart for
having to leave Clifton—this room where C. and
I have sat so happily together in the mornings,
with its city view; where Ch. has come to read
with me—this country where C. and I have had
such glorious walks—these downs where H. G. D.
and I have had strange communings together,
pacing up and down. I have learned, lived,
enjoyed, and grown much in freedom, strength,
and peace, and perhaps knowledge here. Now we
must soon break up our camp. And how little I
have done of any sort! What unattainable moun-
tain-tops above me! How the aspect of Goethe, of
Dante, of Parmenides, of Petrarch, the great souls
with which I have lived, of wind and rain and sunlight and clouds and woods, has filled me with
inextinguishable yearnings and an agony of impo-
tency. I am too full to give forth. " Joy impreg-
nates; sorrows bring forth."

[Symonds started for the Riviera on the 24th
February 1866, and here began the long series of
journeys in search of health, and also a new phase
in his Italian experience. He applied himself to
the serious study of the Italian language. He read

the "Decamerone" by himself, and Ariosto and Dante under the guidance of his Italian master, Signor Belochetto, at Mentone. He reported the progress of his studies to his sister in letters written in Italian. From Mentone he moved on to Bordighera and San Remo, whence he wrote to his father] :—

"We[1] are all together now in the same hotel— Maribella, Mrs. Moore, Catherine, and myself. It is very pleasant, although we none of us think this place can bear any comparison with Mentone in point of beauty. It is prosaic by the side of so much romantic loveliness. I wish I could see little Janet : do you think she might be photographed for us? Auntie wrote that she was small, but I hope she still looks as pretty as she used to be, and that she is not wanting in intelligence for her age. I have been thinking so much of you to-day, and longing to see you again. Life is never so good a thing when I am separated from you by a long interval of time, and what is more, by so complete a distance of daily associations. Catherine made some lovely sketches at Bordighera, where we spent Monday and Tuesday. She has not done anything since she came here, but I hope that we shall not quit the Riviera without her making some studies of

[1] To Dr. Symonds. Hotel de Londres, San Remo, Easter Sunday April 1866.

olive trees. The palms at Bordighera took her fancy, and they certainly are most beautiful—growing with an Oriental luxuriance in groves, or leaning over the city walls. I have also been doing some work—reading Italian and writing an article on Empedocles, which I may try perhaps to publish in the *North British Review*. But as I have made use of the translations which I did for Jowett, I cannot print this paper unless I learn from him more accurately how he means to employ them. I have not received any acknowledgment from him of the arrival of my MS., but I daresay, as it is vacation time at Oxford, that he may not yet have got it. Thank you very much for sending me the *Edinburgh Courant*. I was extremely interested in the abstract of Jowett's lecture. The allusions to the unpaid and persecuted labours of Socrates made me think of Jowett himself. He always seems to me to find a consolation for his own troubles in the thought of great teachers—Socrates and Christ. Conington wrote me the other day a long letter containing much gossip about his and other people's translations, and also about the reception of ' Ecce Homo ' at Oxford. Jowett's party seem to have made rather light of it : Conington himself, as might have been expected from its want of favour with the Jowett school, gives it many kind words."

[Of " Ecce Homo " he writes in a letter to a friend : " We have brought it out to read a second

time together, for there is much in its chapters
which I need to dwell upon; they seemed to me so
new and strange, and raised so keen a desire for
real assimilation in my mind."

Passages in the Diary show how much he enjoyed
the scenery of the Riviera, and how carefully he
noted its beauties in pages which he worked up later
on into his most popular travel sketches. But the
climate, which Symonds found trying to his nerves,
frequently provoked fits of internal depression; and
the unrest was intensified by the continual thwarting of his aspirations through ill-health.]

March 18.[1]—I fret because I do not realise
ambition, because I have no active work, and cannot win a position of importance like other men.
Literary success would compensate me: yet, the
first steps to this seem always thwarted. Intellectual, moral, and physical qualities in combination
are required for this success. I have the intellectual; the physical is always giving way without
my fault, and the moral flags by my cowardly
inertia. I am an over-cultivated being, too alive
to all sensibilities to walk on one path without
distraction, and so keenly appreciative of greatness
in art and literature that I am disdainful of small
achievements. Yet, these gloomy reflections serve
as spurs to goad me on. "Venture, and thus
climb swift to Wisdom's height." A man has but

[1] Diary.

one life to lose; he can but strive; and if he fails
at last and dies with nothing done, an unremem-
bered weed, a sea-wrack on the barren shore, why,
so have lived and died, hoped and despaired,
petulantly struggled and then calmly sunk, thousands before him.

[In reaction from this mood the solicitations of
Monte Carlo attract him; but as in a dream.]

March 22.—After [1] dawdling about Monaco itself
we went round to the "Jeux"—a large gambling-house
established on the shore near Monaco, upon the road
to Mentone. There is a splendid hotel there, and
the large house of sin, blazing with gas lamps by
night. So we saw it from the road beneath Turbia
our first night, flaming and shining by the shore like
Pandemonium, or the habitation of (some) romantic
witch. This place, in truth, resembles the gardens
of Alcina, or any other magician's trap for catching
souls, which poets have devised. It lies close by the
sea in a hollow of the sheltering hills. There winter
cannot come—the flowers bloom, the waves dance,
and sunlight laughs all through the year. The air
swoons with scent of lemon groves; tall palm trees
wave their branches in the garden; music of the
softest, loudest, most inebriating passion, swells
from the palace; rich meats and wines are served in
a gorgeously painted hall; cool corridors and sunny
seats stand ready for the noontide heat or evening

[1] Diary.

calm ; without are olive gardens, green and fresh
and full of flowers.   But the witch herself holds her
high court and never-ending festival of sin in the hall
of the green tables.   There is a passion which sub-
dues all others, making music, sweet scents, and
delicious food, the plash of the melodious waves, the
evening air and freedom of the everlasting hills,
subserve her own supremacy.

When the fiend of play has entered into a man,
what does he care for the beauties of nature or even
for the pleasure of the sense ?   Yet in the moments
of his trial he must drain the cup of passion, therefore let him have companions—splendid women, with
bold eyes and golden hair and marble columns of
imperial throats, to laugh with him, to sing shrill
songs, to drink, to tempt the glassy deep at midnight when the cold moon shines, or all the headlands glimmer with grey phosphorescence, and the
palace sends its flaring lights and sound of cymbals
to the hills.   And many, too, there are over whom
love and wine hold empire hardly less entire than
play.   This is no vision : it is sober, sad reality.   I
have seen it to-day with my own eyes.   I have
been inside the palace, and have breathed its air.
In no other place could this riotous daughter of
hell have set her throne so seducingly.   Here
are the Sirens and Calypso and Dame Venus of
Tannhauser's dream.   Almost every other scene of
dissipation has disappointed me by its monotony
and sordidness.   But this inebriates ; here nature is

so lavish, so beautiful, so softly luxurious, that the harlot's cup is thrice more sweet to the taste, more stealing of the senses than elsewhere. I felt while we listened to the music, strolled about the gardens, and lounged in the play-rooms, as I have sometimes felt at the opera. All other pleasures, thoughts, and interests of life seemed to be far off and trivial for the time. I was beclouded, carried off my balance, lapped in strange forebodings of things infinite outside me in the human heart. Yet all was unreal; for the touch of reason, like the hand of Galahad, caused the boiling of this impure fountain to cease —the wizard's castle disappeared, and, as I drove homeward to Mentone, the solemn hills and skies and seas remained, and that house was, as it were, a mirage.

Inside the gaming-house play was going forward like a business. *Roulette* and *rouge et noir* tables were crowded. Little could be heard but the monotonous voice of the croupiers, the rattle of gold under their wooden shovels, and the clicking of the ball that spun round for *roulette*. Imperturbable gravity sat on the faces of men who lost or won. Several stern-faced, middle-aged women were making small stakes, and accurately pricking all the chances of the game on cards. A low buzz ran through the room, but this came chiefly from the lookers-on like ourselves. Occasionally a more than usually loud trumpet or shrill clarionette sounded from the music hall. Two men attracted my interest.

One was a terrier-faced Englishman, with reddish hair and a sanguine complexion. He staked largely, and laughed at his winnings and losings indifferently. A very astute man, who did not play himself, seemed to be backing him up and giving him advice. The other was a splendid-looking fellow—a tall, handsome, well-made Piedmontese he seemed to be—at least he had a favourable resemblance to Victor Emanuel. His small head, with crisp brown hair, fresh colour, light moustache and long imperial, cold bluish eyes, and steadfast frown, was set upon a little muscular neck, and that upon the body of a Hermes with most perfect hands. There was something innocent in his face; yet the whole man looked like a sleek panther. It would be easy to love him; the woman who should love him would be happy for some days, and then would most probably be broken. But strong determination and cool devilry sat in his face. He seemed once to lose everything. Then he went out and soon returned with bank notes, some of which he paid away and some of which he staked. Then he gained gold, bank notes and *rouleaux*, but he still continued playing with perfect *sangfroid*. When the *rouge et noir* stopped for a minute, he got up and made a large stake at *roulette*, and left a serving man to watch it for him when his favourite game began again. C. said he was like Rolla. Certainly when he is ruined he will shoot himself. At present he is fresh and fair and charming to look at, his great physical and moral strength, though tempered wickedly, being a refreshing spectacle.

The croupiers are either fat, sensual cormorants, or sallow, lean-cheeked vultures, or suspicious foxes. So I term them; yet they only look like wicked bankers' clerks, like men narrowed and made sordid by constant contact with money in a heartless trade, and corrupted by familiarity with turns of luck instead of honourable business rules. Compare them with Coutts' men to note the difference. It is very discernible; for, though in externals much alike, these men of the gaming bank show every trace of a dissolute youth and a vile calling, of low sensuality, and hardened avarice, upon their faces.

We noticed that almost all the gamesters had light blue eyes. No exhibition of despair were visible; yet I saw many very jaded young men, and nervous old men, blear-eyed fellows staking eagerly five-franc pieces. My young Rolla was the royal one—the prince of gamblers in that room—and but for him the place would have had no romance for me. It must be an odd life: lounging and smoking in the gardens, listening to Verdi in the music hall, gormandising in the *salle à manger*, and enjoying every beauty of southern spring, together with the fiery pleasures of that hazard. Eschman says, he had once to pawn his own clothes for a young fellow who gambled away £2000 at Homburg, and then wanted to go back to England. I have not enough continuity of good spirits, of self-deception, and of resolution, to gamble. Under the influence of some kind of passion, I could fancy going into it for a moment, but the yoke would be to me most odious. How nerves can bear it I wonder. But my Rolla's nerves are tigerish, and like the tickling which would rend me to atoms. Perfect coolness and concentration of fever producing calm marked this man. His whole soul was in the play.

[This stimulation of the senses in the imaginative region is worked out, harmonised, and laid to rest, for a time, in such long flights of criticism as this which follows ;—criticism in embryo, it is true, but interesting in itself as a singular *tour de force*,—for a single morning's work,—and valuable as showing how, under the stress of strong feeling, Symonds projected the thoughts which he subsequently wrought into his finished critical judgments.]

Thursday, April 5.[1] — In Wordsworth, Byron, Keats, Shelley, Coleridge, Tennyson, and Browning, the English Renaissance, the Elizabethan age has revived, no longer taking the dramatic or Epic form, but that of narrative and lyrical poetry, passionate, reflective, egotistical, religious, patriotic. The increased interest in Elizabethan authors—Charles Lamb, the Shakespearians — was a sign of this revival. Poets sought Elizabethan phraseology, like

[1] Diary.

Byron in the first Canto of Childe Harold, or Elizabethan richness like Keats. All rules of art, and
French classicisms, were discarded; Wordsworth
preached a natural diction. The two ages [the
Italian and the English Renaissance] are similar;
freedom of religious thought, political freedom, a
new impulse given to all speculation, the movement of the French Revolution answering to that
of the Reformation. During the interval, diplo-
macy had cramped politics, torpor had benumbed
religion, philosophy had crawled upon the lowest
ground of calculation and self-interest, poetry had
ceased to be anything but a mechanical arrangement
of words in obedience to some artificial standard of
correct taste. Men strove in every department to
be as much alike as possible. The sixteenth and
nineteenth century spirit tends to individuality in art
at least. The seven names above are infinitely
different in everything except a common afflatus and
common Elizabethanism. Parallel to this English
movement, there has been in other countries a return
to the fountainhead of literature. The Italians have
studied Dante,—Giusti, Leopardi. The Germans
have created a literature in affiliation to our Elizabethan age. The French have their Romantic
School. What is the essence of Elizabethanism?
In the first place, freedom. Freedom of thought;—
freedom from bondage to great names, like those of
Virgil, or Cicero, or Voltaire; or to great languages,
like the Latin; or to great canons of criticism, like

the Aristotelian unities ;—freedom from servility to
potentates and patrons ; our playwrights are as
liberal as the wind of their words, their Elizabeth is
England : compare them with an Ariosto inspired
by flattery alone ; with the dedicatory poets of the
eighteenth century ;—religious freedom ; notice what
Decker dared to say of Christ, what Heywood spoke
about the Bible in his Chronicle of Elizabeth ;—political freedom ; intolerance of foreign rule, compare
this with the restoration, identification of popular
liberties and royalty, of royalty and popular religion ;
—the freedom of youth, untrammelled, with a bound-
less future and no past, with the luxuriance of young
blood, the consciousness of youthful beauty, the
carelessness of young audacity, the fields untrodden
and the flowers unpicked, a virgin soil and lusty
husbandmen to till and sow and store unbounded
harvests ;—freedom from precedent ; no great ex-
amples to weigh down the wings of genius, no rules
to hamper its flight, no academies to judge, impose,
condemn, and censure.   The result of this freedom
was that every man wrote what he thought best,
wrote from himself, so that individuality marked
every utterance.   And the tendencies of this freedom were regulated by a national spirit, patriotic,
highly moral, religious, intensely human, animated
by a firm belief in reality, careless of books, courageous, adventurous, eager for scientific discoveries,
ambitious of acquiring wealth and power, conscious
of its own energy, martial yet jealous of domestic

peace, assiduous in toil, quick to overleap material barriers, and revel in the wildest dreams of the imagination, manly, delicate, trained in long trials of foreign and civil wars, of factions, of religious persecutions. Elizabethanism is, in fact, the genius of a mighty nation young and free, as manifested in its literature. Further than this in analysis we cannot go, any more than we can analyse the genius of Shakespeare or Beethoven in itself. Yet we may show what circumstances favoured the origin and development of genius, whether in a nation or in a man ; what characteristics distinguish it from other kinds or instances of genius. Elizabethanism is, then, the genius of England, as displayed in literature when England was free and adolescent.

At every period, therefore, of freedom and adolescence, we may expect to find Elizabethanism in England, if literature be not altogether suppressed. And this is why we see it reappearing in the nineteenth century, in that Pleiad, who were stirred by the vast political renaissance of 1790, by the religious renaissance inaugurated by French destructive scepticism, and by the scientific renaissance which opened a new horizon to the world. Freedom leapt aloft, and the English poets answered to her call. New youth flowed in the mother's ancient veins. The winter weeds of two dead centuries were cast aside.

But " Tempora mutantur, nos et mutamur in illis." The dreams of the sixteenth century have been

exchanged for more sober expectations ; there is no
El Dorado now, but California.   Faith has suc-
cumbed to criticism ; religious liberty consists in the
right to doubt, not to believe as we like ; and political liberty in the tranquillity of the individual less
than in the majesty of the people.   We ply our
commerce and preach non-intervention ; we do not
seek to extend our empire or to carry our crusades
against the enemies of our religion or our peace.
We are readers and not hearers.   There is no public
for theatrical display.   The poetry of the outward
world has been exchanged for that of the inner life,
of action for reflection, of passions for analysis of
passions.   All these reasons, and many more, explain
why the renewed Elizabethanism is lyrical and egotistical instead of dramatic and patriotic.   We have
youth and freedom indeed ; but our youth is the
youth of a man, our freedom the freedom of a man
—not the youth of a nation, or the freedom of a
nation.

As a result of illimitable freedom the Elizabethans
fell into the error of extravagance and exaggeration.
This they showed in the expression of their own
sentiments, in their language, in their indulgence of
the fancy, in their profuse ornamentation, in the
characters of their drama, in their preference for
striking incidents and rant, over good taste and
select diction.   No force from without controlled
them, and they had no internal power of self-control.
The motto μηδὲν ἄγαν was peculiar to the Greek

temperament; it has been assumed by other literatures advisedly and in imitation of the Greek. Medievalism had nothing of it, and the Elizabethans were children of the Middle Ages. When the Elizabethan spirit in England gave place to the pseudo-classic, then the good and bad effects of an imposed limit were produced. We had our Dryden, and our Pope, and our writers of limpid prose. But the true genius of our literature was in abeyance, and when it reappeared it brought with it the evils of extravagance and exaggeration.

Yet even in this exuberance and unmeasured fecundity we find one of the excellent qualities of Elizabethanism. Such a wealth of suggestive thought, such a deep sympathy with nature, such a power of expressing the secrets revealed by the outward world to the percipient mind, such a clairvoyance into the innermost chambers of the human soul, never belonged to any other literature, and would not have belonged to ours had the limitations of Art been more regarded, had men thought of the form more, repressed the *élan* of their genius, and sought to prune. Elizabethanism has the spirit of modern Christian art, as typified in music. It is profluent, profuse of emotion, unapt to restrain itself to one note or one series of notes, eager to pour forth its passion in every variety, by means of countless simultaneous instruments, by means of numerous and subtle changes and developments of meaning. It is all iridescent, Gothic, manifold.

Carelessness, want of balance, defective judgment
in the selection of materials or their management,
bad taste, superfluities of every kind, mark the
Elizabethan art.   It is also remarkable for energy,
pomp of language, swelling sound, magnificent im-
provisation, beauties tossed like foam upon the
waves of thought by means of mere collision.   It
has nothing small or mean or calculated.   Its vices.
are the vices of the prodigal, not of the miser, and
of the prodigal whose want of prudence is more near
to generosity than wanton waste.   We forgive its
many faults for its inexhaustible fertility, and lose
ourselves in wondering at its wealth and strength
and liberality.   Every word of this paragraph would
need alteration were we to apply it to the English
of the pseudo-classic age.   If not miserly, then our
genius was very thrifty.   It erred by caution rather
than by haste.   It doled its treasures out as one
who has a purse indeed, but cannot, like the Midas
of the true Elizabethan age, turn all it touched
into gold.

Blank verse and prose are the two vehicles by
which it expresses itself—using both lyrically, governing the periods of both by internal melody and
rhythms, making blank verse more harmonious than
any rhymed metre, and prose more poetical than
the verse of other nations.   The dramatists and
Milton for verse, the greatest divines, Sir T.
Browne and Milton, for prose, are the products
of the first Elizabethan era ; De Quincey, Ruskin,

and even the faulty "fine writers" of the present day, incarnate the new Elizabethan spirit in prose composition. Blank verse, too, has regained ascendancy after the forced reign of the rhyming couplet. But we have few real masters of blank verse. It is in lyric poetry that we excel now.

It is a sign of the Elizabethan spirit never to hesitate or palliate. And the mantle in this also has fallen on the new age. Don Juan, Shelley's Epipsychidion, Browning's Paracelsus and Pippa Passes, Guinevere, and Wordsworth's Poems on Life, set forth aspects of morality as various, as original, as bold, as hazardous as those of the Elizabethans. But they are more analytical, and subjective in obedience to the temper of the age. We have never produced an Alfred de Musset.

The Elizabethan genius first made Nature for her own sake a study. The poems of Shakespeare are full of observations, allusions, elaborate pictures of natural phenomena, from flowers up to the thunder. Nothing was too small or too great for his muse. Seneca says of some hero—"Non circum flosculos occupatur," using flosculos metaphorically; but the sentence may be applied directly; a classic would disdain the enumeration of flowers which we find in Winter's Tale. This quality has reappeared even to excess in Keats and Shelley, but in admirable force in Wordsworth, who gives life to the minutiæ of nature. Byron has been said to have followed her with lust, and Wordsworth professed for her a

raging passion which toned down into philosophy.
And the quality we speak of is now seen most
strongly in our school of landscape painters, musicians, lyrists, writers of sounding prose and various
blank verse in colours, not in words or tones; indeed,
wherever the dominion of the Elizabethan spirit is
felt, this quality is apparent. In France, G. Sand,
De Guerin, A. de Musset, V. Hugo, are names
enough to signalise the true union which subsists
between this devotion to nature for her own sake
and that essential freedom which we regard as the
central point of Elizabethanism. Music, landscape
painting, and a pantheistic sympathy with outer
nature, more symbol-seeking and penetrative than
the old classic pantheism, meet in our Renaissance.

A great difference between the old and new
Elizabethan spirit exists also in the form and range
of thought. Refinements and subtle-subtilisings of
all sorts have succeeded to keen intuitions into
nature, yet we have lost the euphuism of the past;
we are more cultivated in a good and a bad sense,
less able to look directly at things, more on our
guard against mere mannerisms of expression. The
earlier Elizabethans had no " Lazzaretto poetry."
We have very much. There is now far more in-
volution of sentences and laborious effort after
recondite phrases. Again, the subtleties of our
rhythms—Shelley's, *e.g.*—transcend that of the old
Elizabethan; the Wordsworthian vein reveals a new
kind of philosophical and Christian pantheism; the

man of thought is more, of action less; the problems of life are probed with more of casuistical nicety, displayed with less of tragic pomp and human breadth. These parallels might be extended to a tedious length. Read "Adonais" side by side with "Hero and Leander," and note.

This diatribe, being very ill this morning, I wrote to distract my mind from its troubles, to rouse me from a clinging lethargy in which will, memory, physical force, and power of thought seemed all exhausted. I could do nothing—fix my attention on no book, endure no company, take interest in nothing outside. It did me good; and the afternoon spent with C. among the gigantic olives, deep grass meadows, and clear streams of the Val des Oliviers pleased me. I walked in a dream. Scirocco was blowing.

[His fits of depression were cheered by letters from Jowett, whose hopeful, vigorous tone proved now, as always, of immense service to Symonds' diffident sensitiveness.]

"MY DEAR SYMONDS,—Many thanks indeed for the translation of Empedocles. I think that it and the other translations will greatly add to my first volume for the appendix to which I destine them. And if you will do me Democritus I shall be greatly obliged. But I shan't expect this. There is a separate book of Mullach's on Democritus which you might find an advantage in perusing. There is

no hurry, as I certainly shan't want to print them
before the end of the year.   I often feel that I have
undertaken too big a work, and can only hope that
I may survive to do something else.   I hope that
you are better.   I don't suppose that you were
really in any danger.   But I am glad that you took
the precaution of going away.   And I am glad that
you have got a wife to take care of you.

    " I think that you may look forward to a literary
life with good hope and prospect of success.   To
have nothing to do is the best of all lives, if you
only make something real to do.   You escape the
narrowing influence of a profession, and what you
do for others is far more deeply felt.   The point is,
I think, to get a position and occupation, and each
year to look as anxiously to one's own progress as
you would to the coming in of briefs at the bar.—
Ever yours,   B. JOWETT."

    [As summer drew on the Riviera was left behind
for Genoa, Pisa, Lucca, Florence, Ravenna, Milan.
Then the travellers set their faces northward, and
here are some notes of their journey] :—

    " I [1] was glad to get your letter yesterday, and to
know that you are well.   For the rest I wait until I
see you, feeling sure that you will tell me all I want
to hear.   The prospect is very dull to-day.   A thick
raincloud has descended on the Lago Maggiore, and
the islands loom shivering from it with a mournful

    [1] To H. G. Dakyns.   Baveno, May 25, 1866.

cheerlessness. I have nothing to do but to sit and think and write (if I had something to write about), and read Italian. We are weatherbound in a corner of an old inn, with some four or five other people. One of these is a physical philosopher, a scientific man, to whose confession of faith I have just been listening. Ah me! how many faiths are there in the world, and what gods do not ye worship, Israel. He thinks it is but a question of time until we shall know God by means of our senses, and until the Pantheistic Being be fully developed through spontaneous generation. But what the good of the knowledge, that he does not say, nor how the Pantheistic Being subsists. We know just as little about such matters as Empedocles.

"*Sunday*.—I cannot write away from home. You say, and say truly, that perfect communication subsists between people living in the same place and writing to each other. Written words then supplement spoken words. Looks, silences, and tones of voice complete what these leave imperfect. The souls then touch at all points, and, what is of grave import, their physical surroundings are the same. Breathing one air, seeing the same beautiful landscapes, enjoying the same sun, and shivering under the same fogs, nothing from the world outside destroys the sense of sympathy. But when we are so far away—when I in Italy sit by the shore of Verbanus, among the cool ferns, gazing at the distant snow overcast with thunderclouds—when

you in England hear the thrushes, hanging over
those ravines of wood, or listen to the English
sound of Sunday prayer and praise—when I, poor
I, far, far away, am frighted by these madding
powers of nature, incommunicable, sad, weighed
down by forebodings, unintelligible even to myself,
haunted by the past, feeling the present an im-
palpable nightmare, fixing vacant eyes on the
insupportable future—when we are so, and the
arrowy scents of narcissus and honeysuckle mixed
with nightingale music distract my brain if I sit
down to write—how on this Sunday morning can I
feel at one with you or any one in dear far-off England? I know what is passing there. I can enter
the cathedral at Bristol, where they are now chanting
Te Deum, and the coloured light streams from those
southern windows, as it did eight years ago. I can
lie in darkness in the ante-chapel of Magdalen and
listen to the roaring of that tempestuous organ,
or, last of all, I know the stillness of our Clifton
home, the silent pictures, the grave books, the light
and flowers and undefinable fragrance of perpetual
feminine possession. These things I see—see, do
I say?—feel, handle, live among. But I am here,
after all, by the sounding shore of Verbanus; and
the channel of sympathy is cut off, and do what
I will I cannot, by writing to you, stir the load of
mournful presage which weighs upon me. There
is in Marlowe the image of an old king, dethroned
and discrowned, who, waking from sleep and talking

with his murderer, is reminded of his crown, whereat
he cries, 'Where is my crown? Gone, gone, and
do I yet remain alive?'

"The word which tolls in my ears, night and day,
is 'waste.' When I wake from sleep I cry like
the wretch in Persius, 'Imus, imus præcipites.'
My soul is stagnant, and I see no God, no reason
for the world, no vigour in myself, no content in
things around me, nothing but slow-sliding barren
years. Yet I do hate this barren curse of self-indulgent cowardice and wasted youth. I struggle in
my chains and shake the bars, impotent maniac. O
Lord! how long! hast Thou forgotten to be gracious?
Will not Christ come again? 'But if He came,' so
says the voice of the Lord speaking from the depth
of this dead soul, 'art thou one to take His cross,
to preach His creed, to lie in caves, to fight with
beasts, to see the beauty of the purity of holiness
and naked truth, thou whose small intelligence and
little Will have been consumed in useless questions,
enervating feelings, over-cultivation, sickliness, and
sin? Go, saltless soul, go to the dunghill, rot there
thirty years, and wait my time.' Arise: we will
away to the mountains and the snow, and will strive
to forget, moving restlessly from place to place, and
frittering thought away in little things."

[To the mountains, accordingly, they went. The
change from the languid air of the Lakes to the
bracing air of the Alps is indicated at once by the

rise of the spiritual mercury in Symonds' sensitive structure.]

"After[1] two most brilliantly beautiful days our own weather has returned, thunder, mists, and deluges of rain. We are safely boxed up for the rest of the day in a little mountain inn, with a torrent foaming beneath our windows, and the crags towering up above us, wreathed with fleecy clouds among the pines and beeches and brown châlets. It is a real Alpine village, such as I used to long for in London last summer.

"Since I last wrote we have been making a kind of royal progress through these valleys. It is quite absurd to see how the people know and greet Catherine, and with what affection they re-member Mr. North. This began at Baveno, where the landlord and landlady received us with effusion as old friends. While we were there we wrote to Gaspard, whom perhaps you may remember at our wedding. He is landlord of Macugnaga, a very im-portant person in those parts, and a Swiss of more than common intelligence and gravity. He passed three winters at Hastings, and never tires of dis-cussing the North family and its affairs. Well, Gaspard, when he heard that we had come to Lago Maggiore, announced his intention of walk-ing down to see us. We, however, had gone on to Orta before he arrived, and he had to follow

[1] To his sister Charlotte. Fobello, Monday, June 4, 1866.

us, which he did in the incessant deluge. Catherine
and I made an expedition from Orta, and were
returning across the lake. A squall had just begun
to rush down from the Simplon mountains, not a
boat was to be seen upon the lake, the waves
were rising high, and I was wondering whether we
should not have to take refuge on the Island of San
Giulio, when suddenly I spied another nutshell of
a bark upon the waters making way towards us.
A sedate man, with a yellow beard, sat alone
inside it, and Catherine soon recognised him for
Gaspard. Our boats met in mid-sea, and he sprang
on board. He had crossed the Motterone that
morning, and was not content with waiting for us
at Orta, but must needs set out again to find us
in the middle of our excursion. The old proprietor
of the inn at Fobello, called Uccetta, is an old
friend of the Norths, and Uccetta's wife, Maddalena,
has an almost romantic affection for Catherine. She
is not an unimportant person in these parts. She
brought her husband, for her dower, the inn
which they have just sold, and have bought for
themselves a country-house high up among the
pastures, with a garden and an Alp for the cows.
I wish you could see her tall straight figure and
handsome face—such dark bright eyes, and such a
beautiful complexion. I do not know how it is, but
though they work hard, and expose themselves
continually to the sun, the women of this valley
have all of them the freshest colour, and keep their

looks of youth and health far longer than any other mountaineers whom I have seen. I wish also that I could give you the least idea of their costume. You must begin by fancying a Vivandière, for a company of Fobello peasant women resembles a regiment of soldiers in petticoats. They wear trousers of a dark blue, blue shoes edged with red, a short blue skirt, also edged with red cloth, descending to their knees. On their head they have a large red kerchief and ribands, or 'bindelle' as they call them, of any colours that they choose. The dress is completed by a white kind of Garibaldi and a stomacher, curiously wrought with open work of coloured silks, and a strange ugly pouch in front. This pouch contains everything—it is sometimes large enough to carry a baby, like the pouches of the kangaroos ; but I do not think the matrons of Fobello use it for this purpose—keys and money and pocket-handkerchiefs, and knives and thimbles and cotton, being the contents which Maddalena showed us in her pouch. In wet or cold weather they put on a short man's jacket of blue cloth over the Garibaldi, tuck up the skirts to give their trousers freer play, and shoulder a huge Gampish umbrella. Well, fancy the tall, handsome Maddalena suddenly appearing in this dress, clapping her hands, shrieking and laughing with surprise and pleasure, and embracing Catherine. She took possession of us for the day. Uccetta himself was trout-fishing. So we went up to see their new

house, and there she sat us down to drink white
Asti and cream. Two bottles of Asti were opened,
and a huge cream-bowl with a ladle was produced
from the dairy. Each of us had a smaller basin
for our share. To refuse her hospitality was impossible; to drink either Asti or cream in the midst of
walking on a hot day is against all my principles:
to drink the two together at any time shocks all
my notions of propriety. I had often discoursed
to Catherine on the unwholesomeness of sweet
Asti, and the danger of drinking uncooked milk
when one is hot. Yet, here I had, with smiles
upon my face, to finish a huge basin of the one,
together with the larger portion of a bottle of the
other. It was a ludicrous situation, and no ill
results followed. Maddalena kept talking and
laughing all the time with that perfect absence of
self-consciousness and that true good-breeding which
I have always found among the peasants of the
Alps. They get this freedom of manners, combined
with respect, from the condition of society in the
mountains, I suppose. Here there are no differences
of class, strictly speaking. All talk the same patois,
share the same interests, receive the same education, wear the same dress. Wealth constitutes the
only distinction between man and man; a youth
born of poor parents may make money abroad,
and return to spend his later manhood as a village
magnate. These people are not unconscious of
the difference which subsists between them and

us : but the difference of what we call rank is lost
in the difference of nation and habits—they neither
presume upon familiarity, nor do they take it with
that kind of cringing satisfaction which is so odious
in the vulgar of our own country.   When Uccetta
returned from fishing—we met him with his basket
of trout and long fishing-rod by the bank of the
Mastalone—his reception of Catherine was grave
and almost paternal.   Like all truly great men,
and it must not be forgotten that he is a culinary
artist 'meritamente famoso,' he is modest, not
to say timid and retiring.   Such a huge broad-
shouldered cook I never saw : yet, he is gigantically
soft in manner ; as if he were pondering on con-
fections, and as if the heat and study of his art
had made him prematurely grave and old.   I wish
you could have heard the torrents of bad Italian
which fell from us four, Maddalena cackling and
Uccetta drizzling, as it were, in patois, Catherine
and I stumbling and stuttering over our villainous
Italian.   Yet, we managed to make ourselves
enough understood on both sides.   But the best
was when Uccetta began to talk about the new
hands into which his hotel had fallen.   His melancholy touched the true sublime, when he reflected
that he could not cook our dinner for us, and that
we should be served at his own table by the inferior
artist who now lords it in his kitchen.   Each time
I have seen him he has pathetically renewed his
complaint, and on my telling him that I am sure

the present landlord does his best, he shakes his head, and says, 'Vuole, è vero, ma non può.'"

[The travellers reached the Val Anzasca, and the neighbourhood of Monte Rosa; the daily intercourse with that superb mountain as seen from Macugnaga, where the Symondses stayed, evoked the following disquisition, nominally on the art of landscape painting, really on the method of art and criticism in general. It helps to explain that abundance and charm of conversation which was so characteristic of Symonds. The man who had stored all these reflections for his own use on paper, could not fail to flow when tapped by talk] :—

Wednesday,[1] *June* 13, 1866.—I talked a good deal to C. last night about the way in which she ought to approach painting, and, having sermonised so much, it is my duty to render to myself an account of what she said, and see whether it comes to anything.

It seems to me that she is one of those who willingly ignore the human element, who have not recognised those sentiments which alone can touch the hearts of men. They are lost in admiration of pure nature; the exceeding wonder of the world seems enough for them; they do not hear "the low sad music of humanity," among the choruses of Alps and sunlight; they sit down before a Monte Rosa or a Jungfrau and try to put it on their canvas.

[1] Diary.

What is the result?—a more or less accurate portrait of the mountain, very dear to those who know its face, because of the recollections it calls up, but not a poem, not a work of human art, not an appeal to human feelings, and wholly inadequate as a representation of the original when judged by the standards of true criticism. Poets often fall into similar mistakes—they fancy that their admiration of some great scene, and their minute description of the same, will constitute a poem. One such a line as—

"Sur l'Hymette j'ai éveillé les abeilles,"

or

"Qui per saxa volutus
Clarior electro campum petit amnis,"

is worth all their eloquence. (*N.B.*—I am continually falling into this error of cold description, mistaking my own enthusiastic sense of the beauties of a subject for the power of rendering the same to others. A word in season, a single touch, an allusion to some universal vein of human sentiment, a delicacy of cadence, are worth more than myriads of carefully-chosen cataloguing phrases. George Sand will often put a picture on her pages because she is steeped in sentiment, because her characters have taken hold of you, and their emotions make you see the landscape which she would describe). C.'s sketches are too much like these cold efforts of a poet to describe all that he has admired, except that they have the solid advantage of being topographically instructive and true portraits, of beautiful things—whereas his are words—but in point of poetry they do not rank high. A little scrap of larch or rock, or rivulet or cloud, truly felt, would be worth more than Eigers and Jungfraus white against blue sky. They would act by suggestion, just as such a line as " The scent of violets hidden in the grass," acts by suggestion. A Turner may infuse into the whole of a vast picture the burning soul of eloquence and poetry—he may make sunrise or sunset upon his canvas more gorgeous than the real heavens—but smaller artists must be content to compass smaller subjects. To paint Monte Rosa, so as to infuse into it true poetry, is almost as great a task of genius as to write a true Pindaric ode.

But—here I touch upon the most difficult part of the subject—what is this poetry of which I speak, how is it to be attained, how is the transition to be made from prose to poetry ? To begin with, I think there is no doubt that all pictures ought to be the copies not of the landscape merely, but of the landscape as reflected on the soul. And by " reflected on the soul," I mean that the landscape must have impressed itself upon the sensitive, creative mind of man, have stirred ideas there, have gathered round its forms the prismatic hues of fancy, memory, or *sehnsucht*. The image impressed is what the painter ought to represent, and, if he is successful, he will stir the souls of those who see his picture as by the

reading of a poem.   To illustrate this, I remember
going out at Engelberg one evening, and seeing the
evening star above the mountains in a tract of
watery sky, the lines, "Ueber allen Gipfeln ist
Ruh," came into my mind, striking the keynote of a
thousand deep emotions, and I had my picture poem.
Again by the sea, Timon's last words sound in my
ears and transfuse the beach, the foam, the rocks,
the breakers, with a sentiment which, if I were a
painter, I would strive to set on canvas.   C. tells
me that the psalms come into her head all through
a long day among the Alps.   There is the same
thing—she ought to get some waif of them upon
her paper; but she ascends at once to religion, to
adoration, which are the highest pinnacles of poetry,
and not having power to express them, falls back to
earth and simple imitation.

Half our admiration of Nature is passive, inasmuch
as we render no account of it to ourselves, but
are content to look and wonder and rejoice and
praise.   This is all well; nothing is nobler than the
quiet brimful delight of the soul in face of what is
beautiful.   But I do not think that this is the artist's
attitude; a work of art requires the full activity of
the soul, intense reflection on the capabilities of the
subject, a steady aim with regard to the single effect
to be produced, definite sentiments, and an idea
that dominates.   He who desires to paint poetically
must return frequently upon himself, must sit down
patiently before his landscapes, making clear the

thoughts that come into his mind, must never hope to paint a poem unless some definite emotion throws new light upon the object which he sees. He may cultivate the poetic insight in many ways —first, by studying Art, which for this purpose (supposing him to have the "raw" material of emotion, and to need the power of expression chiefly) is better than Nature.   Nature is the order of God's world, Art of man's.   Our study of Art teaches us the mechanism by which man's soul is moved, the great emotions which have always stirred it, and to which all poets have recurred.   Poetry is the most universal of Arts.   Frequent reading of poetry would be good, or pondering on pictures, or feeling music.   The habit of analysis is also useful — to see how artists have wrought, how they have selected their subjects, in what lights they have placed them, how far they have suc-ceeded, what in them is chaff, and what is wheat. Next, there must be continual meditation, a con-stant rendering of accounts to the soul of all that charms us, every attempt to be definite.   Again, the choice of subjects goes a long way.   An artist, who mistrusts his powers, should paint nothing but what suggests to his mind some feeling—he should choose the mists and glooms, and wild lights and fantastic details, and suggestive wayside bits of Nature, which are lyrical, instead of those great landscapes which are epical.   I pre-suppose that he has technical ability.   Again, what is very

necessary is the study of style. Ruskin seems
to me to have done some harm by making people
exchange style for mere imitation. I do not want
them to falsify Nature—I would only have them
remember that many poetical effects are only to
be produced by manipulating Nature, by suppres-
sing, heightening, deepening, in obedience to the
inner rhythm which desires to strike a peculiar
chord. If Nature could be perfectly copied—which
would be the same as making a new nature—that
would be the best, perhaps. But we cannot do that.
We must be content with modification. Style consists in making that necessary modification subserve
poetic purposes. Use your knowledge and technical
ability, not merely for the purpose of accuracy, which
often impedes poetry, though it makes honest prose,
but also as the servants of an inner and idealising
faculty. Which is of more value, a yellow primrose painted by Hunt, or a poem on a primrose
written by Wordsworth? Suppose we say the former—what is its value? All the spring days we
have spent among mossy lanes and woods, spring
hopes, the valley by Mentone, &c. Yes; but a
primrose itself would serve better. It would, if
we could always get one; but the primroses only
bloom in spring, and the picture abides for ever.
I grant you; yet you can say no more of Hunt's
primrose. After all, it is but a substitute for the
flower, and as a substitute happens to remind you
of pleasant things. But there are hundreds, city-

born, or men like Conington, whom it reminds of
nothing. Now the poem speaks to all of these,
is more imperishable than the flower, and is just
as suggestive of spring days. Moreover, those
who see nothing in a flower get no instruction
from the picture; from the poem they are taught
to love flowers, to see more in them than they
saw before, at least are thrilled by the poet's
moral.

I would give a byeword to the spirit of criticism.
While looking at a picture of the Sun god, the critic
may say, his muscles are too large, or his throat is
too fat. "Goodness! what does that matter now?"
I cry, "I am trying to understand how Raphael has
conceived the Phœbus Apollo, the Greek god,
the fiery shooter of sunbeams." Every boy who
has gone through his first course of anatomy
knows that Raphael, or the engraver of his pictures,
has made the neck and muscles wrong. Go to
the poetry, the soul, seek the important things;
don't tithe your mint and cummin, and forget the
weightier matters of the law. So of Claude. The
critic sees Radicofani, Cecilia Metella's tomb, a wood,
a river, the sea, some Roman soldiers on a bridge,
the ruins of the Claudian aqueduct, sea-weedy trees,
and leather dock-leaves, all in one picture. At these
he turns up his nose, instructed by Ruskin and the
spirit of the nineteenth century. But the poem has
escaped him, the large peace, the bounteous air, the
melody of afternoon. Yet Claude has lived three

centuries, and will live. Our grandchildren, who
will know even better than ourselves all about
anachronisms, and the way to paint trees and docks,
will still admire Claude.   Technical accuracy will
seem to them so trivial and easy and methodical,
that they will forget that Claude did not possess it,
lost still in admiration of his sweetness.   I do not
mean to say that criticism is not right, that Ruskin
is not right, to explain his defects in order to purify
style and break down what is pernicious in long-
established models.   But, having once learned the
lesson, let us be humble; seeking beauties rather
than defects; acknowledging Claude's childishness,
or Blake's extravagant sins against anatomy and
good taste—and trying to grasp the spirit of
poetry which lies above and beyond, and in spite
of these material defects.   It is the privilege of
the educated to ignore defects, or rather to make
allowance for defects without danger.   The imperfectly educated cannot afford to do so; they
must throw away wheat and chaff together for fear
of mistaking chaff for wheat.   So none but the
purest models should be given to students.   But
having learned, we are able to part and prove, and
say, "This is good in feeling, and, allowing for
its technical defects, a work of genius," or "This
is faultily faultless, correct, but adds nothing to our
ideas."

But after all, there are very few poems made
in the world, very few to be made.   We are most

happy if we feel a poem once in four months,
and thrice happier if we can succeed in executing
it, however imperfectly. The only duty is to try,
to try hard, ceaselessly. And this trying is so
difficult—it ends almost always in wishing. We
are like men who sit at a window and want to get
far away to a hill-top; there they sit and look, and
seem to forget that the hill-top can only be reached
by walking—or, like those who beat their breasts
and long for salvation, but do not go into the
convent and fast, and pray, and watch, and scourge
themselves. I know this—how hard it is to improve my style, to get fresh keenness of insight,
and more gravity of judgment, to purge away my
affectations, to brace up my language, to base my
criticisms on more fixed foundations. The only
way is never to neglect the question, to turn it
over in the mind, to think often "how can I do
better?" That asking "how" is of some good—
one day one side light, another day another side
light comes. And, after all, if you die with un-
accomplished aims, and a name written on water,
it does not matter. To have felt poems, to have
striven for expression, to have done your best, that
is something.

[The stimulus of the Alps, and above all, the
delight in Macugnaga—"a place where happiness
has come upon us, we might almost say unawares,"
is made sufficiently clear in the joyous, vigorous,

dithyrambic pages of the Macugnaga journal. But
it had to come to an end. The Symondses left on
June 17th, and went by Ivrea to Courmayeur, and
thence by Aosta over the St. Bernard to Ouchy,
and finally, to Mürren. There, in a place which had
proved of such importance in his life, Symonds, as
was very usual with him, takes stock of his position.
"It is dangerous to revisit places which we have
loved very deeply, and at critical times of life. I
felt this for a moment here, but yesterday Mürren
reassumed all its own power. I find it hard to
write about the mixed emotions which possess me;
but one thing is clear,—in three years I have grown
older, stronger, steadier, more contented, happier.
I am neither so dejected nor yet so ambitiously
expectant as I was then. If I consider what I
have gained in point of knowledge and intellectual
power during these three years, I find it nothing.
But my views of life are more settled and defined.
I wish that I could command poetry: oh, how
deeply, fervently I wish it. Then I might speak
out somewhat of that which is within me." In this
important passage Symonds takes a characteristically modest view of his intellectual achievement
so far. Writing towards the close of his life, however, he judges this period more liberally and more
justly; he recognises that the year 1866–67 was
"important for my literary development. I did a
great deal of careful, yet instructive work, which
helped to form my style." And he approached the

three main subjects which were to be the field of
his literary labours, Italian history, Greek poetry,
and Elizabethan Drama.

But the passage just cited is of higher moment
in the delineation of Symonds' intellectual and
spiritual attitude, for it shows us his major desire
in the field of literature to be a poet, to express
what he had to say, not in the form of critical
analysis, but in the guise of creative art—and it
indicated expressly, for the first time, that strong
conviction which governed the whole of his career,
that life is more than literature. In the chapter
wherein Symonds sums up his literary achievement,
it will be seen to what extent the desire to be
an artist, and the doctrine that life is more than
literature, crossed, thwarted, hampered each other.
The whole attitude is, indeed, highly characteristic
of the man. He wished to be and to do everything; to be a poet, to be a critic, to be a student;
to live a life of action, to live a life of pleasure;
to know whatever has been known by men, to
see, as he says, "*I vizi umani ed i dolori*"—an
attitude which he used to sum up in the one word
—curiosity.

This memorable journey ended intellectually in
a second reading of "Ecce Homo," and a critique
on the nature of faith; emotionally, with these
words, "I am writing within sound of the lapping
Lake of Neuchatel—on the last verge of Switzerland. I love Switzerland as a second home—

hoping to return to it, certain that I am happier, purer in mind, healthier in body there than anywhere else in the world. I would not take Rome, Florence, and Naples in exchange for the châlets of Mürren."]

CHAPTER VIII

MANHOOD. SPECULATIVE LIFE

Return to London.—On method in writing poetry.—Visits to Rugby and Oxford. — Visit to Clifton. — Bad health. — Goes abroad with his sister.—Rouen.—St. Ouen.—*Saxifraga pyramidalis.*—The Columbine. — On Gothic architecture.—Norman buildings. —St. Etienne at Caen. — Bayeux. — Depression. — St. Lo.—Coutances.—His philosophy.—His religion.—Mont St. Michel. —Emotional strain. — Returns to England. — Ill health. — Mr. Henry Sidgwick. — Writes poetry. — Longing for the Alps. — The necessary conditions of life.—Speculations on life.

[THE house in Norfolk Square was not a favourite with either Mr. or Mrs. Symonds. They had lived so little in it, that it had never acquired the atmosphere of home. They reached it on the 24th of August, 1866, and the malaise of London settled down again upon Symonds, and showed itself in such remarks as these—" To some men God's gifts come like dew and sunshine; whatever good others obtain is pressed from them by upbraidings of conscience and throes of self-condemnation and anguish, of self-disdain and jealousy and discontent." As these phrases will probably indicate to those who knew him, Symonds was, at this time, writing a considerable amount of poetry as well as prose, and this important passage on method occurs—"When engaged on a subject, it is good to throw off casual jottings, and short essays, *infimæ species*, as it were, in the order of composition. These ought, however, to be frequently inspected, so that their results may be wrought into unity; in time a number of preliminary syntheses, *media axiomata*, would thus be gained, and all lead up to the organic view. This, at least, is the idea of my method. Another way would be to keep all in solution in the mind until the final process of crystallisation. No doubt this would be the most vigorous and artistic way." The London life was varied by visits to Rugby— of which there is a glowing account—and to Balliol, where, on his arrival, he finds Jowett "half asleep on two chairs in the dusk;" with Jowett he discusses the idea of a "History of the Renaissance in England." The Diary of these visits closes thus: "These swallow flights ventilate my thoughts; and the concussion of ideas with Arthur, Jowett, Green, adds to their depth, rapidity, and freshness."]

In[1] March, 1867, at Clifton, I caught a bad cold, from which I did not recover easily. Nevertheless, we went back to 47 Norfolk Square. My father was so anxious about my state of health—I was suffering from the chronic trouble in my head, a permanent malaise and nervous sensibility, which made me incapable of steady work, together with

[1] Autobiography.

the sub-acute pneumonia in the left lung—that he thought it best to send me off upon a journey at the end of May. My wife was unable to travel, expecting her second confinement in a few months. So my sister Charlotte kindly volunteered to bear me company; and very good company she was during our ramblings in Normandy.

I find a collection of letters written to my wife upon this tour, parts of which she copied out into a MS. book. From these I mean now to make extracts. They clearly indicate the state of my mind and emotion at that epoch.

ROUEN, *May* 29, 1867.—We travelled slowly through the orchards and meadows this morning, by the side of shallow transparent rivers golden with iris on their banks. It is a pretty rural land-scape; but the village houses are tiled with a very black slate, which spoils them.

Services were going on in all the churches here. I never really, enjoy a cathedral without music. It seems to set the mute hymns of the arches and the clustered piers to melody, to interpret the stories of the blazoned windows, and to fill the spaces of the aisles with invisible presences. Without this living accompaniment and commentary, architecture seems to me cold and dead. Are the harmonic ratios of form and sound really so sympathetic as mutually to elucidate each other? Or is it a matter of association—the religious purpose and solemn character of organ music tuning our mind to the proper key for comprehending sacred architecture?

The church of St. Ouen might be almost called provokingly perfect—a full-sized, elaborately-designed Gothic cathedral, finished on one plan down to its minutest details. Some of the romance of old church building is lost by this completeness. The precise way in which it has been isolated from surrounding houses, and planted at one end with pleasant trees, destroys the pathos of the picturesque. Nothing is left to the imagination. But, for gaining an insight into the working of the medieval brains which planned these structures, St. Ouen is invaluable. Here the veriest child can see that the spirit of Gothic art is not anarchy, but symmetry and order. Only the parts here forced into correspondence are almost infinite—not, as in the case of Greek work, select and few.

While I am writing, the curfew is tolling over the town — a fine, deep, melancholy bell — and the towers of Notre Dame, just now so rosy, are fading like the Alps at sunset into a dead greyness. Like the Alps! it does not do to think too much about them. Alas, I know that health is awaiting me there if only I could get to them. It is pitiable to be so much feebler than I was this time last year. Where were we then? At Macugnaga, reading S. Beuve's "Causeries de Lundi," under the scarcely fledged beech boughs, within sight of melting avalanches fringed by crocuses and soldanellas.

This morning (Feast of the Ascension) we heard service in three churches. There seems to be a renascence of old, dry, ecclesiastical music in France, as elsewhere. It fills me with infinite sadness to stand in one of these naves, and to hear these reiterated adorations and supplications, and to think of the hundreds and thousands of colossal temples of the past—Egypt and furthest Ind, the deserts of Palmyra and Baalbec, Persia and China, and the tangled forests of Mexico—not to speak of Judæa and Phœnicia and Greece and Carthage and Italy, nor of all the regions of the north—fruitless altars and vain prayer-stations, raised to the inscrutable, unapproachable God, the sphinx of Being called by a myriad names. Those rites have vanished—the voices of the priests and chanting choirs are silent—the barbaric bands are mute—the prayers are forgotten—the ceremonies have ceased. Only our form of worship still exists for us, for us "the foremost nation of the world," for us who think ourselves so wise, and dream our creed the final one. Our particular small faith still lives, destined ere long to be merged in other equally impotent attempts to reach the source of aspirations.

I do not sleep much. Below my fourth-floor window are roofs of all colours, jumbled up in all ways, flowers growing on the sills of dormer windows, cats asleep; above all, the cathedral and its booming bell.

CAEN, *May* 31.—Yesterday, while we were

walking in the flower-market at Rouen, something
brought you [his wife] vividly to my mind. I saw
five or six pots in one stall, holding what plant, do
you think? Our great saxifrage.[1] Yes, there it was,
with its plume of flowers and cushion of green leaves.
But the wonderful wild thing had been tamed by
cultivation. The leaves were more numerous, and
sprawled asunder; the blossoms were whiter and
less fantastically thick upon the sprays; the stalk
itself had a duller, greyer hue. To complete the
poor plant's slavery, it was trained upright along
a stick, which the woman who sold it called a
"tuteur." Horrid pedagogic name. I tried to tell
her of the black gorges and river banks and windy
waterfalls where we had seen it last year.[2] Curiously
enough, there were several large tiger-lilies in bloom
by the side of the saxifrage; so that all Varallo and
the Val Anzasca seemed to have been tamed and
travestied together in that prosy Rouen flower-
stall.

If I had to choose a flower, I think I should take
the columbine. It is so wonderfully finished in all
its details, both of leaves and blossom, so graceful
in carriage, so varied in colour, so perfect in drawing. Then the associations I have with it are
many. Luini's picture at Milan, the foreground of
Titian's Bacchus and Ariadne in our gallery, the
dark-brown garnet-coloured beauties of San Salva-

---

[1] *Saxifraga pyramidalis*, of which Symonds was particularly fond.
[2] In Val Anzasca.

dore, the white ones of the Colma, the lilac flowers in Leigh Woods.

The columbine has started me on sad reflections. If there were but only one strong and perfect thing in me I should feel worthier; I might perhaps let youth ebb away, and weakness get the upper hand more contentedly; but when I regard my past life, I find so many broken arcs and no full circle: so much ignoble selfishness and the folly of sentimental ideality: at the same time, such vulgarity of soul, cunning, want of faith in the highest things, that I am ready to sit down and cry for my futility. I am brought very low indeed now, stretching out my hands and praying that this perpetual weakness of the body, and this weary mental suffering, may not quench my best chance of rising to nobler things through life.

CAEN, *June* 1.—This is a pretty little place, more homely and friendly than Rouen, with several interesting churches. Caen stone is of a pure rich white—in tone and colour like our Bath stone, but harder in grain. It takes a pleasant mellowing with age, so that the houses are not so dead-grey as those of Bath. The town, too, is planted with avenues of limes, just coming into flower, which clasp the grim Norman turrets in greenery and fragrance.

It seems almost incredible that the Normans, the Germans, and the Italians—to omit other nations, Flemish, Spanish, &c.—should have started from Romanesque as their common point, and have run

a parallel course upon the same lines to similar conclusions, during the same period of time.   What we
call the Gothic style, emerging from the Romanesque, seems to have been developed independently
by each people, obeying one law of growth, and to
have passed through the same successive stages, in
each case exhibiting the specific genius of the race,
together with the general characteristics of the type.
It would be interesting to analyse this matter in
detail, and to discover, if that were possible, what
caused this simultaneous progress from the early
pointed to the decorative manner, and from the
decorative to the decadent, until the style was
thoroughly worked out.   Perhaps the last stage in
the evolution of Gothic would be the most instructive in its bearing upon national character.   We
might select the formal cross-bars and perpendicular
lines of St. Mary Redclyffe, or the flattened roof of
King's College Chapel, the sinuous and flame-like
traceries of the façade of Notre Dame at Rouen,
the exquisitely graceful classic foliage of Siena, the
thorny intricacies of the Nürnberg Lorenz-Kirche,
the vicious scrolls and writhing lines of the town-
halls at Ghent and Louvain.   I am sure that the
last chapter in the history of Gothic architecture,
arrived at in each case upon a line of parallel progression, in each inevitable, and determined by the
previous stages of the art, reveals a deeply-rooted
national quality of genius.   English prosiness and
common-sense—French subtlety and plasticity—

Italian feeling for decorative beauty and the classic past—German grotesqueness and idealising symbolism—Belgian bourgeoisie and prosperous comfort. But this would involve long studies, and technical acquirements, philosophical analysis. I cannot hope to undertake it. I must content myself with throwing out an *aperçu*.

I do not feel as though I knew enough about the Normans, or had enough sympathy with what I do know, properly to appreciate the rude vigour and pride of strength in their great churches here. The forms of Romanesque in Italy,—Lombard façades, Tuscan pilastered rows of shallow galleries ascending to a peak, slumberous memories of decadent Papal and rudimentary Christian culture blent upon the Adriatic coast, mosaics and marble panellings,—they seem to me nearer than these spruce, perfectly correct, humanly repellent structures, which, in an odd sort of way, remind me of the Prussian Government.

St. Etienne is very simple. Its barren towers are so grand, the interior is so impressive, that I am subdued by the exhibition of pure mental force and character. Charm has not to be demanded. We feel that the sons of the old Norsemen knew not the graces, or else that they refused to pay them homage. The tale of the Niblungs, the story of Gudrun, survive in these churches. Humanity is left to freeze and suffer, or to expand, according as it can—but mostly in a tragic way—among such art surroundings ; just as it does amid bleak unsympathetic nature.

What most attracted me at St. Etienne was the structure of the towers; tall, fearless, square towers surmounted by beautifully shaped pyramids, and flanked with smaller turrets of the same spiry form. This ground idea, which is feebly carried out in our Oxford Cathedral, serves for a distinctive mark of the Caen churches.

BAYEUX, *June* 2.—We came here to see the tapestry and the cathedral. We have seen them. One cathedral does not differ much from another, except to the antiquary. I hope I shall never come to say that one mountain does not differ much from another, except to the geologist. Nature increases, art diminishes, as we grow older.

I cannot guess what so subtle poison it is that has passed imperceptibly into me, and sucks out all my force. It is terrible to face the prospect of a languid inadequate life of enforced idleness. You speak about my becoming, after all, a strong man. That may be. It may even be that I shall strangle ambition in myself, give up the desire to do and be something, acquiesce in letting the years slip by in peace until the peace of death comes. At present I am plagued by the constant desire to use my brains for work, to store up knowledge for future writings—baffled by the terrible incapacity of a naturally weak constitution, and health broken by mismanagement. I am twenty-six years of age this summer; I have for all intents and purposes been idle during the last three years, those years in which I ought to have acquired stores of useful knowledge; and my enforced idleness has been an idleness of pain and illness. Are we to look forward to endless "peregrinities," and the lingering death of me after some few years more of flitting to and fro consumptively?

St. Lo, *June* 3.—I did not do Bayeux justice. On a second visit to the cathedral, by dint of staying there in quiet for two hours, I harmonised my mind to its severe and heaven-aspiring beauty. This church has the bloom and freshness of adolescence; the strength of the old Norman with the delicacy and luxuriant loveliness of early Gothic. The huge round arches of the nave are adorned with diapers and traceries, not yet formed into flowers or foliage, but rich like figured brocades. The transept and the choir expand into the beauty of clustered columns, soaring to a vast height, and feathering with fantastic leafage, while the long pointed windows of clerestory and chapel hold wheels, cut into hexagons and quatrefoils by pure crisp cusps, the very models of expanded summer blossoms.

Of all the places I have seen this journey, St. Lo appears to me most capable of picturesque description. It stands on a hill of solid grey rock overhanging the Vire, a stream not unlike

our Avon, which winds through wooded slopes
of dark red ironstone and limestone, curving a
gentle course towards the open plains and the not
far distant sea.   The valley, the river, the woods,
the gardens on the hill-slopes, and the richly-
meadowed land beyond, can all be surveyed from
the cathedral square.

This Val de Vire was one of the most favoured
regions of old Normandy.   Here a local poetry
flourished, not altogether unlike that of the Pro-
vençals, a lyric poetry of spring and love and
flowers, with interludes of martial clangour.   For
England was close at hand.   You hear plenty about
the English in the songs of Val de Vire.

I have bought a collection of fourteenth and
fifteenth century songs of this country, the Co-
tentin and Val de Vire.   If after reading them,
I find they have sufficient substance, I may write
something about the town and its poets.

June 3.—In Coutances I have at last received
a true and profound impression from architecture.
The cathedral is superb: moreover, it is not
"swept and garnished," but still remains in its
time-honoured state of cobwebs, dust, and green
mildew.   The windows are labyrinths of blue and
crimson, not tapestried in gigantic pictures like the
clerestories of Rheims, but broken into jewellery
and sparks of passionate dyed flame.   This is the
kind of glass I love.   There is some of the same
sort at Strasburg.   It is finer even than the glowing

paradise of Florentine rose-windows, the one at St. Maria Novella, you remember.

Like all the best Norman churches, Coutances Cathedral has two massive western towers, rising into spires, and a central lantern. The nave and transepts are much shorter than is common in our English churches, but much higher, so that the proportions are entirely different. The whole is terminated by a chevet, or double-apse, divided into chapels radiating from the semicircle. These fundamental forms seem to be universal in Normandy; but each church shows some particular features of construction. At Bayeux it was perhaps the chaste beauty of the later Romanesque style, and the majesty of the four great columns, that support the central tower. Here the predominant effect is gained by the lantern, which from inside resembles a second church suspended in mid-air. The clumsy attempt at Siena to raise a dome above a Gothic building, has here been realised so skilfully, as to combine external and internal beauty without sacrificing the least detail of architectural coherence. From every point of view this lantern, with its bold groining and glorious line of pointed windows, adds loftiness and grandeur to the church. I could have wished for greater breadth in the side-aisles, a bay or two more in the nave; but this would have suited the spirit of English, not of French building.

Coutances might be compared to Lincoln. Both

towns stand on the tops of hills, crowned with three
noble church towers.   But Coutances is surrounded
by a country prettily wooded and undulating, not
by the bare impressive Lincolnshire flat.

A citizen of Coutances gave a large garden on
the hill-slope to his townsfolk.   It is laid out in
terraces and walks.   Before we found it out, we
met two old women sitting on the steps of a church
and gazing across the house roofs to the lands
below.   They had a young man with them,
slender and graceful, with a wistful look in his
grey eyes, as though they were sweeping the
horizon in search of something sweet and far
away he had not yet discovered.   Charlotte asked
them where the public garden was.   They rose
at once to show us the way, and the young man
sauntered at their side, half bold, half shy.   A
singularly magnetic youth, with a force in him
"eligible to break forth," and only too ready to
do so.   The simplicity of the two old women, in
their prim white caps and blue check gowns, formed
a curious contrast to the passionate suppression
of the boy, alert for adventures.   I hummed to
myself "Non so più cosa son, cosa faccio."   They
grinned from ear to ear.   He, their son and
nephew, as it turned out, kept appealing to me
with his eyes, and asking mutely whether I too
did not want something more than this.   It was
pleasant to see so much enjoyment of the simplest
things in the old women, such gaiety and good

humour, such kindly artless manners. Yet I fancy
that they have their troubles. The mother told
me she had only come to live in Coutances since
le dernier S. Michel. Her husband was an old
man of seventy-five; and her son had a fancy
for the town, he was a young man, a *fils unique*,
and this was his pleasure. Her sister still lived
in the country. She became so sad at this
point, and the lad lowered so disdainfully, that
I changed the subject. However, I should have
liked to know more about him. He must have a
story; for his manners were excellent, and he knew
some English, and his intelligence in seizing the
nuance of what one said was perfect. These meet-
ings with passing strangers, these magnetisms of
one indifferent person by another, are among the
strangest things in life. Well, when the conversation flagged .between Charlotte and me and the old
women, one of them would say, " Ah, quelle heur-
euse rencontre. Nous nous êtions là assises sur
les marches de l'église. Nous nous attendions à
rien. Et violà que vous êtes venus. N'est-ce pas,
François ? " And François only smiled a little
sadly. I, for my part, felt how idiotically human
life is made. Charlotte delighted in the kindly,
hale, hearty, sweet-tempered, plain-featured, innocent, hospitable, elderly old ladies. They liked the
amusement of walking with two English tourists.
But the young man and I, we wanted to be comrades,
if only for a day or two in passing—he to hear of

my life, I of his. And things are so arranged that this may not be, though I cannot, for the soul of me, see why they should not be.

AVRANCHES, *June* 4—We have had a day of diligences. This morning we left Coutances in the *intérieure* of a fusty old omnibus, which jolted us to Grouville—a curious port, built upon a mass of black granite projecting into the sea like a formless Monaco. The houses are of grey granite and black slate, sometimes whitened. That is all I remember of Grouville. Yet I carried another memory away, a thought rather than a recollection. It was a dreamy fancy of the many young men who have set forth from this port for distant voyages, for the fisheries, for Iceland perhaps, leaving their mothers and their sweethearts behind them, and some of them returning never, their beautiful strong bodies and white faces tossed to sleep on unfamiliar waves —the vast water-ways of the monstrous world, which Grouville surveys unmoved from her station on the sea-commanding promontory.[1]

I hope that this travelling does me good. I have more of animal spirits than I had. But the least noise keeps me awake, and we live in the midst of diligences. These pretty country places are more full of foolish bustle than London or Paris. Perhaps one attends to it more here. Perhaps it would be better for me if I could fraternise with the people, drink with them, and go to bed narcotised. The life

[1] *Pêcheur d'Islande* had not been published then.

of a mere brain-being is bad. I do not touch, or else I shrink from the coarse human nature round me. Yet I cannot say how I long to meet with a man, a comrade, the first face and hands responsive to my own. Why? I do not know. I hate the sophistication of my existence, the being penned up in a cage of archæology and literary picture-making. All this has nothing to do with the ties, inviolably sacred, which bind me to my home, and make me feel my centre there in you.

AVRANCHES, *June* 5.—You forecast the future far too much. For all the great occurrences of life I am strong enough; it is for the little things, the daily ennui of my tired brain and eyes, the help-lessness and inability engendered by my state of health, that I feel myself feeble. We ought not to sit down like the German girl in the cellar, watching the hatchet which might some day fall on her, forgetting the ale that kept running from the cask.

No one is happy who has not a deep firm faith in some ideal far beyond this world, in some law of majesty, beauty, goodness, harmony, superior to the apparent meanness, ugliness, evil discord of the present dispensation. How difficult it is to live the life of the spirit thoroughly, to be per-manently interested in the eternal things, the durable relations. This is why so many of us are not happy. I have a great deal of faith in my soul, vague, not reduced to a creed. But what I have

sustains me in the obscuration of my energies. To
this I owe my happy moments—to the support I
draw from nature, books, and art—the imperishable
thoughts of men, the everlasting mysteries and
glories of the world—finally from that, whatever
that is, which underlies all this, and is the real
reality, the truth and unity of the whole. Those
who are not "tenoned and morticed" upon something indestructible, must be rendered wretched
by the changefulness and barrenness of daily life.
They may not know exactly that they are poor and
miserable. Or they feel it vaguely, like the sullen
Roman nobles, so magnificently painted for us by
Lucretius, hurrying from one palace to another
to escape the gloom of boredom. It is wonderful
that we are at all contented with the transitory
interests and trivial occupations which fill up the
inexorable years—each year leading us, at so short
a distance, to the bourne of death, and after death,
if anything, then either endless change or continuity
of eternal being. In either case the soul needs a
refuge from the things that pass like a show, to
some reality above them and beneath them. This
I feel with all the force I have. The all but mortal
blow which prostrated me three years ago, since
when I have been like a clock suddenly stopped,
marking the time with moving fingers no more,
has taught me so much.

The misery of scepticism, of intellectual doubt, of
worldliness, of mental indolence, and moral inactivity,

consists in this—that men have to suffer cares, ill
health, ennui, and often the greater evils of life, without a calming prospect, without any hope that
the wrong will be made right, the broken pieces
joined into a perfect whole hereafter.   I verily
believe that a robust vice, an energetic state of
sinning, if it inspires confidence in some reality, is
better than the condition of negation.   If the world
is to live without faith and to become conscious of
the vanity of things—that is, if men take to seriously
thinking upon the facts of this life without a
religious trust in God—a simultaneous suicide might
almost be expected.   What people call pessimism—
the philosophy of Schopenhauer, for example—
implies and virtually professes this conclusion.

Is it the misfortune or the fault of folk in this age
that they are so often denuded of belief in God—I
mean of the personal and vividly-felt God of Christianity?   No one can really doubt that some God
animates the world.   "Quis Deus incertum : est
Deus."   I have no living God in constant relation
to myself, no father, no future host and friend and
master in the immortal houses.   At times this very
disbelief appears to me as an illumination and a
martyrdom, because I know that it has not been
brought upon me by the desire to elude the law of
God, and because it is actually painful.   At other
times I cannot maintain that attitude, when I consider
how poor the purposes of my life, what difficulty I
find in rising above trivial thoughts and passions.

The ideal seems so far away from me. Compared with other people, I may not appear as sordid as I feel; but every man ought to compare himself with what he might be, with his own best self, before he thinks of applying the standard of other people.

In these difficulties I fall back on a kind of Stoical mysticism—on the prayer of Cleanthes, the Proem to Goethe's "Gott und Welt," the phrase of Faust, "Entbehren sollst du, sollst entbehren," the almost brutal optimism of Walt Whitman. I cry to the Cosmos, "Though thou slay me, yet will I trust in thee." Can a religion be constructed out of these elements? Not a tangible one, perhaps, nothing communicable to another heart. But a religious mood of mind may be engendered sufficient for the purpose of living not ignobly.

I have no will to sprawl contentedly, or the reverse, like the common herd and children. You shall see me die or become idiotic through ennui or soul-sickness first. It is not good for men to sprawl. Let us say :

> "Je souffre; il est trop tard; le monde s'est fait vieux
> Une immense espérance a traversé la terre;
> Malgré nous vers le ciel il faut lever les yeux."

Let us say this and make the best of it we can.

You and I together must be strong in the world; be it what it is to be for us—or if we are weak, we are still together. I clench my fists, and refuse

to be beaten. I gather strength in myself, when
flung down to the lowest, and find wings in the
futility of my nature. Pain, grief, despair raise
men above the condition of dumb creatures and
infants. There is a dignity in endurance.

Do not imagine that I am writing all this like a
sermon on commonplaces. I am feeling it very
intensely. For to-day has disappointed me much.
I thought I was getting stronger. But two hours
of real interest and keen attention at the Mont St.
Michel brought back my worst brain-symptoms. I
sat for half-an-hour on the steps of the monastery,
quite stunned with mere nervous annihilation, staring
at the stonecrop, hyssops, and lichens; and the
drive back to Avranches was very doleful. Grievous
to have the very mainspring of all sensations and
thoughts broken.

AVRANCHES, *June* 6.—It was well that we went
to Mont St. Michel yesterday. To-day the rain
descends in deluges, and I shall employ my time in
writing an account of one of the most impressive
places I have ever visited. I am afraid that I
cannot do justice to my own impressions. The
wretchedness of yesterday still lasts, though it has
abated more quickly than I could have hoped for
in London.

Mont St. Michel, at first sight, is one of those
places which you seem to know by heart, and
scarcely want to look at. The conical hill of granite,
rising from a flat expanse of sand and salt water;

the buildings crowned with Gothic pinnacles and turrets ; the bastions descending to the sea by zig-zags. All this has been often painted. No less familiar are the houses of the township, attached like swallows' nests to ledges of bare rock, nestling beneath the massive masonry of the monastic strong-hold like the mud-dwellings of those building bees you see on ancient monuments. To complete the sensation of being in a picture, as we approached the mount across the Grève an appropriate group of fishermen and fishwives, with bare legs and blue jackets, had gathered just outside the town-gate, bargaining about the sale of whelks and cockles. They made the necessary foreground. Breezy clouds and stormy strips of light, with wheeling gulls, gave value to the distance.

The gate is rudely carved from the granite of the island, and enclosing a portcullis, it bears upon its ample front a long deep undulatory slab of sculp-ture, imaging the waves of the sea, wherein are fashioned fishes diving. The symbolism of the steadfast granite, the shifting tide and treacherous sands, might be elucidated at greater length than I can spare. Such as it is, this portal forms, as it were, a frontispiece to the whole mount. For that is consecrated to St. Michel, in the peril of the sea, to religion and to knighthood, to the ark and strong rock of the spirit in the midst of even more destructive waves than Neptune's.

The sea has played its part of havoc on the

dreary Grèves around St. Michel. At one time a forest stretched from the mainland to the Channel Islands, surrounding the mount and its sister islet of Tamberleine. But in the year 709 A.D. the sea rose, swollen by tempestuous winds, and swept through the forest at high tide, converting its bed into a swamp, which, since that time, has remained waste, partly the sport of salt water, and partly an unfruitful flat of sand.

Mont St. Michel is a primeval haunt of human worship. Who shall say how many gods have dwelt there? The Druids consecrated the mount as a high place of their forest-cult. The Christians gave it to St. Michael—Michael, the prince of the legions of the air, the conqueror of Lucifer, the destined chainer of the dragon, the successor of Bel and Heracles, the tutelary deity of elevated, sea-commanding, lightning-smitten sites. The adoration paid to this archangel, who is also the minister of judgment at the last day, has elements of peculiar charm for our imagination. In England the highest churches are dedicated to him. Dundry is an instance. He inhabits hill-tops, round which winds battle and the clouds chase; which commune with the stars, and give resting-place to the feet of celestial couriers; which invite the lightning, and stand like watch-towers for the armaments of heaven to overlook the outspread land, and see what wars may there be waged against the evil one.

The exterior of the feudal and monastic buildings

of St. Michel cannot easily be spoiled. Their
Romanesque and Gothic masonry is overgrown
with yellow lichens, stonecrop, white hyssop, wild
pinks, and red valerian. The archæologist will not
scrape these off, as he has torn the flowering shrubs
and creeping tapestries from the Colosseum and the
Baths of Caracalla. It is not worth his while here.
Sea winds have eaten the solid blocks of granite,
red and grey, into honeycombs; or, where the
stone-work resists their efforts, have painted it with
weather-stains. The colour, therefore, of the whole
structure is very delicate and varied.

You enter by a dark and massive tower, pierced
with a gigantic opening, guarded by double battle-
ments and a portcullis. It is the gate of a castle
and a prison; for Mont St. Michel has been both,
as well as a monastery. This door leads into what
seems utter darkness, until the eye becomes accustomed to the little light that falls from the northern
windows and lancets of a vast hall. The guide led
us through two noble halls. In one of them the
monks distributed alms and entertained pilgrims.
For more than two centuries it has been called the
Salle de Montgomerie, because it was here that
nearly a hundred soldiers of the Huguenot chief
were slaughtered, one by one, as they climbed at
night into the convent fortress. They expected to
carry death and treason with them; but they found
these waiting for them, and were destroyed, each
by himself, without the knowledge of his doomed

successors. The next is called Les Écuries. It is a vaulted Romanesque chamber of immense height and length, in which the Knights of the Order of St. Michel stabled their horses. A postern gate at the extreme end, from which one can see the shore and tufted rocks below, gave entrance to the chargers. Standing there in gloom, gazing out into the bright light upon the broken cliffs, I pictured to myself those horses scrambling up the rocky path, led by the squires, panting, armed, and bleeding perhaps from combats waged upon the sandy tracts around the mount.

Above these two halls are another pair of equal size and greater architectural beauty ; the Salle des Chevaliers, where the thirty-six knights, founded by Louis XII., held their chapters, and the old Refectory. The one is a piece of late Norman work, severe, simple, yet elegant; the other is a very refined chamber of pointed Gothic. Both have been defaced during the period when the Mount was a prison—walls pierced for windows, pillars sawn through, carved work broken down. Still the general effect remains.

Above these is yet a third tier of buildings ; the dormitory of the monks and their cloister. It would be impossible to imagine a more exquisite specimen of Gothic than these cloisters are. Their narrow lancets, slender shafts and graceful foliage belong to the best period, while their windows command a view across the bay, the Grèves, the distant ocean. The wind howls terrifically at this altitude ; for the cloisters stand 400 feet above the sea. This prevents there being any galleries open to the outer world after the fashion of Italian *loggie*. The central court, however, is quite free to the air, and not roofed over. Among the foliated capitals and spandrils I noticed one figure of Christ upon the Cross, turned westward, facing the sunset and the sea, opposite the largest of the windows. Some saints were grouped on each side of the Cross. I thought there was something pathetic, a fine touch of poetry, in setting this crucifix to front the ocean with its infinitude, and the sunset with its illimitable yearnings.

All the buildings I have described together make up what has been called La Merveille. They deserve the name because of their marvellous position on a narrow ledge of cliff, which has been strengthened and enlarged by buttresses and sub-structures of immense power, yet light and airy in appearance. This is the triumph of the Gothic style, to be both strong and graceful, like young Galahad armed *cap-à-pie*, but at the same time fair. The name of Merveille might have been given for a different reason, since the building is a miracle of human perseverance. This rock, at the verge of the ocean, in the midst of a great plain, surmounted by spires and pinnacles, was continually attracting the lightning, and being burned down and rebuilt. The belfries were reduced to ashes, the peals of bells molten, the woodwork consumed, the masonry riven by the two-edged sharpness of the levin-fork. Yet quietly and obstinately the monks renewed their habitations, without taking it amiss that St. Michael, general of the hosts of heaven, should be unable to divert from his own house-roof the fiery darts of the fiend.

This letter has been the work of a long wet day. Tired as I am, I feel the better for writing myself out. Had I not written, the details of the Mount would have vanished from my memory after some years. Nothing would have remained but the moment of pain when I sat exhausted on those granite steps, and stared at the stonecrop, after trying to comprehend and feel too much. What I have done by writing has only this value—that I have been talking to you, and resisting my besetting weakness. We must make the machine of the brain go. It does not do to let it stop. Whatever happens, energise—even if the result be only like a diluted page of Murray's Handbook. This, by the way, I have not with me ; and what I have said about Mont St. Michel is probably wrong in a multitude of details. "Mir ist's gleich," as the Germans say. Clumsily, heavily, I have recorded my impression, and put pressure upon myself.

CHARTRES, *June* 9.—It is a blessing to be fond of books. They are a resource and a relief when all else fails. I wish you understood what it is to make

a friend of such a book as the "Divine Comedy."
Nature is more refreshing; but you cannot always
have recourse to her consolations. I repeat what I
said before, that nature becomes more to me and art
less. This is the secret of Walt Whitman's influence over my mind. I do not quite know what you
mean by art requiring an effort. All great things
make demands upon our sympathies and our intelligence: none more than grand landscape, which, I
believe, requires a long and patient apprenticeship
for its comprehension. So do great characters,
great statues, great buildings, great symphonies,
great pictures. I suppose it was the effort you
speak about which broke me down at Mont St.
Michel."

On the whole, I returned to England worse than
I went. Such a fortnight was enough to fatigue
any one. Not only did I try to feel and understand
everything I saw, but I scrutinised my own soul
at every spare moment.

After a short visit to Hastings, where we stayed
until June 23, we returned to London, and lived at
27 Norfolk Square. I could not shake the lung-
mischief or the brain-weariness off; but grew worse
and worse during the hot weeks, panting continually
to be in Switzerland.

Henry Sidgwick, whose acquaintance I had
recently made, was also staying in London, philo-
sophising, going to spiritualistic séances, and trying
to support himself (for an experiment) on the

minimum of daily outlay. Our acquaintance ripened rapidly into a deep and close friendship, which has been to me of inestimable value during the last twenty-two years.

This summer and the year that followed were of such importance in my life, that I must relate the incidents in some detail, and illustrate them by extracts from note-books and letters in my possession.

I began writing poetry again during the hot summer weather. The second half of "John Mordan," "Diego," "Love and Music," "The Headmaster," together with a great number of dithyrambic pieces in the style of Walt Whitman, belong to those months. Yet I find myself constantly doubting my own literary faculties.

"Art is very long. I have not yet vigour of nerve enough to give to composition that patient and incessant application which results in form. I have the molten fluid in my soul; but the strength to fashion the mould for it is wanting."

"Whether I am a poet or not, I am haunted by certain situations and moral tragedies which demand expression from me. I suppose that this arises from what I have myself suffered in the past—emotional distress that has indelibly impressed my nature, and which reproduces itself in the shape of dreams or dreamlike images. Long ago I crushed the tendency to write these situations into poetry, as being injurious to my health of mind and body. Besides,

I had no belief in my artistic faculty. Yet, for all this, the tendency to do so remains and gathers force; the ideas have never left my mind, but have acquired distinctness and durability with my growth."

"There is a passive and an active imagination. The one creates, the other sympathises. The one makes new things for the world, the other appropriates whatever has been made, informing the past with something of fresh life. To men who are not in a true sense artists, it is a solace thus to retrace the history of the world. Like Dürer's Melancholy, they sit brooding, their minds a mirror, their wings down-drooping, their arms sinewless, their back unbraced."

No wonder I grew weaker and more ill. It was my one craving to be off to Switzerland. Instinct told me I should regain health there ; for since those weeks I passed at Mürren, in the year 1863, I had never failed to feel a peculiar well-being among the mountains. This craving expressed itself in dithyrambic incoherent prose.

"In London, when I rise in the morning and go to bed at night; walking the streets and squares, deafened by the roar and dazzled by their movement; when I pace the hot hard flags, or sit beneath the blackened branches of the trees; when the bricks at night give out their stifling odours, and the breathless dawn goes forth through over-burdened air ; when the passing crowds confuse me,

and wretched faces, under wet lamps, make me sick ;
when the canopy of tawny smoke is stretched all
night above the noise and sin and worry of the
house-roofs ; but mostly while I lie awake and listen
to my laboured breathing,—the thunder of the town
is heard outside, the gaslight slants sideways through
the window-chink, there is quarrelling and singing
in a public-house hard by. But before daybreak all
is still, and the leaden-hearted morning, sick and
sorry, climbs the jaded sky—then, mostly then, do
I fly away on wings of thought to Switzerland. In
my yearning I exclaim : ' Now creeps the rose of
dawning down the snows of Monte Rosa. A solitary watchman rings the dawn-bell in the church
tower. Light mist lies along the flowers and
streams—the glacier rills have not begun to flow.
Silently the glory of the sunrise floods the snowfields ; the blue behind them glows into violet ; the
rose-bloom rises to gold, and, after gold, the saffron
and the white light of the morning come.' I turn
on my pillow and clasp my hands, but shed no tears,
and find no rest. It is of no use. I try to put these
thoughts aside, but they come crowding back again.
' In the majesty and simplicity of the high mountains there is peace. The mowers go to their labour
over shadowy lawns. The goat-herds and the cow-
herds, who have seen the stars fade through the
roof-chinks of their chalets, lead their flocks afield.
The dews dry upon the flowers, the rills begin to
trickle, from the valley rise up fleecy mists and melt

into the air.' Then I remind myself that the
mountains are not always so idyllic, and that I
have not always been happy or at rest among them.
'Well am I reminded of these things. I have not
forgotten the misery of Engelberg, the anguish on
the Brünli, the self-abandonment of grief at Unter-
seen. Pitiless are the everlasting hills in their unsympathetic sunlight and sarcastic splendour, their
imperial immobility, inaccessibility, indifference to
life, their cruelty and wastefulness and never-ending
dying. Inexorable are they as nature's laws. The
stars at night are not more cold, the earth's rotation
is not less friendly.' And so I vainly interpose a
little censure of my own ideal. It is of no use. I
love the mountains as I love the majesty of justice.
I adore God through them, and feel near to Him
among them. I cannot breathe in this city."

I very rightly connected my present discomfort
with past experience of sorrow and repression. But
I did not know how to cure myself. Perhaps I
could not just then have cured myself in any way
except the way I wanted—change of scene, return
to the vital Alpine atmosphere. I find myself
writing thus to Henry Sidgwick—

"Now that you are gone, and I am not to see
you again until we meet in the dim distance of the
Riviera, I feel that much which I have told you
about myself must seem painful. My past life has
been painful in many ways, and I bear in my body
the marks of what I have suffered. With you, with

my wife, with friends like Arthur and Graham, or
when I am writing verses, I can treat those troubles
of memory with cheerfulness. But at times, when
my nervous light burns low in solitude, then the
shadows of the past gather round, and I feel that
life itself is darkened. Oppressed thus, I am often
numb and callous ; all virtue seems to have gone out
of me, the spring of life to have faded, its bloom to
have been rudely rubbed away. I dread that art and
poetry and nature are unable to do more for what
Dante with terrible truth called, 'Li mal protesi
nervi.' These darknesses, which Arthur calls my
depression fits, assail me in splendid scenery, among
pictures and statues, wherever, in fact, I ought to
enjoy most and be *most alive*. It is only the intercourse of friends which does me really any good."

Large portions of these diaries and note-books
from which I am now quoting, consist of criticisms,
reflections upon art, religion, morals, proving that,
despite of so much physical and mental *malaise*, I
was forming my own mind.

"'Im Ganzen Guten Schönen resolut zu leben,'
'To me to live is Christ, and to die gain.' How
much simpler is the latter phrase! It looks like
a motto for children. But how much larger, really
sounder is the former. It is large as the world,
a motto for adult souls. We cannot in this age
believe that St. Paul's utterance is the whole truth.
We cannot burn our books like the Ephesians ;
we ought not probably to sell our goods and give

to the poor. Those were impulses of incipient faith. We have now to co-ordinate ourselves to what is, and accept the teaching of the ages."

"What is left for us modern men? We cannot be Greek now. The ages and the seasons of humanity do not repeat themselves. The cypress of knowledge springs, and withers when it comes in sight of Troy; the cypress of pleasure likewise, if it has not died already at the root of cankering Calvinism; the cypress of religion is tottering, the axe is laid close to its venerable stem. What is left? Science, for those who are scientific. Art, for artists; and all literary men are artists in a way. But Science falls not to the lot of all. Art is hardly worth pursuing now, so bad are the times we live in for its exercise, so faulty our ideas, so far more excellent the clear bright atmosphere of antique Hellas. What, then, is left? Hasheesh, I think; hasheesh, of one sort or another. We can dull the pangs of the present by living the past again in reveries or learned studies, by illusions of the fancy and a life of self-indulgent dreaming. Take down the perfumed scrolls; open, unroll, peruse, digest, intoxicate your spirit with the flavour. Behold, there is the Athens of Plato in your narcotic visions; Buddha and his anchorites appear; the raptures of St. Francis, and the fire-oblations of St. Dominic; the phantasms of mythologies, the birth-throes of religions, the neurotism of chivalry, the passion of past poems; all pass before you in

your Maya-world of hasheesh, which is criticism.
And Music? Ah, that is the best anodyne of
all. But, alas, not even slumbers of the critic
and dreams of the music-lover are undisturbed
by anguish. The world weighs on us. Nature
and conscience cry: 'Work, while it is yet day;
the night cometh when no man can work.'
Heaven goads us with infinity of secrets and
torments of innumerable stars. The spirit thrills
us with its chidings. Hasheesh is good for a
season, *faute de mieux*. But this is no solution
of the problem. Criticism, study, history, artistic
pleasure will not satisfy the soul. 'Therefore to
whom turn I but to thee the ineffable name?'
Ever onward toward infinity I voyage, demand-
ing only what is permanent, imperishable in the
world of reality."

"Drudgery, too, is a kind of goddess, worthy of
worship for the gifts she gives ungrudgingly. A
Cinderella-sister of Semnai Theai is she, clad in
homespun, occupied with saucepans, sweeping up
man's habitation, a besom in her horny hands. She
is accessible, and always to be found. The anodyne
of fatigue is in the greasy leather wallet at her
girdle. All men should pay vows at her shrine,
else they will surely suffer.

"I wonder what morality is; whether eternal justice exists, immutable right and wrong, or whether
law and custom rule the world of humanity, evolved
for social convenience from primal savagery. I am

led in my actions by impulse, admiration, regard for the opinion of my fellows, fear of consequences, desire for what in moments of happiness I have recognised as beautiful, dislike of what is vile, mistrust of low and impious men, but never by fixed principles. I do not know what these are, and I very much doubt whether any one is guided by them. I pardon a vice for its sister virtue's sake. I feel coldly toward a virtue because of its stolid insipidity."

END OF VOL. I.

Printed by BALLANTYNE, HANSON & CO.
Edinburgh and London

www.ingramcontent.com/pod-product-compliance
Lightning Source LLC
Chambersburg PA
CBHW071356050326
40689CB00010B/1663